AUTHOR

WHITAKER, T.W.

CLASS

Y44

TITLE

North country ghosts and legends

Terence Whitaker lives in Burnley, his home overlooking the brooding bulk of Pendle Hill, famous for its associations with the seventeenth-century witch trials.

Although born in South Yorkshire, he has spent most of his life in Lancashire. He was educated at Morecambe Grammar School, and had a varied career in the theatre, as a merchant seaman, a prison officer and a civil servant, before becoming a full-time writer and broadcaster.

He has presented several local radio series, and has taken part in national radio programmes on Radio 2 and 3, including 'The Stuart Hall Show' and more recently 'Gerald Main Time' from the Ideal Home Exhibition at Earls Court. He has also broadcast on local radio stations as far apart as Radio Oxford and Radio Cumbria.

Several appearances on the regional television magazine programme 'Northwest Tonight' resulted in his own television series from Manchester, when his first book *Lancashire's Ghosts and Legends* was adapted successfully for television.

Apart from books, magazine and newspaper articles on ghosts and legends, Terence Whitaker has written on such diverse subjects as the double murderer Dr Buck Ruxton, the theatre and the River Lune, as well as writing an award-winning comedy play. He also lectures and runs evening classes on local history, legends and folklore.

Married, with a daughter at Leeds University, he is currently preparing material for a further television series.

By the same author

Books

Lancashire's Ghosts and Legends
Yorkshire's Ghosts and Legends
Dr Ruxton of Lancaster
The Ghosts of Olde England

Play

He'll Have To Go, Mrs Lovejoy

Radio

'Ghosthunt'
'The Timeless River'
'Christmas Ghosthunt'

Television

'Ghosts and Legends'

TERENCE W. WHITAKER

North Country Ghosts and Legends

GRAFTON BOOKS

A Division of the Collins Publishing Group

LONDON GLASGOW
TORONTO SYDNEY AUCKLAND

Grafton Books
A Division of the Collins Publishing Group
8 Grafton Street, London W1X 3LA

A Grafton Paperback Original 1988

Part One (*Yorkshire's Ghosts and Legends*)
first published in Great Britain by
Grafton Books 1983

Copyright © Terence W. Whitaker 1983, 1988

ISBN 0-586-07474-0   03546667

Printed and bound in Great Britain by
Collins, Glasgow

Set in Garamond

In memory of Ruth Bates

Contents

Contents

Foreword

Ever since I stayed in a haunted house in my late teens I have had a healthy respect for ghosts. Although I am well aware how lively one's imagination can be in the wee small hours of the morning, seeing is believing. Much can be explained away by perfectly natural causes, we all know, but there remains the inexplicable: when the impossible can no longer be ruled out and the unbelievable becomes the acceptable.

Terence Whitaker has devoted much of his life to chasing this unbelievable; to ruling out reason and to finally accepting that all around are mysterious ghostly phenomena which defy all human explanation.

Born in Yorkshire and living in Lancashire, Terence has found more than enough to interest him in his own counties. Two of his previous books, *Yorkshire's Ghosts and Legends* and *Lancashire's Ghosts and Legends*, have more than whetted the appetites of the sceptics and fascinated the open-minded.

A well-known broadcaster, Terence's cheery face belies his haunting pursuits. A more down-to-earth man it would be hard to find. His ghostly interest has led him to some interesting corners and corridors of our county. When a ghost in Chipping walked through a wall in a public house, it was later discovered that once, long ago, there was a door in the wall leading into the kitchen at the very spot where the ghostly serving wench had disappeared.

And, as one ghost leads to another, there is still a wealth of material – or should we say 'ectoplasm' – for him to explore; legends handed down from generation to generation to be verified. Whether you believe them or not, they make fascinating reading. Read on and let Terence Whitaker convince you.

Joan K. Laprell
Features Editor, *The Lancashire Magazine*

Preface

Ghosts, ghouls – call them what you will. But what are they? Well, for a start, they are world-wide phenomena which have been recorded throughout history, appearing in a variety of shapes and forms and without seeming, in many cases, to have or serve any purpose.

The most widespread, of course, is the ghost of a human being, appearing sometimes as solid-looking as one's neighbour, or as a mist-like entity, roughly human in shape, which will disappear just as suddenly as it appeared. Yet, despite investigation, many reported sightings remain a complete mystery, and any explanation as to the reasoning behind the most persistent haunting is, at the most, theoretical.

And many theories abound. The most widespread popular belief is that ghosts are evil manifestations of the dead, a belief which carries with it the supposition that ghosts are intelligent in some way.

Another popular theory suggests that the spirits of some dead persons must remain earthbound for one reason or another, perhaps to atone for some earlier misdeed, or to avenge themselves for some crime committed against them during their lifetime. Perhaps the spirit does not realize it is dead, or perhaps the person so loved the place in life that he cannot bear to leave it even in death.

Is a ghost some form of energy left behind at the point of death? One theory suggests that it could be, for it is a well-known fact that energy cannot be destroyed. This same energy makes us walk, move, breathe, eat, yet on death the body suddenly becomes devoid of energy. What happens to it? Where does this energy go if it cannot be destroyed? Is this what causes the paranormal movement of objects to occur? The Greek philosopher, Athenodus, thought so when he put forward the theory nearly 2,000 years ago.

However, more modern evidence points to another, more plausible theory. Ghosts can be likened to television images. Such recorded images have no consciousness and therefore have neither good nor evil intent, and the circumstances in which they are seen seem to suggest that they are simply playbacks of incidents and strong emotions from the past, triggered off in the percipient's own brain, possibly by some type of impression left in the ether or the fabric of the location by the person whose ghost is seen. Perhaps a strong emotion experienced by the individual at the time of death, who later appears as a ghost, caused some impression to be stored in some way, only to be transmitted again, given the right conditions. No one really knows.

In the majority of modern reports, ghosts appear as living people, as solid-looking as you or I. In fact they can look so real that it is only their unnatural behaviour – such as floating above the ground, or walking through solid walls – that tells us that something is going on which is not quite right.

However, not all ghosts fit into these categories. Many were invented or based on some ancient legend to cover up various nefarious activities. Stories connected with haunted graveyards, for instance, are often of eighteenth- and nineteenth-century origin, intended to cover up the activities of body-snatchers, and many an old manor house has an associated ghost story, intended to account for the shadowy figures and flickering lights which might have been seen in the grounds at the time when Roman Catholics were cruelly persecuted, or to cover up the activities of coin-clippers or smugglers.

When asked for his views on the subject of ghosts, Samuel Johnson considered it to be, 'One of the most important that can come before human understanding. A subject which, after five thousand years, is yet undecided.'

I don't expect, through this book, to settle the argument one way or another, but bearing in mind the evidence of over thirty years' interest in the subject, and the fact that it has been estimated that one person in ten will see a ghost in their own lifetime, then either a large number of people – and I include myself in this category – have been the victims of some kind of delusion, or ghosts really do exist.

Whether you believe in the supernatural or are a hardened sceptic, I hope that many of these stories will help you accept that not all supernatural phenomena are figments of the imagination, for many of these stories are the first-hand experiences of people I have met, or who have written to tell me of the apparitions they have to live or work with in their daily lives. Besides, let us admit it, we all enjoy a good ghost story. We all enjoy being frightened – always providing, of course, we are in the company of others and in warm, convivial surroundings.

As ever, so many people have been responsible for helping me write this book that it would be impossible to acknowledge them all by name. To my friends at BBC Radio and Television; to the many newspapers and magazine editors and the countless librarians who have gone to a great deal of trouble on my behalf; and to the many individual contributors, I offer my humble and sincere thanks.

There are three people who deserve a special mention: my wife Marjorie for her helpful suggestions, patience and understanding; Joan Laprell, for giving up her valuable time to write the Foreword; and Ruth Bates, a much-loved friend, who generously gave of her time to arrange some interviews on my behalf. Tragically she died during the preparation of this book.

To Ruth, and to all who helped or contributed in any way, this book is dedicated.

Burnley
1987

Yorkshire's Ghosts & Legends

Spectral Workmates

A broadcasting studio would, one might think, be the last place where one might meet a ghost. Not so, for the studios of BBC Radio Sheffield, built over a hundred years ago for a prominent citizen of the city, have a history which is beyond explanation, for amongst the modern, sophisticated equipment and the non-stop working atmosphere of today, something or somebody lingers.

I am indebted to Ralph Robinson, senior producer of BBC Radio Sheffield for allowing me to quote his article in the *Radio Sheffield Magazine*.

Says Ralph, 'It is one of the standing jokes of the station that the ghost may be somebody who was separated from a visiting party and expired whilst trying to find the way out.'

The building in Westbourne Road has a pleasant, rambling quality that can flummox many a first-time visitor. By day it can be eerie enough, but at night, with the wind rustling through the trees and the occasional owl hooting eerily in the branches, Ralph says, 'It can make Dracula's castle look like a Wendy house.'

Whoever or whatever the ghost might be, it is not a malevolent presence. Two people have claimed to have seen something, whilst others have heard it or sensed it. One young lady, who lives in Derbyshire, spent a late evening in Sheffield and had to get up very early in the morning to do an early shift at the studios. Instead of going home, she bedded down at the radio station but an hour later she got up and drove home because she felt she was not alone.

Ralph himself says that he has walked out three times late at night: once because strange things were happening to signal lights on electronic equipment and twice because he felt he was being watched.

A freelance reporter, Richard Hemmingway, was entirely on his own in the newsroom when he heard the front door open and footsteps go through the hall and up the stairs. He went to see who it was and found himself alone. Later he heard lights being switched on and off.

Not only is the presence felt late at night. One Sunday afternoon, engineer Peter Mason noticed that a recorded programme which was being broadcast had become barely audible. He hurried to the studio and found that a volume control knob on the main control panel had been turned down. No one had been in the studio and when he tried to reproduce the fault, he failed.

Two people, Gerry Kersey, BBC Radio Sheffield theatre critic, and Phil Baldy, former sports producer and reporter, have been closest to the ghost.

Gerry Kersey often works into the small hours and has become used to the clicks and bumps in other parts of the station, but one night he was really scared. He was passing a cupboard, when the door suddenly sprang open and tape spools started to come out, one at a time, as if being thrown. Gerry thought someone was having a joke at his expense. He flung the door wide open and was amazed to find no one there. On another occasion he was alone in the building at 2 A.M. and while editing a tape, he happened to glance up at the studio door. There is a square porthole in every such door at the radio station and Gerry swears he saw a shadow pass across it. He went out and called, but there was no one there.

Phil Baldy had the closest encounter of all one night in August 1978. Having finished the late news shift and feeling tired, he went to the door of the newsroom, which looks out on to the main stairway and an archway. At that moment, something white fluttered across the archway. It was no particular shape, just a white form, but there was no way in which Phil was going to investigate.

Shaken, he switched out all the lights; the last at the glass-panelled front door. The switch is four or five yards from the door and, having switched off, one has to grope for the door latch in the dark. Phil was unable to find the latch. He fumbled frantically in the dark while panic mounted. Finally he got the door open and with a sigh of relief, closed it behind him and turned to double lock it from the outside. The glass panels of the door reflected the yellow street lights in Westbourne Road behind him. He could see his reflection . . . except that the face he saw was not his. Needless to say, he fled.

Ralph said that when Phil told him the story the following day, he said that the face he saw was that of an old man. Phil was a young man!

The premises of the firm of Air Heating Limited, of Yeadon near Leeds, are subject to paranormal phenomena usually ascribed to poltergeist activities. The incidents were first reported in 1970, having been occurring over a period of eight or nine months.

The building, according to the records, was originally constructed as a church in 1834 and later it became a church school. At the turn of the century, a brewer's dray ran out of control and collided with the building. The driver was thrown through a window and died instantly. This could possibly be the cause of the present phenomena but more likely is the fact that during the Second World War, when the building was turned over to industry and became a sheet-metal workshop, the owner was interested in spiritualism and it is said that he often held seances there.

During certain hours of the day it was impossible to do any work in one particular office, because of the inexplicable happenings which took place. A tin of paint was mysteriously flung across the office, denting a door and bursting open on the carpet. A heavy desk moved right across the room of its own accord, telephones were dashed against the walls and heavy cabinets toppled over.

A local vicar exorcized the place and although these occurrences are not as frequent, nor as drastic as on earlier occasions, strange things still happen from time to time, I'm told.

The showrooms of the Yorkshire Electricity Board in Mexborough have a record of odd happenings, which have taken place over the past twenty-five years or so, according to Mr C. R. Pocklington, who worked for the YEB in various capacities for twenty-seven years, until his retirement in 1974. He spent the last sixteen as a salesman in the Mexborough shop, and says:

'Over the years a lady assistant became such a bag of nerves, she had to retire early. A male assistant, who though normal enough when he commenced at the shop, soon required intensive psychiatric treatment and a young female assistant who was married at the age of twenty-one, became a widow less than three weeks later.'

Mr Pocklington himself had very little time off work through ill health, but in 1959 he suffered a stroke which robbed him of the use of one eye and put him off work for nine weeks. He continues: 'We eventually brought these happenings to the attention of the Area Manager, because we felt they were too much of a coincidence and because we felt there was something malevolent about the shop. The Area Manager was sceptical and said that these things could have happened anywhere.'

Some time in 1969, Mr Pocklington was alone in the shop, the other two assistants having gone to lunch, when a man came in and made a purchase from the 'small items' counter on the left of the shop floor. Mr Pocklington took the cash from the customer and, as he did so, saw a lady bending over a display in the centre of the shop floor. He told me: 'She was dressed entirely in a black, shiny material, with a broad hem on the jacket and three parts of the skirt. She wore black stockings and a good pair of black shoes. I couldn't see her face.'

Telling the lady he would only keep her waiting a second or two, Mr Pocklington turned around to put the cash from the man's purchase in the cash register behind him, a mere two or three seconds, and then turned back to serve the lady, but she had disappeared. She could not have gone out of the shop in the length of time it took to put the money in the cash register and although Mr Pocklington searched the shop and looked outside, he says he could find no trace of her.

Was this the malevolent spirit which had caused so much distress in the past? Or was it the ghost of some previous occupant of the site? It appears, so far as I can ascertain, that the premises were built in 1936 on ground which was barren with no record of any previous building on the site. Mr Pocklington told me that as a boy he used to walk over the land occasionally on his way to the local grammar school during the period 1924–8. So we will probably never know the origin of the spectre, nor who or what caused the mysterious sounds of movement on the lower level of the showroom floor, or why the shop would sometimes go very cold for no apparent reason. At the time of writing, the YEB have moved to new premises and this shop is now empty.

Not far from the centre of Huddersfield there used to be a cinema which rejoiced in the title of 'The Grand'. Over the years it has seen a number of changes, graduating from a dance hall and bingo hall, until today it is in use as a night-club. Some time ago, Mrs Madeline Dannott and her husband were employed at the club and she related a number of rather unusual experiences they had while working there.

On more than one occasion they heard footsteps on the balcony, but on investigation found no one. Doors opened and closed by themselves and the sound of breaking glass was often heard, but again on investigation, nothing appeared to have been disturbed or damaged. Mrs Dannott told me: 'It was alleged in the local newspapers that only men heard these noises, but I know that I too have heard them.' What causes these ghostly noises?

It is thought to be the ghost of an elderly woman and goes back to the days when the club was a bingo hall. Apparently, in those days a person having a large win at bingo had to return at a later date to collect their winnings. The lady in question appears to have won quite a sizeable amount, but it seems that the excitement proved too much for her and she was called to her Maker, before she had time to call for her winnings. So now she haunts the passage near the room where the money would have been paid out, supposedly seeking her night's winnings. A dedicated bingo fan indeed!

The Leeds Library, which was founded as far back as 1768, is the oldest organization of its kind in the country and it was in this old and dignified building that the ghost of a former librarian, Thomas Sternberg, was allegedly seen late in the last century.

Thomas Sternberg was appointed librarian in 1857 and died in office in 1879. He was a fine, handsome man with a good head of hair, close-cropped beard and moustache; erect, suave and very courteous. He was, in effect, a ladies' man who was well liked and respected by staff and public alike. Following his death, John MacAlister, sub-librarian of the Liverpool Library, was appointed as his successor and it was he who was to have the first sighting of old Mr Sternberg's ghost.

Late one evening in the spring of 1884, MacAlister was alone in the library. He was working in his office, which was separated from the main library by a short passage. In those days the building was lit by gas and, as the main room was in darkness, MacAlister had to use a lamp to find his way from his office, through the main room which, like his office, was on the first floor, down the stairs and through the ground-floor room to the street when he was ready to leave. Noticing the late hour, he decided he must leave at once if he was to catch the last train home to Harrogate.

Picking up his lamp, he turned into the passage leading to the library proper and, to his surprise, he saw at the far end of it what appeared to be a man's face. His first thoughts were that a thief had broken into the building. He turned back to his room and took a revolver from his safe and then, holding the lamp behind him, he made his way along the passage and into the room. He saw no one at first, but as he moved cautiously past the rows of bookcases, he saw the face peering around the end of a row. It had an odd appearance, as if the body were inside the bookcase with just the head sticking out. The face was pallid and hairless and the orbits of the eyes were very deep. He advanced towards it and as he did so, he saw a man with high shoulders who seemed to rotate out of the end of the bookcase and, with his back towards him, walk with a rather quick shuffling gait, from the bookcase to the door of a small lavatory.

He heard no noise and following the man quickly into the lavatory was surprised to find no one there. MacAlister confessed later to experiencing then, for the first time, an eerie feeling. Quickly he left the library, only to discover he had missed his last train.

The following morning he mentioned what he had seen to the Rev. Charles Hargrove, a member of the Library Committee, who after listening politely suggested that the description fitted that of Thomas Sternberg. The ghost was seen several times after that by various members of staff, but to my knowledge it has not been seen this century. Why it should suddenly appear and just as suddenly cease to haunt the library is beyond me. Perhaps it is sufficient to relate that the ghost was never seen again after 1887, when John MacAlister left to take up another appointment in London.

Another library which provides us with a more up-to-date ghost story is that at the York Museum, where at 7.40 one Sunday evening in September 1953, a strange thing happened which was to result in a great deal of publicity in the national press.

On the evening in question George Jonas, the caretaker, was waiting for a meeting to finish and was sitting enjoying a quiet cup of tea. Eventually the meeting ended and after seeing everyone off the premises, Mr Jonas set out to make a final check on the building before leaving himself. As he left his room, he heard footsteps and thinking the curator was still in his office, went to speak to him. However, instead of finding the curator, Mr Jonas was confronted by a complete stranger, busily engaged in searching for something in the museum office.

The man was bent over in the far corner of the room. He straightened up as the caretaker walked in, turned round and walked out of the room, passing Mr Jonas as he did so. Mr Jonas at first thought that it was someone who had stayed behind after the meeting. He followed the man out of the room, remaining a few steps behind him. He later told the press, 'I noticed then that he was dressed in a frock coat and drainpipe trousers, rather like an old professor; and wore elastic-sided boots. I noticed this quite distinctly, as there were no turn-ups on his trousers.' Mr Jonas then went on to describe how he had followed the figure into the library, turning on the lights as he did so, and heard the man speaking slowly, as if to himself, saying, 'I must find it – I must find it!'

The figure moved about from bookshelf to bookshelf, rummaging among the volumes and Mr Jonas went up to him and said, 'If you want to see the curator, I'll escort you across to his house.' As he spoke, he reached out to touch the man's arm, but as he did so the figure simply vanished, much to his bewilderment. Before vanishing, the man dropped a volume he had withdrawn from the shelf, the title of which was *Antiques and Curiosities of the Church*. The caretaker left the book where it had fallen and the following morning told the whole incredible story to the curator.

Four Sundays later Mr Jonas saw the apparition again. The figure of the old man crossed the hall and simply faded through the locked doors and into the library. Again, a month later, Mr Jonas and a friend heard the turning of pages and saw the identical book drop to the floor. It now became obvious that proper investigations should be carried out to determine just who the phantom reader was and, as a result, six people gathered in the museum's library one Sunday evening in December 1953, and sat waiting for the ghostly apparition. A careful check had been made beforehand and all present, a doctor, a solicitor, Mr Jonas and his brother and two representatives of the press, agreed that any form of trickery was out of the question.

On previous occasions the ghost had appeared at exactly 7.40 P.M. but on this occasion it was 7.48 when the first phenomena occurred and the gathering heard a rubbing sound and saw a book slowly withdraw from the shelf and drop to the floor, remaining in an upright position. No figure was seen, but the watchers felt their legs become uncomfortably cold up to the knees and all present were convinced that they had been witness to the activity of a supernatural agency.

Whose ghost was this? Theory had it that it was the apparition of Alderman Edward Wooler, a Darlington solicitor and antiquary who had died in 1921 and who had owned the book in question. However, since that night in December 1953, the ghost has never been seen, so it has not been possible for positive identification to be made. Several people have investigated in recent years, but have reported nothing other than the feeling of unnatural coldness.

* * *

While I was on a visit to Hull in 1972, a relative, knowing of my interest in ghosts and the supernatural, took me to a smart hairdressing salon in Whitefriargate, not far from Paragon station in the city centre. I don't know whether the salon is still there, but at that time the ghostly activities of an anonymous and noisy phantom were causing something of a stir in the town.

If I remember correctly, the owners were then a Mr and Mrs Hardy or Hartley. They had become so disturbed late in 1971 by mysterious noises coming from an upstairs room that they had called the police. The sounds, which had been heard by customers and staff alike, were those of someone slowly pacing the floor of the empty room and dragging something towards the door. This was followed by further shufflings and scuffling.

The police had to admit that they were baffled by it all but they locked the door and fitted trip wires. They were even more baffled when the sounds continued and when, on opening up the room, they found it remained undisturbed, although the lights had been mysteriously switched on. Investigations by the police, the local press and others, including the author, have failed to come up with any reasonable explanation for the unaccountable noises which continued for some time after that and, for all I know, are still being heard.

The *Wharfedale and Airedale Observer* of 1883 tells of a mysterious happening which took place in a small cobbler's workshop in the village of Timble, on the southern slopes of the Washburn valley, in 1825.

In that year, a young shoemaker called William Holmes rented a small house and workshop, where he lived and worked alone. Like most cobblers and shoemakers of that time, he used a glue which was kept in a sizing tin. In the course of time, he noticed that on some mornings the sizing tin, which he had left empty the previous night, filled with leather parings and odd scraps from his workbench. Soon it began to be filled regularly and he noticed that on top of the tin there were always two long strips laid crosswise.

At first William Holmes thought it was the local village lads playing tricks on him, so he began to lock and shutter his windows at night as well as his door, and he made sure before he went to bed each night that the glue tin was empty. However, the next morning the tin would again be filled.

One night he balanced the tin on an upright iron rod which he had driven into a wooden block. The slightest touch would upset it. Needless to say, the following morning the tin was found to be filled, but remained undisturbed, precariously balanced, as he had left it the previous night.

Next, Holmes decided that each night he would sweep up every scrap of leather left over from his day's work. It made not the slightest difference, except that now the tin was found to be full of an assortment of broken glass and bits of wood and it still had the usual cross on top. William Holmes was, to say the least, perplexed. He went to discuss his problem with the local vicar, who agreed that, with his friend the village tailor, he would stay the night at the house and try to solve the mystery.

So, a few nights later, the vicar and the tailor stayed in the house, sitting up all night while William got some sleep. The next morning, both the vicar and the tailor testified to hearing a noise during the night which sounded like quick, short breathing. They also shamefully confessed to being too afraid to go down to the workshop to investigate. Holmes said he slept soundly all night and heard nothing. The tin in the meantime had been filled up again.

Some weeks later, Holmes having finished his evening meal decided to go and visit one of his near neighbours. He went out of the house, locking the door behind him. On returning later that night, he was surprised to find the tin was partly filled, and for the first time he began to feel frightened. He gave up renting the house and moved to lodgings elsewhere and the mystery of the tidying-up ghost, or whatever it was, was never solved, although William Holmes, in later years a successful farmer, told the story up until the day he died in 1850. He always maintained that the ghost was that of Tommy Kaye, an idiot boy who had lived in the village, but had died several years before these events took place. Even as late as 1883 there were still a number of people living in the village who remembered the curious incident.

RAF Lindholme at Hatfield, near Doncaster, was haunted by the ghost of a big man in aircrew uniform. It first made its appearance in 1947 when a group of airmen returning to the base saw it walking out on the marshes nearby. It soon became known as 'Lindholme Willie' by both airmen and local people, several of whom have seen it in more recent years.

The villagers of Hatfield believe the ghost to be that of an airman killed in a crash on the marshes during the Second World War and every description of him has been the same. In November 1957, a corporal in Air Traffic Control at the base reported seeing 'Willie's' misty shape walking on the runway, having come from the direction of the marshes. Knowing an aircraft was due to land and thinking someone had strayed on the runway, he radioed control to alert them, but before he could take a closer look, the figure vanished.

Another ghost, which sets off a burglar alarm for no apparent reason, is giving the staff at one town hall in North Yorkshire the creeps. Members of the town hall staff say it could be the pranks of a ghost called 'Oscar'. Even security experts cannot guess what makes the flashing-light alarm at the town hall go haywire from time to time. The Mayor has said that the warning lights go on in the town hall, but not in the local police station as they should. Some people who have investigated have reported seeing a strange figure lurking in the shadows.

Who was 'Oscar'? My own enquiries lead me to believe he was a man who was arrested for fighting in a drunken brawl sometime during the 1880s and who hanged himself in the police cells, which used to be below the town hall, now probably trying to get his own back.

On a June night in 1956, seven workmen settled down to sleep in makeshift beds and sleeping-bags which had been provided for them on the ground floor of Watton Abbey, near Driffield. The owner was selling up after a tenancy of over thirty years and the workmen had come up from Retford in Nottinghamshire to help with the three-day sale of furniture and fittings of the old abbey.

A fierce June wind howled around the reputedly haunted building as they slept. Then, at about one o'clock in the morning, above the high wind could be heard the eerie tolling of a bell.

Every one of the workmen awoke at once and sat bolt upright in their beds, spines tingling and the hair rising at the back of their necks, for they knew that the abbey bell had been removed many years before.

One man was so afraid that he dived head first through a window, injuring himself when he landed in a flower bed. The auctioneer's foreman in charge of the men grabbed a shotgun, loaded it and fired off both barrels skywards. This had the desired effect and the bell suddenly ceased its tolling. As one, the men picked up their beds and bedrolls and spent the remainder of the night in a large marquee which had been erected in the grounds of the abbey to hold the auction. They were taking no chances, for there was no doubt in their minds that the ringing was the work of the headless ghost of Watton, the nun, Elfrida (see 'Ghostly Monks and Phantom Nuns', page 92).

As I began this chapter with a haunted broadcasting studio, so I will end it.

'The staff at BBC Radio Leeds have for years worked alongside a ghost, and flying kettle lids and eerie footsteps are accepted nowadays without question.' So says Caroline Woodruff, now of BBC Radio Manchester.

The BBC took over Broadcasting House in Woodhill Lane some time in the 1930s, and even at this time members of staff were claiming to have seen the hooded figure of the so-called 'Grey Lady' gliding across the gallery into studio two and disappearing through the opposite wall. The 'Grey Lady' apparently gets her name from the fact that she has never been seen in colour, but in varying shades of grey and black. She moves just above the ground, something which is accounted for by the fact that the ground levels of the building were altered when the 'Beeb' took over. Today, no one claims to have witnessed the ghost, but other unaccountable sights and sensations have led a number of employees to refuse to work alone in this part of the building.

Seventy-six-year-old Albert Aldred recalled working at the studios during the Second World War and hearing footsteps in the gallery at night when no one else was in the place. He said they sounded more as if they were walking on carpet, rather than on the present stone floor. He knew a lot of the staff in those days used to hear things and some of them actually resigned through fear.

In December 1978, Sharon Carter began work at the studios as a part-time receptionist. Now she refuses to enter the upstairs restroom. She said, 'I wouldn't go into that room again after what happened to me.' Apparently, one Sunday evening just before seven o'clock, Sharon was in the restroom talking to a friend on the telephone. There was a kettle on the floor and for no reason at all the lid suddenly turned round and flew across the room, landing in the sink at the other side with a resounding crash. Sharon said, 'There was no one else around and I certainly didn't put it there. The room had been very cold where I had been sitting, but it was really warm in the area around the sink.'

Caroline Woodruff told me that when she was working at Radio Leeds, a member of the Radio Leeds newsroom staff arrived for work early one morning to find tapes and papers strewn across the room for no apparent reason; and a typewriter had been overturned. Many of the staff find the building a little eerie at night and Caroline, then a station assistant, was working there one Sunday night when she got a distinctly cold feeling about her. She told me: 'I was not imagining things. Although it was eleven o'clock at night and I was the only person in the place, I got the feeling that I was not alone. I jolly soon picked up the tapes I was editing and took them down into the studios to finish them.' Caroline said that, after that, she would not edit at the studios at night, nor would she go into studio two, next to the gallery, at night either.

Investigations have consistently failed to shed any light on the ghost or its origins. There is, however, a theory that the 'Grey Lady' is in some way connected with the Quakers who occupied the building before the BBC took it over. She does seem to appear most often on a Sunday, so perhaps she feels that the staff would be better engaged in religious activities rather than working on the Sabbath. However, the present staff do not view her as a threat in any way.

What one might call a 'radio active' ghost, perhaps?

Mysterious Grey Ladies

The visitor to Yorkshire is well catered for when it comes to stately homes, castles, country houses and halls. Nearly all of them have their resident grey lady. In many cases the reason behind the haunting has been lost in the mists of time, or the details have become distorted over the years in the re-telling. Even the identity of the ghost in question is often shrouded in mystery or in a mixture of fact and fantasy. Many of the ghosts in this chapter have never been seen by anyone within living memory, but others, the ghosts of older private houses and farms, have been seen recently and will continue to be seen for some time to come.

Rose Cottage stands in a small village near Halifax and was for some years the home of the daughter of Mr C. Robinson of Norton Tower, Halifax, to whom I am indebted for the following story.

It appears that the cottage was built on the site of an old Quaker chapel and when, in the course of time, parts of the cottage were knocked down and a kitchen extension and bathroom were built, this encroached on the old graveyard and may have been the cause of the frequent manifestations which the family afterwards witnessed.

Mr Robinson told me: 'When my daughter was expecting and towards the end of her pregnancy, she was unable to sleep too well at night. So as not to keep disturbing her husband, she decided to sleep downstairs on the large settee. One night she woke up and was surprised to see a lady, dressed in a long dark dress with white collar and cuffs, standing at one end of the settee, looking down at her.' She was not in the least frightened by this and even forgot about it, neglecting to tell her husband.

Some time later the cottage was sold to a couple who had lived for many years in Australia, and who had returned to this country on retirement.

Mr Robinson continued: 'A few weeks after moving in, my son-in-law happened to meet the new owners and they asked him why he hadn't mentioned the ghost to them. Tony, my son-in-law, had not experienced it and admitted he knew nothing about it.' Apparently, the ghost of the woman had been seen quite frequently by the new owners. She would just appear and stand looking at them for about a minute, before fading away. Their fourteen-year-old niece had also seen it and a nephew almost walked into the ghost in the passage.

'One weekend,' said Mr Robinson, 'the wife took ill. Her husband spent the first night of her illness in the small bedroom and awoke in the early hours to find the ghost of the woman standing at the foot of his bed. Her arms were folded and she appeared to be shaking her head as if to say, "I am very sorry." The man was most alarmed at this, for he took it to mean that something was going to happen to his wife.'

It didn't. The ghost was in fact referring to him, for exactly two weeks later the poor man collapsed and died!

A far happier spectre was seen by eleven-year-old Philip Lawton one winter's evening in 1945 when, with his parents, he lived on a farm above Huddersfield. Parts of the building dated back to the sixteenth century. Mr Lawton told me: 'I lived in one of the farm cottages, across the yard from the old farmhouse itself, which was occupied by my uncle. On this particular evening I was asked to take something across to the house for my uncle. In crossing the yard, I had to pass an old coach house, the huge doors of which had long since disappeared.'

Passing the entrance to this old building, he happened to glance in and a movement from inside caught his eye, causing him to stop and look closer. Coming out of the doorway was a stout woman, wearing a long blue dress over the front of which was a white apron. On her head she wore what he could only describe as a 'mob cap' and she was carrying a large basket containing what appeared to be laundry. Mr Lawton continued: 'I can see her now in my mind, so clearly. She came to within a yard of where I was standing and then she just smiled at me and vanished. I can clearly remember the scent of her cleanliness, a soapy odour which surrounded her. Her arms were fat and red, as was her face.'

He said he was not the least bit afraid. The whole thing lasted for no more than half a minute, but it was, to his young mind, a pleasant and in a sense a comforting experience. The identity of the ghostly lady remains a mystery, but does it really matter who she is? To house such a friendly shade of the past just adds to the attraction of these old Yorkshire farming communities.

Standing on the right-hand side of Thornhill Road in Rastrick are two delightful cottages, which are thought to have been converted from an inn, built in 1690 on the site of earlier premises. My family and I spent a pleasant afternoon here in the spring of 1980, discussing with Mr and Mrs Auty, the present occupiers, some of the strange goings-on which had occurred over the past six years.

Marilyn Auty told me that the occurrences began shortly after they had moved into the house in November 1974. At first she used to hear a low whistling noise which continued on and off for several weeks, until it became loud enough to be heard over the noise of the television and was accompanied by an annoying tapping sound, which seemed to emanate from the lounge ceiling and move from one end of the room to the other. It continued for periods lasting several hours.

More recently a figure had been seen and a mysterious fine film of swirling smoke. Mrs Auty said, 'My husband had just retired to bed one night recently and I was tidying up downstairs before going up myself. As I went to turn out the lounge light, I saw what appeared to be a fine film of smoke near the front door, which swirled for a few seconds before disappearing.' Some days later she was vacuuming upstairs, when from the lounge came a loud tapping noise as if someone was knocking with a coin on a pane of glass. Thinking someone was at the front door, Mrs Auty went downstairs only to find no one at either the front or back door. Puzzled, she began to go back upstairs and on nearing the landing saw a 'long, thin, filmy, cloudlike thing' glide straight past her and cross the top of the stairs from one landing to the other. By the time she reached the top it had vanished.

That evening, over dinner Marilyn Auty started to tell her husband of her experience. For a while he listened politely and then suddenly his face changed. She said, 'He looked straight past me and fixed his gaze on something behind me.' This was at a very large and very old picture on the wall which was visibly swaying from side to side.

Her husband told me that he always felt as though someone was watching. There was often a strange atmosphere on the stairs and Mrs Auty's sister refused to go up them whenever she visited the house. People had told them that while they were away from the house, a figure was seen peering through the bedroom window at the front. Was this the same figure that had been seen by Mr Auty? He told me, 'Marilyn was in hospital at the time. I had been to visit her and arriving home at about 8 o'clock, I made myself a snack and sat on the settee to eat it. Suddenly, from the door leading to the kitchen a woman in grey floated across the room and vanished near the front door. She wore a cloak over her grey dress and appeared to have been cut off at the knees.' The floor in this room had been raised by Mr Auty, who is a joiner, with the original flagged floor remaining intact beneath it. During our visit I made several attempts to photograph Mr and Mrs Auty near the doorway where the figure entered. On each occasion my flash-gun failed to operate and it was only after I had asked them to sit in a different place that I was able to obtain my photograph.

About a week after our visit, Marilyn Auty wrote to me to tell me of an incident which happened just after we had left. She said, 'After your visit, my husband went to do some work in his garden whilst I remained in the lounge. About an hour elapsed, when I heard someone call my name. As I got up from the chair I heard it again, very clearly and sounding most perturbed. Thinking it was my husband, I rushed into the kitchen only to find it empty and I could see him busy digging at the bottom of the garden.'

Who or what haunts this cottage is obviously friendly towards the young couple and although these occurrences startle them from time to time, they are in no way afraid. Why should they be? The house has a lovely friendly atmosphere about it.

More recently, I again interviewed Mr and Mrs Auty for my 'Ghosthunt' series, when Marilyn told me of other experiences – such as neighbours complaining about a bell ringing in the early hours of the morning.

'The neighbours asked who kept ringing a bell in the small hours. But we said it could not have been coming from here. However, they persisted so we agreed to ring every bell we have in the house. It was to no avail, they couldn't recognize the sound of any of them,' she told me. 'Then I remembered a bell at the top of the stairs, although this had been broken by my nephew, who had lost the clapper out of it. But, just to check, I rang it with a pen and to our amazement, they agreed that this was the sound they had heard!'

Most of the incidents seem to centre round the staircase, which was put in when the cottage was renovated. Mr and Mrs Auty believe that there may have been a room here at some time in the past for this has been the scene of the strangest events. None stranger than the day Marilyn suddenly found herself at the bottom of the stairs, not knowing how she had got there. She told me: 'I picked myself up after coming to with a sharp pain at the back of my head. I had been getting ready to go shopping and was going to catch the two o'clock bus into town. When I did eventually get to the bus stop, a neighbour asked me what bus I was waiting for. I told her and she said that it had gone long since – It was twenty past two!' She still has no idea what happened to her in those lost twenty minutes.

Not so with Greenfield Lodge though. Greenfield Lodge, well known amongst hikers and cyclists for its cuisine, stands high above the reservoirs on Rishworth Moor near Scammonden dam. It is a fifteen-roomed Georgian house with Victorian additions and when originally built was called 'Red House'. In 1847, it became known as Greenfield Lodge and then, around 1860 when a barn and stables were added, it was renamed 'Parkfield Hall', although for some reason it has reverted to the name of Greenfield Lodge.

During the past twenty-odd years, while it has been occupied by its present owners, a number of strange incidents have occurred. Until recent years when they began to keep cows for their own milk production, milk was delivered from a farm nearby. One morning, the lady who delivered it was making her way to the Lodge in her Landrover and had the feeling she was not alone in the vehicle. When she pulled up outside Greenfield Lodge, she was terrified to see the passenger door open and close by itself, as if an invisible passenger had got out. On another occasion, the screech of brakes on the road outside late at night caused the occupants of the Lodge to dash to the bedroom windows to see what had happened. I was told that a car had come to a grinding halt in the middle of the road and the driver, a man, was examining the orchard gate, directly opposite the house. The gates were securely fastened, but his passenger, a young woman, appeared to be very frightened for she was heard to say, 'Come on, let's get out of here,' and, pointing to Greenfield Lodge, 'It came from out of there.' The man got into the car which sped off noisily into the night.

Could this have been a recurrence of something which happened twenty years earlier? When the family were moving in, the husband had brought a trailer-load of furniture from their home in Rotherham and as it was rather late he decided to bed down for the night at Greenfield Lodge.

He was awakened during the small hours by the sound of children. It seemed quite light outside and on looking out of the window he saw a group of children singing and shouting in the forecourt and completely ignoring the car and trailer parked there. He watched as the group then walked down towards the Brown Cow Inn a few hundred yards away, across the road to the gates of Mount Pleasant Farm and then back towards the stables of Greenfield Lodge, before vanishing as if into thin air. No one knows to this day who those children were, but later investigations show that many years ago the Lodge had been inhabited by an order of monks who used it as a children's home and the ten stables, now in ruins, had been in use as dormitories.

The house itself has a more interesting spectre, thought to be the ghost of Elizabeth Emmet who, in 1834 (as far as I can make out from the mass of legal documents I was allowed to examine during my visit to the house), either came into possession of Greenfield Lodge or died there during that year. The ghost invariably appears whenever some work is about to be undertaken, or when alterations are made to the house. She wears a long grey skirt and a high-necked blouse with a row of buttons down the front. Her hair is parted down the centre and fastened in a bun on the top of her head. However, it is not possible to make out her features, for invariably her hands appear to be covering her face as if she is weeping uncontrollably.

On another occasion, the family were away and a friend of theirs was staying to look after the house. She was sitting alone on the settee in the dining room, when the kitchen door at one end of the room opened and closed. She sensed someone or something cross the room, which had turned extremely cold, and then, to her utter amazement, the door which leads into the hall opened and closed.

For many years, the house has had one room which is used as a café. One afternoon, a coachload of women arrived for afternoon tea. As they were about to leave, a woman was seen to come out of the living room, where no one should have been, and go upstairs. The bus driver called to see if all were on the coach and he was told to wait because someone had been seen going upstairs. Investigation proved that no one was there, although there was no way in which she could have got out again without being seen.

Many times visitors to the house have heard noises upstairs, as if a person is moving about. These noises occur at all times of the day and night. A woman's voice can often be heard, although muffled, repeating a single word. In one corner of the living room, the lovely aroma of fish and chips can often be smelled, as if wafting up from the cellar underneath where some old fire ovens have been discovered recently. The sound of a car stopping outside when the road is empty and other mysterious happenings which one is hard put to explain, make this one of the most interesting houses I have visited during my researches. And although the family are exceptionally warm and friendly people who made me more than welcome, I got the feeling that the house itself is not friendly towards prying strangers. Even though it was a nice warm day, the house felt chilled and I regret to say that I was not sorry to turn my back on it.

Mrs Constance Drake of Halifax related an interesting story concerning a close friend of hers whose husband was the resident caretaker of Kirkby Hall, near York.

The Hall, the seat of the Crowther family, was built about 1750 alongside a Tudor dwelling which became an integral part, although most of the Tudor fabric was pulled down around 1949–50. Parts of the house surrounded an old cobbled court-yard and all the bedrooms that were in use overlooked the courtyard and outbuildings. In what is now called the dairy there is often a lovely smell of fresh baked bread, suggesting perhaps that this might have been a kitchen or bakehouse in days gone by. In the stone-flagged passageways on the ground floor the sound of running children's feet and the delicious rustle of silk, as if someone is chasing them, has been heard on several occasions.

Once, Mrs Clark, the caretaker's wife, expecting members of the Crowther family to return from a holiday, went into the library with the intention of giving it a good clean and polish and was more than horrified at the sight which met her eyes. The room looked as if a hurricane had blown through it. Papers were scattered, books had fallen from the shelves, ornaments appeared to have been thrown about, and on a small table lay a battered book, opened at a poem which she paused to read. Later, having tidied up, Mrs Clark fastened the room up and went about her other duties. Later in the day, she had occasion to go to the library for something and was dismayed to find that again it was in a state of disarray and the book was again lying open on the table, at the same page. No one has ever been able to explain the significance of this.

By far the most interesting experience happened several months later. Mrs Crowther had received a letter from an elderly lady who lived away from the area and who had been associated with the house in her younger days. The lady said that she would like a last look at the house before she died, as it had such happy memories. As Mrs Crowther knew the lady she replied that she was most welcome to look over the house again, but that she herself would not be at home and the caretaker's wife would receive her.

Mrs Clark was instructed that the elderly lady would be driving herself up to the house on a certain day and she was to be made to feel at home, be shown round the house and be given a cup of tea. The day duly arrived and as it wore on, it seemed that the visitor was not going to call after all. By 11.30 that night, Mrs Clark knew there was no chance of her coming that day and retired to bed.

At about two in the morning Mrs Clark was awoken by the sound of a car and saw the reflection of headlights in the room. Getting out of bed and looking through the window, she was surprised to see a Standard Vanguard draw up in the courtyard and a white-haired lady get out and close the car door with a bang. Mrs Clark opened the window to call out that she would come down to the front door, when the woman suddenly got back into the car and drove off. It was only afterwards that Mrs Clark realized the car had driven straight through the locked gates!

The following morning Mrs Crowther telephoned and Mrs Clark told her what had happened, that the visitor had come late in the night and had driven off before she could open the door. Mrs Clark was quite taken aback when she was informed by Mrs Crowther that it was not possible, for the old lady had been killed at two o'clock the previous afternoon, when her Standard Vanguard had been in a collision with another vehicle.

In 1934, a nineteen-year-old girl whom, to respect her wish to remain anonymous, I will call Gemma, went to work at Nafferton Hall, between Driffield and Bridlington, as a domestic maid. She told me: 'It was in the middle of winter. I knew very little of Nafferton, coming as I did from some miles away and I knew very little about the Hall.'

As was customary for maids of that period, Gemma was given a bedroom in the attic. The Hall had been converted to electricity by this time, but the cellars and the servants' quarters had not been connected up and therefore they still had to use candles. Gemma continued: 'On going to bed on my very first night there, I had an odd sort of feeling. I can't say I felt frightened, more uncomfortable really. I did not like the room I had been given and after a few nights I took the precaution of wedging a penknife in the latch, so that it could not be opened. We had no locks on the doors. One night I felt so uncomfortable, I lit my candle with my eyes shut as I was afraid of what I might see in the dark.'

She says she had the same feeling in the cellars, in particular the apple cellar. She hated going in there. There was a large slab in the cellar floor with a ring in it, which was said to be the entrance to an underground passage. The door to the apple cellar was always open and this frightened the young girl, who had to pass it every time she went to the dairy. However, more of this later. After a while, Gemma made friends with the cook and mentioned to her the feelings she had both in her room and in the cellar. The cook told her that she had heard tales of a 'white lady' haunting the Hall. Gemma says, 'I never saw her, but I got the feeling she was connected with my bedroom in some way and that she was watching me whenever I was in there.'

The following summer, two young men came to spend the weekend at Nafferton Hall. They were students and friends of the family, who used to be invited quite often. On this particular occasion, they were to sleep in the empty room immediately beneath the attic room where Gemma slept. She said, 'During the night, I suddenly heard them jump out of bed and go racing downstairs. I heard a window open and the chain and bolt of the front door rattle. All was quiet for a short time and then the window was closed and I heard the students come back to their room.'

Serving breakfast the following morning she overheard a member of the household saying she had heard the two students opening the door during the night. To which the students replied that they had not, they had gone through the window as it was quicker, and followed the figure of a white lady across the lawn, where she suddenly disappeared. Gemma heard no more of this particular conversation as she had to return, rather reluctantly, to the kitchen. She said, 'I gathered they had slept in that particular room with the intention of sighting the ghost of Nafferton Hall.'

Time passed and Gemma could not shake off the feeling of

being watched. By October of that year she had become very nervous and decided that she must give in her notice. While she was working out her notice, she was in the house alone one afternoon, having been given strict instructions to have the tea ready at a certain time for when the family returned. She began to prepare the tea when she discovered that there was no butter or milk and she would have to go down into the dairy, in the cellars. Taking up a candle, she set off into the cellars and as she passed the apple-cellar door, which was again open, she paused to close and fasten it. 'It fastened with a chain and padlock,' she said, 'although I did not padlock it as that would have meant trouble from the family. I just put the chain over the staple and hooked the padlock through.'

Feeling much better with that door shut, Gemma went on her way to the dairy. On her way back, however, she nearly fainted when she saw that the door was once again open. She hadn't heard the chain fall, which she says she would surely have done if it had come open by itself.

Gemma dashed terrified to the kitchen, leaving her candle to burn itself out in the dairy as she dared not go back for it. Needless to say, she was in trouble when the family returned for not having got the tea ready, but she did not tell them why. She tells me that this is something that she has regretted ever since, for had she asked, she might have learnt the story behind the ghost of Nafferton Hall, although she says, 'Perhaps I was too afraid to want to know at that time.'

Another strange incident occurred just before she left which has mystified her ever since. One night she heard a noise which she tells me sounded rather like a cockerel, but with a funny crow. She says that she heard the noise two or three times, but could never make up her mind as to just what it was. One thing Gemma is sure about though, she was very relieved to leave Nafferton Hall. She said finally, 'I did not see a ghost, but there was something very uncanny there. I had never been afraid of attic bedrooms before or since, whether they were lit by candle or electricity. As a matter of fact, I would sit in the dark by the open window and listen to the owls hooting, so I couldn't understand why I shouldn't like Nafferton Hall.'

* * *

So much for the personal stories, but what about the other, better known, grey ladies who haunt Yorkshire and whom we all know about, but very few of us can claim to have seen? For instance, the ghost which haunts the fifteenth-century home of the Metcalfe family, Nappa Hall at Askrigg, which has been recorded as being seen wearing a Tudor-style dress and cap and is generally thought to be the pathetic and heartbroken spectre of that lovely, but unhappy royal prisoner Mary Queen of Scots. She is said to have spent a couple of nights here, sleeping in the massive oak bed, which has been preserved. Although she is known to have been kept a prisoner at Bolton Castle for about six months in 1568, there is some doubt as to whether she did actually stay at Nappa Hall, or indeed whether this ghost is really hers. Like her cousin Elizabeth I and Anne Boleyn, Mary's alleged ghost is one of the most popular phantoms in the country.

East Riddlesden Hall, a seventeenth-century manor house situated within a few yards of the busy A560 at Keighley, is haunted by an unidentified female, wearing a long blue dress which can be heard swishing about as she walks aimlessly along corridors and in and out of rooms. This old hall was originally owned by the Rishworth family, and in one of the rooms can still be seen a carved wooden cradle, used for rocking their children. I was told recently that this cradle has been seen rocking, without being touched by human hands. Perhaps these were the hands of the mysterious lady in blue.

Mrs A. Townsend of Keighley related an interesting experience she and her daughter had while visiting the Hall about ten years ago. She told me: 'After looking round the house and the grounds, we went into the old barn where an old stage coach was kept. As I made to go towards it to have a look inside, I suddenly went very cold and felt as if something was holding me back and I was not able to go any further. My daughter shouted for me to come out as she didn't like it in there and felt very much afraid.'

Another correspondent, Mr M. Atkins of Whitby, had an even more unusual experience at the Hall in December 1963. At the time, Mr Atkins was a taxi driver and one night he was called out to pick up a fare from the Hall. He said, 'There is a large stone porch and when I got there it was quite dark with no lights either in the porch or the grounds. I couldn't find the bell-push in the dark, so I went and peered through one of the windows nearby.'

He was surprised to see, inside the room, a lady in period dress, but as it was near Christmas he assumed there must be a fancy-dress party going on. Going back to the door, he found it was not locked so he let himself in to the large reception hall. There was no one about and he thought how strange it was for a party to be going on, yet the place as quiet as a church, except for some music coming faintly from somewhere down a long passage. Following the sound he found himself in the caretaker's room where he found a lady waiting for him to take her home in his taxi. He continued, 'In the taxi I said to the lady I thought there was a party going on and told her what I had seen through the window. She sat quiet for a time and then said, "Do you know, you have seen a ghost."' Mr Atkins said to me later that he is not a very good story-teller, nor is he a great believer in ghosts, but as he said, 'One thing I do know, that woman was there in the Hall all right.'

Had Mr Atkins seen the lady in blue? If so, who was she? Was she a member of the Rishworth family or was she a nanny who, like many an unfortunate young woman before and since, met a tragic end?

Another lady in blue, this time elderly, haunts Temple Newsham House, near Leeds. Lord Halifax, who lived there until 1922, is said to have observed her when, on a winter's night in 1908, the firelight in his bedroom revealed a woman with a shawl draped over her shoulders, crossing the room and vanishing into an adjoining one. Screams of agony have also been heard in this part of the house. The house, which is said to have been the birthplace of Henry, Lord Darnley, husband of Mary Queen of Scots, has many other ghosts to its credit including a small boy who has been seen stepping out of a cupboard in the room where Darnley is thought to have been born.

* * *

An old house in Kirkgate, Wakefield, was said to have been haunted by a woman who had been locked up in one of the cramped little attic rooms, high under the chimneys, and who starved to death when whoever locked her in forgot about her, either by accident or design.

While in the Wakefield area, mention should also be made of the ghost of old Lady Bolles of Old Heath Hall who, when she died in 1661 at the age of 83, left a very detailed will. £700 was left to be spent on mourning and £400 to cover funeral expenses. It must have been some funeral! Old Lady Bolles also left strict instructions that the door to the room in which she died was to be permanently sealed.

The room remained locked for a good number of years, but eventually a new occupant of the Hall, possibly not knowing of the old woman's wishes, opened it up again and in doing so disturbed the vengeance-seeking spirit of old Lady Bolles. Angry at her orders being disobeyed, her ghost haunted the Hall for the next two hundred years or more, until its demolition. Her most favoured haunt was the banqueting hall at Christmas time, where she was seen several times by a number of soldiers billeted there during the Second World War.

Now all that is left of her old hall is the door to Lady Mary's bedroom, which is on display at Wakefield Museum. And her ghost? That was said to have been laid by a local vicar at a place called Bolles Pit, on the River Aire.

Castlegate House, close to York Minster, has a grey lady who has been seen climbing the stairs. Two other ghosts, thought to be former occupants, haunted Thornton Watlass. One was said to be dressed in eighteenth-century clothes and the other, a Victorian woman dressed in grey. Countersett Hall, near Hawse, is haunted by an unknown ghostly female, and an unknown ghost seen at North Kilvington, on the A19 north of Thirsk, was clad in white. Local gossip said she was the wraith of the seventeen-year-old daughter of Roger Meynell of Kilvington Hall, who was killed by soldiers in the Chapel of the Hall at the time of the Dissolution, and whose body was thrown into a stream.

Heights Farm at Rishworth is haunted by a ghost known as

'The Lady of the Heights'. A figure dressed in late Victorian clothes and thought to be the ghost of a lady who died there some years ago, has been seen quite frequently in the area.

Snape Castle, near Bedale, boasts a regal ghost, thought to be Catherine Parr, the last wife of Henry VIII. Over the past century, several people have claimed to have seen the ghost of a young girl in Tudor-style dress, with long fair hair showing beneath a small white lace cap. She is said to appear happy and contented.

Spofforth is a charming little village between Wetherby and Harrogate, on the A661, and its castle was for centuries the home of the notorious Percy family, until things became a little too hot for them in these parts and they moved to Northumberland. William the Conqueror held William de Percy in high esteem and he provided him with a number of manors in Yorkshire, as payment for services rendered during the Conquest. Over the years the family's influence spread throughout Yorkshire and the North of England.

The castle, more a fortified manor than a traditional castle, has been a ruin since it was damaged by the Yorkists during the Wars of the Roses after its owner, the Earl of Northumberland, died in Towton. It then fell into decline during the early Tudor period and parts of it were dismantled. It was little more than its present ruin by the time of Elizabeth I. The tower, which still stands, is haunted by a spectre which has been seen quite often over the years and, indeed, was seen quite recently. The spectre appears at the top of the tower and after standing quite motionless for several minutes, it appears to throw itself off and plunges to the ground where it disappears. Only the top half of the figure is ever seen, and those who have seen it claim it is female.

According to Mr William Foggitt of Thirsk, a restless lady haunts Thirsk Hall, the home of Captain Peter Bell and his wife Hilary. This apparition has been seen several times by visitors sleeping in the huge four-poster bed in the bedroom overlooking the parish church. The ghost is thought to be that of a young woman who, through committing suicide, was refused burial in consecrated ground and was most probably buried beneath the Georgian hall.

Similarly, a poor victim of an insane and jealous husband roams about the ruins of Skipsea Castle, which stand near the junction of the B1242 and the B1249 between Bridlington and Hornsea. This is the ghost of Lady de Bevere, niece of William the Conqueror, who roams the castle in the vain hope of leading some hardy soul to her last resting place. It has been said that once someone follows her and retrieves her bones to give them a decent Christian burial, her tormented soul will find eternal rest.

Bolling Hall, a lovely old manor house near Bradford, boasts an anonymous ghost of a grey lady who was responsible for saving the lives of the whole population of the town during the Civil War.

In 1643, the Hall was owned by Richard Tempest, an ardent supporter of Charles I. It was beneath his roof that the Earl of Newcastle stayed the night after issuing grim orders for the massacre of every man, woman and child in Bradford. The town was a hotbed of Puritanism and lay under siege by the King's forces. The Earl of Newport had been killed during the laying of the siege and Newcastle was so incensed by this he issued the now infamous order that, on the following day, his soldiers should 'put to the sword every man, woman and child, without regard to age or distinction whatsoever'.

That night the Earl slept badly, for he reported that three times the clothes were pulled from his bed and a ghostly female form appeared, dressed all in white, which appealed to him in 'piteous and lamentable tones' to 'pity poor Bradford'. Sceptics said the Earl was drunk. Others were not quite so polite and suggested that the female was not a ghost but a venturesome wench who lived nearby. Whoever or whatever it was, however, succeeded in persuading the Earl to cancel the previous day's order and thus spare the poor citizens of Bradford.

One man who resided in Bradford during the siege was Joseph Lister, who was to write later, 'It was generally reported that something came on the Lord's Day night and pulled the clothes off his bed many times.'

* * *

There is nothing anonymous about the final ghost in this chapter, for she is perhaps the best known grey lady in the whole country. She is, of course, the ghost who haunts the old hall at Burton Agnes on the A166, a few miles from Bridlington.

Burton Agnes Hall, the seat of the Boynton family, dates from about 1600 and was built by Sir Henry Griffiths. Old Sir Henry had three daughters and it is the youngest, Anne, who still haunts the Hall, 350 years after her death.

History records that Anne was attacked by footpads when returning from a visit to the home of the St Quintin family at Harpham. She was so badly injured that she died five days later. (At this point some historians disagree and say that the house itself was under attack by marauding thieves and Anne was mortally wounded in the struggle.) However, as she lay dying she asked her sisters to preserve her head at Burton Agnes Hall.

Despite their promises, this wish was not carried out and Anne was buried in the yard of the old Norman church at Burton Agnes. Not long afterwards were heard loud crashes, bangs and moans. Doors slammed and the disturbances became so frantic that the distracted family decided the girl's body should be disinterred. When the coffin was opened the head, already a grinning skull, was found to be severed from the shoulders, yet neither the limbs nor trunk showed any sign of putrefaction.

The skull was taken back to the house and for a time all was quiet, until one day a servant girl threw it out of the window. It is said to have landed on a passing cart and the horses stopped, refusing to move an inch until it had been removed. Since then, all attempts to bury it in consecrated ground have led to all sorts of trouble. After being kept on a table in the great hall for many years, the skull was finally bricked up in a wall where it remains to this day, but Anne's ghost, known familiarly as 'Awd Nance', is still said to haunt the house she loved so much, apparently inspecting the furniture and making sure the house is kept up to standard.

Knights of the High Toby

The great age of the highwayman was between the mid-seventeenth century and the early nineteenth century, a period of about 150 years. Although they were rife along the main roads, many in fact preferred the lonely roads and country lanes. It was to serve the stagecoaches that major highways like the Great North Road were built and they were to serve the purposes of the highwayman admirably. The Great North Road had an unsavoury reputation and people travelled it at their peril.

The ghosts that haunt this particular stretch of the Queen's Highway and the surrounding country lanes are of men who were legends in their own lifetimes and local folk have told terrifying tales ever since the highwaymen were a source of terror to travellers.

Dick Turpin, of course, lends his name to many of the old pubs and inns along this route and any room where Turpin and his contemporaries might possibly have hidden is almost certain to have a ghost story attached to it. His legendary exploits cover a wide area, but although his ghost has been seen on the A5 near Nuneaton and on the B488 at Woughton-on-the-Green near Bletchley, it has never been seen anywhere in Yorkshire. In fact legend has made far more of Dick Turpin than there really was. His greatest success was not as a highwayman but as a cattle stealer, near his father's home in Essex, and he was hanged, not for highway robbery, but for stealing a horse. However, be that as it may, any spectral horseman seen on the A1 since has been dubbed 'Dick Turpin'.

More authentic are the stories of the highwayman's ghost to be seen at various points between Scotch Corner and Boroughbridge, about six miles south east of Ripon. This ghost is without doubt that of Tom Hoggett, self-styled 'King of the High Tobeymen of the Great North Road'.

Hoggett was a real dyed-in-the-wool villain whose success in lifting purses over a wide area earned him quite a reputation. He was eventually caught by troopers sent out from York, at the Salutation Inn one stormy, moonless night and kept under guard until he could be taken to York on the mail coach the following day. The ever-resourceful Hoggett bided his time and during the early hours of the morning was able to escape from his captors. He made a dash for the nearby River Swale, hoping to cross it at Langdon Fords, but in the darkness he stumbled into a pond and drowned. The pond still bears his name and it is said that no one who falls into it will survive.

Many stories are told of how, on moonless and stormy nights, Hoggett's ghostly figure can be seen, hatless and wearing a caped coat reaching to his ankles, gliding alongside the road at considerable speed, his coat glowing dimly, as if illuminated by a feeble lamp.

Further north at Ardwick-le-Street, a copse known as the 'Hanging Wood' was the favourite resort of another of Yorkshire's infamous sons, William Nevison. It was Nevison, not Turpin, who made the epic ride to York in 1678, covering the distance from London in the incredible time of fifteen hours and thirty-five minutes on the same black horse, the famous Black Bess. Despite this feat which was achieved to establish an alibi, Nevison was arrested and placed in York Castle, from where he managed to escape after bribing his jailer.

Charles II offered a reward of £20 for his recapture and it was not long before he was caught and subsequently hanged on the York Tyburn. His ghost is said to haunt the area around Batley, where in 1681 he was involved in a fight and killed a man called Darcy Fletcher.

A couple of miles north of Hornsea is the village of Atwick. Here an unknown headless highwayman has been seen on a number of occasions and at Hickleton, near Goldthorpe, the ghost of an unknown highwayman terrified the author many years ago.

In those days I lived with my grandmother in Thurnscoe and worked at Doncaster, about eleven miles away. Because I didn't finish work until after 10.30 at night and the last bus left Doncaster at 9.30, I had to cycle home every night.

Leaving Doncaster, I would cycle up Barnsley Road through Scawsby and Marr and then begin a gradual uphill climb to Hickleton. Hickleton is neighboured by coal pits but it is an island of charm really, with a fine church at the crossroads and behind it, the seventeenth-century home of the Halifax family. Apart from that, several small cottages make up the remainder of the village.

On this particular night, as I cycled up the tree-lined road towards the church, I could see, between the trees on my left, the road which would cross my path outside the church. There was very little traffic along here in those days, but had anything been approaching the crossroads from my left, I would have been able to see it quite well. I was surprised to see a figure on horseback, trotting quite leisurely towards the junction. I remember thinking to myself, 'What a funny time for someone to be out on a horse,' for although it was late June and quite light, it was after eleven P.M.

The horseman came to the crossroads and stopped, looking down the road up which I was cycling, until suddenly the horse shied and I was able to distinguish quite clearly a billowing cape and tricorn hat. That in itself was bad enough, but then to my absolute terror both horse and rider vanished before my eyes. I was no more than fifty or sixty yards away by this time and I think it would be an understatement to say I was frightened, I was terrified. In fact, had I not been so near to home I would have turned back to Doncaster. As it was, I put my head down and pedalled furiously past the spot, covering the last two miles or so in record time.

Since then, while doing research for my books on ghosts, I have had one or two other frightening experiences, but I don't think I have ever been so terrified as I was that night in 1953.

When I reached home and had fully recovered, I told my grandmother of my experience, thinking she would accuse me of being over-imaginative, but she just listened quietly and then suggested I have a word with one of the neighbours who had been a policeman and used to patrol that area on his bike some years before.

The neighbour told me that he had seen the ghost himself on one occasion and that several people living in the village had reported seeing it, but no one knew who it was. One theory was that it was the ghost of a man ambushed by troops and killed on that spot. Research over the years has failed to bring any fresh evidence to light, but I understand the ghost has been seen as recently as 1977 by a lorry driver, who braked hard on reaching the crossroads when a figure on a horse suddenly appeared from nowhere and vanished just as quickly.

On 2 July, 1644, Cromwell defeated the Royalist army under Prince Rupert, at the battle of Marston Moor, just under a mile away from the village of Long Marston. Ever since that terrible day, tales of ghostly Cavaliers fighting it out with Roundheads have been told. Some people have claimed to have seen the battle silhouetted in the sky, while others tell of seeing ghostly survivors of this memorable clash trudging by the wayside.

Back in November 1932, two touring motorists, lost in their search for the Wetherby road, found themselves travelling along the A59 which runs through the site of the old battlefield. Ahead of them they noticed a small group of perhaps three or four ragged individuals, stumbling silently along the ditch. Realizing there was something odd about them, they slowed down to look more closely. The figures were dressed as Cavaliers, with wide-brimmed hats turned up and fastened with cockades and long, flowing locks. At first they thought they must be actors from some carnival event.

The figures, moving in the same direction as the car, with their backs to it, suddenly staggered to the centre of the road and into the path of a bus approaching in the opposite direction. It was obvious that the driver of the bus could not see them as he did not even slow down and appeared to the two observers to drive straight through them. They stopped the car and searched the road on either side, but were unable to find a trace of anyone.

Today one still hears of solitary figures haunting the battleground. As a point of interest, the Old Hall at Long Marston which was used by Cromwell at the time of the battle of Marston Moor, is said to be haunted by his ghost.

A ghostly army was said to march through the Forest of Knaresborough and last century three farmers swore to seeing men clad in white, led by a commander in a scarlet tunic, their swords flashing in the sunlight.

Four miles north east of York, at Stockton-in-the-Forest, divisions of a large army were seen silhouetted in the sky. The A64 between Pickering and York is haunted by a spectre called Nance, whose sole aim appears to be to help travellers in distress.

Nance, who was a farmer's daughter, came from Sheriff Hutton and was engaged to be married to a mailcoach driver on the York–Berwick run. In the case of Nance, however, absence failed to make the heart grow fonder and she found solace in the arms of another, eventually running off with him.

About a year later, the coachman was shocked to see Nance waiting at the side of the road, with a baby in her arms. She was so weak and ill, she could hardly stand. Stopping the coach he lifted her and the baby on to the seat beside him and as they continued their journey to York, the poor girl told him what had happened to her over the past year. It appears that the lover had abandoned her when the child was born. He was not only a married man, but also a highwayman to boot.

The coachman took Nance and her child to the Black Swan Inn which used to stand in Coney Street, York, but both she and the baby died the same night from exhaustion and starvation.

Some years later, the coachman was again approaching York when he ran into dense fog, forcing him to take a postilion to lead the horses at a snail's pace. Suddenly, the reins were jerked into the air by invisible hands and the horses set off at a frantic gallop. Looking round in terror, he saw Nance seated beside him, whipping the horses on, dressed as she had been on the night she died. She drove the horses flat out to York and into the yard of the Black Swan.

Nance can still be found on the A64, particularly on foggy nights, a lithe, young ragged girl, moving swiftly in the glare of the headlights. Any driver who cares to trust her can be confident that, for as long as he can see her, he is safe. She will glide faster when the road is clear and will slow down should hidden dangers be ahead. The cat's eyes in the centre of the road will gleam clear through her body.

Drive along a certain street in Scarborough and you may come across the ghost of Lydia Bell, walking in the pink gown she wore on the night of her death. Lydia was the daughter of a well-known York confectioner who was found strangled on the beach at Scarborough in 1804. The street where she and her parents stayed on that fateful holiday has been haunted ever since. Also, while driving through the town, keep a look-out for the Black Horse of Scarborough, which has haunted the town for almost 800 years. Back in the twelfth century, reports of a black horse being seen galloping near to the town were made to the authorities. Over the centuries hundreds of people have claimed to have seen it and their accounts haven't varied much. A black, riderless horse passes, the sky suddenly goes black and there is a violent thunderstorm accompanied by hailstones.

At Sutton a ghost can be seen, said to be the spectre of Tom Busby, who was hanged and gibbeted in 1702 for killing his father-in-law. The story behind this ghost is that Tom married the daughter of a counterfeiter called Daniel Auty and, after the wedding, became Daniel's partner-in-crime. One day, during an argument over how the money should be shared, Tom lost his temper and beat Auty to death with a hammer. The gallows where his body was left to rot stood opposite the Busby Stoop Inn and it is at this spot a figure has often been seen, with lolling head and a knotted rope still around his throat.

Another ghost, which has terrified many a lonely traveller, is that of the wicked Lord Wharton, which can be found on the A685 near Kirkby Stephen.

As Lord of the Manor, Lord Wharton presided at the peculiar Court of Ravenstonedale, a position which allowed him to exact extreme penalties. His list of crimes against tenants and wrong-doers makes even Stalin fade into insignificance. No one was in the least surprised when retribution struck, suddenly, in the form of blindness as he rode home alone.

When he died his ghost groped its way, with outstretched hands, along the same road.

The Yorkshire Moors provide a number of ghosts which the wary driver should look out for. For instance, the ghost of Kitty Garthwaite can be seen on the moors near Gillamoor. Kitty, a local girl, was courting a boy from the nearby village of Hutton-le-Hole. When she became pregnant by him he deserted her and in despair she drowned herself in the River Dove one Sunday evening in 1784. Some days later her ex-lover was found dead in the same place and it was not long before local people reported seeing Kitty's ghost, sitting naked under the tree where she and her boyfriend used to meet. Needless to say, it was always the local men who saw her and many of them were lured to a watery grave.

Another moorland ghost is said to be that of Emily Brontë who haunts the stark windblown moors near Top Withens farm, thought to be the scene of her most successful novel, *Wuthering Heights*. She can be seen in broad daylight, walking alone along the narrow path which leads to the Brontë Waterfall, a small fall about two miles from where she was brought up at the parsonage at Haworth, and which was a favourite spot for her and her sisters within sight of Top Withens.

Legend tells us of a tragic ghost which can be encountered in the streets of Swinton, near Mexborough. Many years ago, there lived in the town a farmer, and his wife, Mary. Mary was a good wife who took good care of her husband, despite the fact that he spent most of their hard-earned money on drink, afterwards coming home roaring drunk and very often beating the daylights out of the poor woman.

One night the farmer came home, drunk as usual, and demanded that Mary make him a good supper. The poor wretched woman was beside herself as there was no food and not a penny in the house with which to buy any. She decided her only salvation lay in slaughtering one of the two pigs they kept. Now the farmer loved one of these pigs, probably more than he loved Mary, and it was unfortunate for her that this was the one she should choose to kill. The farmer was furious and in his rage he picked up a large knife and chased her out of the house. Blind with fear she stumbled into the River Don nearby and drowned. Every year since then, she is said to ride through the streets of Swinton on the back of the wild boar, both of them screaming in terror.

Yorkshire also has its fair share of phantom coaches which are quite often witnessed on the county highways. A spectral coach driven by six horses is said to have been seen racing down a fellside in upper Wensleydale, and a coach and four has been seen on the old road leading from Settle to North Craven.

At Beverley, a ghostly coach and four, reportedly driven by the ghost of old Sir Percy, son of the 4th Earl of Northumberland, has been seen racing ever onward to eternity. Some people claim the horses are black and headless and the carriage contains a solitary passenger, a skeleton.

A further spectral carriage can be seen at Aislaby Hall, near Whitby, while in the same town, yet another might be glimpsed careering along the road near the cliffs over which it plunges on reaching a certain point. Also in Whitby, in the area around Prospect Hill, has been seen the ghost of a man strolling along a path, carrying his head under his arm.

Although to my knowledge they have never been seen, spectral horses can be heard galloping in the dell near the cricket pitch at Bramham Park in North Yorkshire. They are thought to be the ghostly echoes of those who fled from the Battle of Bramham Moor in 1408.

Middleham Moor is said to be haunted by a woman wearing mourning clothes. Legend has it that in life she had two suitors and her plans to elope with one were discovered by the other who, in a jealous rage, murdered her on Middleham Moor. In the last century, a skeleton of a woman dressed in the remains of a black dress was discovered high on the moor by peat-diggers.

Another 'Lady in Black' can be met at Woodhall. Apart from her black clothes, she wears white gloves and carries a walking stick. She can be seen at any time of the year, day or night, and I am told that apart from her clothing she looks as normal and as solid as the trees around her.

*   *   *

Recently, after investigating an alleged haunted site near Wennington, I drove home rather late in the evening by way of Giggleswick and then the B6478 to Gisburn, where I would join the A682 to Nelson. Leaving the village of Wigglesworth I spotted a signpost for Tosside, which brought to mind a ghost I'd heard of and which I fervently hoped never to meet. This is the ghost of a young girl who lurks around the Tosside area and has been held responsible for causing numerous accidents.

According to local legend, many years ago, on a dark snowy morning, a young servant girl who had been sent to fetch water from the stream, fell in and drowned. It is claimed that this is the ghost that lies in wait for a motor car to approach and then runs directly into its path, causing the motorist to swerve violently, usually ending up in the ditch.

Another spectre associated with water is that of a woman who haunts the banks of the River Ouse near Beningbrough, about eight miles from York. She was said to have been murdered here in the late seventeenth century. She was the housekeeper to the family at Beningbrough Hall who, it is said, spurned the advances of the steward of the estate. Because of this, he paid a local poacher, William Vasey, to murder her. Vasey was caught and hanged at York, but the housekeeper's ghost still haunts the spot where she met her end, presumably from drowning.

The anonymous ghost of a woman can be seen at Lady Well in Melsonby, up in North Yorkshire. Little is known about her, except that she is minus a head.

Should the reader be in Skipton and see the ghost of Lady Anne Clifford riding up the main street in her spectral coach towards the castle gateway, then he can expect to hear within days of the death of the Lord of the Honour of Skipton.

Mrs M. Hall of Fartown, Huddersfield, is convinced that she and her mother had a close encounter of the spectral kind when returning from a visit to New House Hall in the latter part of 1936.

She told me: 'We were walking home arm-in-arm up Wiggan Lane, which in those days was lit by a solitary gas lamp. There was a full moon and I remember it was a crisp, clear night.' About halfway up the lane they suddenly saw a young woman dressed in white and wearing what appeared to be some kind of veil on her head which flowed out behind her. She seemed to float across the road in front of them, through a stone wall and disappeared into the field beside the road. Mrs Hall said, 'We took a tighter grip on each other and, picking up courage, looked over the wall into the field, but there was no one there. I firmly believe we had seen the ghost of the young woman who is said to haunt the Hall.'

A similar experience happened to Mrs Adele Lathom of Batley a few years ago. She was returning home by car from the cinema at Leeds with three friends when they lost their way. Two of the friends were asleep in the back seat and Adele was sitting in the front with Mandy, the driver. Suddenly, ahead of them, they noticed what appeared to be white steam in the centre of the road. She told me, 'At first I thought it was either a collection of steam from some factory or other, or else a large polythene bag. But as the car approached, it appeared to rise and float up over the top, silently. I was terrified and for no reason at all I felt tears rolling down my cheeks.' She noticed that Mandy's cheeks were also wet with tears. Neither of them could understand why they were crying, nor could they fathom out what the shape was.

'The following day,' she continued, 'we were told at work that the mother of one of our friends had died at about the time we saw the object on the Beeston–Cottingley road. We were even more astounded to learn that at the time we saw the apparition, for that is what it was, we were passing the crematorium where she was to be cremated later in the week.'

As Mrs Agnes Kelly of Fartown, Huddersfield, drove her car into a sharp bend, the glare of oncoming headlights picked out the figure of a young, fair-haired boy. Horrified, she swung the steering wheel over as the boy's freckled face loomed up in front of the windscreen. That single act probably saved her life. She crashed into a parked car, but suffered only shock. As she waited for an ambulance, she anxiously asked a policeman, 'Have I killed the boy?' But there was no boy.

A court heard, in January 1981, that what Mrs Kelly saw as she took the bend in Somerset Road, Huddersfield, was a vision of an eight-year-old child, who had been knocked down and killed by a car on the same spot many years before. After the case she said, 'But for that vision I am sure I would have driven straight into the car coming up the hill towards me. I most probably would have been killed.'

Finally, the story of a ghost that appeared to be so natural at the time that the young man who was witness to it still cannot believe that what he saw was a ghost.

Back in the mid-1930s young Robert was cycling home from school along Dewsbury Road, Leeds, and approached the traffic lights at the crossing near Meadow Lane. As the lights were against him, he pulled up behind a tramcar and, as he did so, happened to glance across to the other side of the road where he saw his grandfather approaching from the opposite direction. The lights changed and Robert pulled away behind the tram and, as he passed his grandfather, called out to him, 'Hello, Grandad.'

The old man raised his walking-stick in acknowledgement and, smiling, waved back at him. Robert was quite used to seeing his grandfather at this particular stretch of Dewsbury Road once or twice each week, because the old man used to visit a friend of his who ran a tobacconist shop there, buy his tobacco and stop for a while to catch up with the latest gossip. Robert rode on home, trying to catch up with the tramcar, so he didn't bother to look around again and, so far as he knew, his grandfather carried on towards the shop.

When he got home, Robert put his bike in the back yard, washed his hands and set about ravenously eating his tea, as all schoolboys do, pausing only to mention quite casually to his parents, that he had seen his grandfather in Dewsbury Road. His parents stopped eating and looked at each other in silence for a moment or two, before his mother said quietly, 'Your Grandad died, late last night.'

Robert was to say many times later, 'There was no mistake. I could have recognized him anywhere – his distinguished appearance, waxed moustache and walking-stick. I know it was my grandad that I saw and that he recognized and acknowledged me.'

Things That Go 'Bump'

Most people tend to think that ghosts only haunt rambling old houses. I would agree that the atmosphere of some of these old places is often conducive to imaginative sightings, but it is quite misleading to think ghosts cannot haunt a modern home, because in my experience many truly authenticated ghost stories come from such places. As I said in *Lancashire's Ghosts and Legends*, my own home, built in 1904, is comparatively modern and is haunted by a delightful Edwardian of a most likeable disposition, who exists quite happily side-by-side with my down-to-earth family. Unfortunately, other people are not always quite so lucky.

Miss Joy Bailey had two rather unnerving experiences: the first, in 1971, was when she lived with her parents in an old terraced house in Masbrough, near Rotherham. Going to bed as usual one evening, leaving her parents to sleep downstairs as they often did in the cold weather, she snuggled down into her warm bed and quickly fell asleep. Miss Bailey said, 'At about 3 o'clock in the morning, I awoke for no reason at all and was surprised to hear footsteps crossing my parents' room and then go down the stairs.' Thinking that perhaps one of her parents had been taken ill, she called out, but there was no reply. Plucking up courage, she hopped out of bed and went downstairs to see if all was well. Both her parents were fast asleep. She continued, 'I woke my father and told him about the footsteps and he, thinking it might be a burglar, searched the house thoroughly. All the doors were bolted still and there were no signs of any disturbance.'

Miss Bailey said that she always had the feeling that someone was watching her whenever she went into the small bedroom.

Her mother agreed there was something about the house which she could not quite understand and that she too had been surprised to hear footsteps about the house when she had been sitting alone at night.

The second incident occurred in a house in Scrooby Street at Greasbrough, on a hot Saturday afternoon during the summer of 1978. At the time the house was empty as it was undergoing extensive alterations and Miss Bailey, out of curiosity, decided to have a look around to see how the alterations were coming along. She said, 'As soon as I entered the house I could sense something was wrong. It is very hard to describe the feeling which came over me, but I should say it was a mixture of fear and sadness; and cold, intense cold.'

Reaching the top of the stairs she went to look at the bathroom, but these feelings became so intense she froze at the doorway, unable to open the door. She decided to get out of the house as quickly as possible.

Later, she happened to mention to her mother that she had been looking over the house, but took care not to mention her experience. Her mother, to her surprise, told her that she remembered how, during the Second World War, a woman who lived at the house had been accidentally electrocuted in the bathroom.

A more distinctive, but none the less frightening spectre, made life intolerable for Mrs Frances Mills and her parents when, as a young girl, she lived with them at Allinson's Cottages in Mexborough. The cottages have now been demolished, but they stood on what was known as Crossgates.

Mrs Mills told me: 'My parents had been troubled by this spectre for some length of time and I saw it at least three times. My father worked the night-shift at the local colliery and therefore each afternoon he would go to bed. Many times he rushed downstairs to see which of us children had been clomping up and down them, when all the time we had been playing quietly in the back room.'

Once, while her grandmother was staying with them and sleeping with the children, they all felt something pass over the foot of the bed. Likewise, when an aunt stayed with them, she was making the bed in this same room when something touched her on the shoulder. 'Needless to say,' said Mrs Mills, 'she didn't stay much longer after that.'

The first time Mrs Mills actually saw the ghost she saw only part of a face peering round the top of the stairs into her bedroom. She had been sent to bed for some minor incident, but she soon started shouting out in fear, bringing the rest of the household quickly up the stairs to see what was wrong.

Twice in later years she saw the figure again, quite plainly. It was the figure of a man. 'In those days we slept in an old iron bed with old-fashioned brass bedsteads, which are much in demand today,' she said. 'I woke up one night and saw the figure of a man quite plainly. Actually I thought I was dreaming and put my head under the bedclothes, but when I peeped out again he was still there.' The figure was not very tall, in fact his head just cleared the bottom rail. He had a long nose which was quite noticeable on such a short man; and he appeared to be wearing a night shirt, or possibly a shroud. The figure stood motionless, pointing into the corner to the right of the bed.

Mrs Mills's mother awoke one morning to see a blue light dancing from side to side in the wardrobe mirror. She got out of bed and opened the bedroom curtains, but there was nothing to account for it. No amount of investigation could account for the hauntings, but it is believed the figure may have some connection with the two men who were the previous occupiers of the cottage.

Mr W. D. Mather of Sheffield related a similar phenomenon, although at the time he did not recognize it as such. It was some time between 1908 and 1910 and Mr Mather was living with his family in a Victorian house which contained the old-fashioned system of bells. These had to be pulled manually, a series of wires from each of which went up through the attic and back down to the kitchen, where a set of eight or nine iron clappers were attached to the wall just below the ceiling.

He said, 'One evening, the family were all sitting around the kitchen fire, when all the bells began to ring at once and continued to do so for several minutes.' His father explored the house from cellar to attic, but was unable to trace either a human or an animal which might have tampered with the wires. Mr Mather continued, 'As we had an aunt staying with us at the time, who had come over from her home in Paris to visit us, the whole incident was dismissed as a welcome peal to her, on her return to her native city.'

This incident made a profound impression on Mr Mather which has never left him, although the idea of the supernatural would have been ridiculed by his parents, who were very Victorian and would not admit to there being such 'unholy' things as ghosts.

Mrs Jeanne Shackleton, of Huddersfield, had a rather unnerving experience during the Second World War. At that time she was in her early twenties and living in an older-type terraced house. She told me: 'There was a passage between my house and the house next door, with the staircase on the farther wall and so, when I heard footsteps in the early hours of the morning, I knew they just had to be on my staircase.'

The footsteps stopped just outside her bedroom door. Thinking it was an intruder and worried about the safety of the children asleep in the next room, Mrs Shackleton got up and taking a large, heavy naval torch went to investigate. There was no one on the stairs, the children were safely asleep and after going through the whole house, checking the doors and windows and finding nothing, she went back to bed rather puzzled.

She continued: 'I lay in bed listening and a short time later, I heard the same footsteps again and began to count them. There was one step that always creaked when anyone came up the stairs, so I knew just how far the footsteps had come when I heard it creak. They really were on my staircase and again they stopped outside my bedroom door.' This time she was too afraid to check again and lay in a state of fear for the remainder of the night.

The next morning a very worried Jeanne Shackleton discussed the previous night's events at her mother's home. She learned that before she took the house, it had been occupied by two elderly spinsters and their brother. One night the brother hanged himself from a hook in the kitchen and shortly afterwards the sisters had moved out.

Someone suggested that the next time Mrs Shackleton heard the footsteps, she should open the bedroom door boldly and demand to know who or what was bothering her. She went on to say, 'When I next heard them I was all for doing what had been suggested, but I was young then and if the spectre of the man was to appear looking all horrible and with his neck all twisted, I'm sure I would have died – of fright. So, to my eternal regret, I never opened the door to ask what was, I suppose, a vital question.'

A similar, but rather more sinister experience befell Mrs Bould of Wakefield, a number of years ago. Mrs Bould told me: 'I hadn't been married long and my husband and I lived in an old house in the middle of Tavern Street, which was situated in Kirkgate. My husband was in the habit of going out with his pals most nights, leaving me at home with our little girl.'

The night in question was a Monday. The little girl was in bed with measles and, as usual, Mrs Bould was alone downstairs. Being Monday, it was, as it has been for generations of Yorkshire Mondays, washday; and she was tidying up after putting the clothes out ready for ironing. She continued: 'There was no gas or electricity in the house. I took a candle and went upstairs to see if my daughter was all right. Having satisfied myself, I crept quietly down the stairs carrying the lighted candle in front of me.'

Nearing the bottom of the stairs, a figure, which she describes as 'black shrouded', came through the living-room door and appeared to glide through the wall into the pantry. Mrs Bould said the figure was that of a man wearing a black, hooded cloak of some kind, with his arms folded inside the cloak. She said, 'I let out a shout thinking my husband had come home early and was playing a trick on me. I went to the pantry intending to tell him just what I thought of him – but the pantry was empty. Needless to say, I went outside and stood at the garden gate until I saw my husband coming up the street.' There is no apparent explanation for this ghostly visitation and it was not very long afterwards that Mr and Mrs Bould moved to another house.

*   *   *

A more recent haunting was experienced by Mrs A. K. Vaughan-Morris of Featherstone in March and April 1980, which is all the more remarkable because she has seen the ghost in two different places, her daughter's home and her own.

During the Christmas holidays, Mrs Vaughan-Morris was staying at her daughter's, sharing a top-floor bedroom with her little grandson. She awoke one night feeling cold and was surprised to see a little figure walking towards her. It was a girl of about seven or eight, wearing a long dress and pinafore, with golden curly hair and holding an old-fashioned stool in front of her. At first she thought it was one of the grandchildren out of bed, until the figure came closer to the bed and suddenly disappeared.

The matter was forgotten and Mrs Vaughan-Morris returned to her own home where, she says, the little girl again materialized on 6 January, 1980, beside her bed, dressed as before, but this time she was minus the stool. After this things began to happen regularly, as follows:

5 March: A man's figure appeared and just as suddenly disappeared, following which a bouquet of flowers fell on to the bed and disappeared also. Mrs Vaughan-Morris fell asleep, but later in the night awoke feeling cold. She was astonished to see a baby's arm, clad in a blue sleeve, with frilled cuff and the little hand held out towards her. It disappeared towards the door.

14 March: Woke up with a shivery feeling around the face and saw what appeared to be a basket floating towards her face, only to vanish after a few seconds.

19 March: Again, Mrs Vaughan-Morris woke up shivering and feeling that someone was leaning over her. The basket-shape reappeared accompanied by what can only be described as a folded bolt of cloth of varying colours. It appeared to fall off the bed and when she reached over to pick it up, again there was nothing to be seen.

21 March: The basket appeared again. Mrs Vaughan-Morris cried out, 'Go away. I don't like you.' At which the basket appeared to float away sideways, before disappearing.

These and similar related incidents continue right up to the present day. Mrs Vaughan-Morris wrote to me on 11 April,

1980, following a further night of interrupted sleep. That night she had awakened to find the basket, filled up with what appeared to be twigs, resting on her chest. She reached out to touch it but, as before, there was nothing there. Each time these incidents occur the room temperature drops rapidly, her face feels icy and she is conscious of somebody nearby.

Mrs Vaughan-Morris wonders whether the child might have any connection with her grand-daughter, who was born prematurely on 1 October, 1970 and died five hours later. On 19 February, 1977, her husband died suddenly. As they were very close, it could well be that because of her present heart condition, he is worried about her health. There seems to be no other explanation.

Fifty years ago, when Mrs J. Halstead of Sowerby Bridge was a child, she experienced something which she has remembered ever since. She told me: 'My mother was in hospital and father had washed my sister and me and told us to sit by the fire in the large wicker chair, whilst he and my brother made the beds. Suddenly, my sister, who was two years older than me, whispered to me not to make a noise. In a terrified whisper she told me to look under the table.' Looking through the back of the chair, Mrs Halstead could see a large, white, filmy shape, not actually a man or a woman, but more a vague outline. She said, 'I was not in the least scared. As "it" drifted towards the cellar door, I said to my sister, "Don't be frightened, Mary. It's only a ghost!" At this Mary screamed and rushed to the bedroom door. She had frightened me by this act and I rushed after her, screaming too.'

Many years later, the girl's father told them that often he heard noises during the night. Thinking one of the girls might be sleepwalking, he would take a candle and go downstairs, only to find that the noise was caused by the old rocking-chair, gently rocking on its own in the corner.

Mrs L. Hagell of Leeds had a similar childhood experience when, at the age of four, she lived at Goring House, near Wakefield.

She says that as far as she can remember, the man who built the house was so disappointed with the final result that he hanged himself. She told me: 'I think I remember someone saying he had hanged himself from the banister in the hall, but my sister says he hanged himself in the cellar.' Whichever way it was, he was considered to be the cause of the strange night-time noises, sounding as if he was tapping his way across the hall with his stick, on what sounded like a parquet floor. No shade was ever witnessed so far as I can make out, but doors were often seen to open and close of their own accord.

Mr John Harris of Halifax related to me a number of incidents which took place in 1962, when he lived in an old house in Southowram.

Mr Harris had married in 1958 during his National Service days, but it was not until 1960 that he spent much time in the house, except during his short periods of leave. However, in February 1962, following demob, his wife went into hospital to have a baby. Mr Harris said, 'I decided to take the opportunity to do a few home improvements while my wife was in hospital. At the time I was working the 2 P.M. to 10 P.M. shift, so when I started putting some shelves up on this particular night, it must have been after 11 P.M. Because of the thickness of the walls, I knew it would not disturb the neighbours.'

Having finished the shelves in the small hours, Mr Harris decided to shampoo the living-room carpet and banked up the fire, in order that it would dry reasonably quickly. He continued: 'I had no idea of the time, but it must have been in the early hours of the morning. The fire was roaring and the carpet was drying nicely. The old cat was curled up on the hearth and I sat by the fire to have a mug of tea, feeling highly pleased with my night's work.'

Suddenly there was a resounding crash, rather like a heavy door slamming shut. The cat leapt up and appeared to fly around the room several inches from the ground, howling in terror. 'I thought someone had come in at the front door and had slammed it behind them, but when I went to look there was no one about and the door was still bolted. I unlocked it and looked outside – nothing, but the cat shot out of the house and disappeared up the hillside, where it remained for several days.'

Returning to the living room rather puzzled, Mr Harris

suddenly became aware of what he could only describe as 'giant footsteps' crossing the room overhead, from one corner to the other, slowly and very loud. Breaking into a cold sweat, he forced himself to go up to the bedroom and investigate, but he found nothing.

The following morning he called on a neighbour in the hope of finding some explanation, but the woman replied that if he intended staying in the house he would have to get used to the strange noises, for she too had heard them quite often, over the years.

There are two possible explanations for the mysterious events that took place in this house. At some time previously, a firm of builders had done some excavating on the land behind the house and they had unearthed a plague pit containing a number of skeletons and thought to go back to Cromwellian times, for it is understood that Cromwell camped at Southowram to avoid the Halifax plague. Could they have disturbed some spirit from these times? Perhaps, but the second theory seems to be nearer the mark and Mr Harris also subscribes to it.

Mr Harris discovered in a tattered old book about the area that the original buildings were known as 'Blaithe Rood' and had been in turn a monastery, a plague house and a farm (Blaithroyd Farm). They were then converted into five separate dwellings. The author described how he had in fact visited Blaithe Rood and had been very impressed, not only by the magnificent stone fireplace at one end of the hall, but also by the stained-glass windows at the opposite end, which depicted a one-legged man. 'This,' said Mr Harris, 'could explain the peculiar walk which, on reflection, could have been of a person with a limp or an artificial leg. This would explain why the footsteps were heavy and well spaced, but who the one-legged man was, I have not been able to discover.'

Mr Albert Paradise has lived in Stainland, Halifax, for sixty-three years. Before moving to his present address a few years ago, he had lived with his father, until his death, in a cottage a few hundred yards down the road. Mr Paradise told me: 'The building was erected in 1705 and we ourselves moved in about 1920. My father had a fear of gas and electricity, considering it to be highly dangerous and so, from 1920 up until after his death in the late 1950s, we survived with nothing more than a coal fire for cooking on and oil lamps and candles for lighting.'

In all the thirty-odd years he and his father had lived in the cottage, they had never seen or heard anything, but after his father's death a number of mysterious events took place, culminating in one particular incident which, Mr Paradise said, 'frightened me half to death'.

It was New Year's Eve, 1956. Because he didn't have electricity in the house, he used to go to bed reasonably early and listen to an old accumulator-operated radio set. He did not drink and in fact still doesn't, so cannot be accused of having been celebrating the New Year. He said, 'Because it was a moonlit night, I left the bedroom curtains open and lay in bed fully awake, listening to some classical music on the radio. The bed was facing the fireplace and over the mantelpiece was a picture, which was quite old. Suddenly, a face seemed to appear in the frame in place of the picture and then, to my absolute terror, a figure appeared, as if walking out of the fireplace from the house next door, and floated towards the bottom of the bed. His face was a ghastly white. He had sunken eyes and long, flowing hair, which was as white as his face.' The figure appeared to be playing a violin, his head moving from side to side, long hair shaking as if in time to the radio. Mr Paradise admits to racing from the room in sheer terror.

A couple of nights later, he was making his supper in the kitchen when he got a distinct feeling that someone was standing behind him. Too afraid to turn around, he shouted, 'Oh, not tonight. Go away, please.' He tells me he sat in the kitchen all night, too afraid to go to bed. There does not appear to be any record of other incidents in the house prior to these and I am told that once the fireplace had been bricked up and electricity was installed, there were no further incidents.

The bed-time antics of a sexy spectre frightened a young mother of four towards the end of November 1980. She became so upset she called the local vicar to bless her house in a bid to be rid of the saucy spook.

Mr and Mrs Ken Batty and their family had been haunted by

a series of eerie happenings since they moved into their council home at Thurcroft, near Rotherham, early in 1980. But it was the incidents of November of that year that were the most unnerving. Mrs Batty said, 'I was in bed one morning when I felt the blanket being pulled down from my chin. Then I felt my chin being tickled and I naturally thought it was my husband back from work – I was pleasantly surprised but, when I looked up, there was a weird face with staring eyes and no teeth, grinning at me. When I screamed, it suddenly vanished.'

Previous incidents in the Batty household had involved cups being hurled across the kitchen, lampshades vibrating violently and the sound of footsteps when there was no one else in the house.

No one can shed any light on the identity of the spectre, or why it should suddenly turn up as, so far as I can ascertain, it had never troubled any previous tenants. The local suggestion is that this is the ghost of an old retired collier who lived in the house some years ago but, as no one else has yet seen it, this can only be pure speculation. One thing is certain though: Mrs Batty knows she was not imagining things.

About nine years ago Mrs E. Parker of Brighouse moved with her husband into a house which had been converted from an old pub, the Black Bull, at the top of Elland Edge. She told me: 'On going into the house for the first time I was immediately aware of a very strange and frightening atmosphere. I stood in the hall at the bottom of the wrought-iron staircase and, for no reason at all, called out, "You're welcome to stay if you don't frighten me." Why I said it still puzzles me, but I knew somehow that the place had a ghost.'

On their very first night there, they were disturbed by footsteps. Her husband, who was a farmer and as down-to-earth as they come, felt sure that someone had broken in so he got up to investigate, without success. Time after time, night after night, the footsteps could be heard, clomping all over the house.

Mrs Parker continued: 'I was always the last to go to bed and one night I was annoyed by a curious tapping which seemed to come from the wall beside my chair. This went on for several nights, sometimes being so continuous as to drive me to bed. Other times I would tap back, only to receive an answering tap.'

Some time later, Mrs Parker says, she had a vivid dream which she still remembers quite clearly, in which a fair-haired lady in a blue dress came into the bedroom and beckoned for her to follow her into one of the cellars. Here the woman pointed to a loose stone in the wall and indicated to Mrs Parker that she should remove it. She said, 'The dream was so vivid. The next day I realized that the part of the cellar I had dreamed about was immediately beneath where I heard the tapping most nights.'

A couple of days later, she could stand the strain no longer and told her husband of her experiences and her dream. She was convinced there was something in the cellars, but for some reason had always been afraid to go down there. Her husband said there was no harm in looking, particularly if it would give her peace of mind. He went down, put on the light and then called to her to come and show him where the woman had been pointing. She said, 'It was uncanny. It was exactly as I had seen it in my dream, loose stone and all. There was nothing behind the loose stone except an empty cavity, but after that day when we left the stone in the middle of the cellar floor, I was never bothered again by the tapping. The thing is, though, did I let some force loose into the house, for often after that I heard footsteps down there, and my dogs wouldn't stay in the house at all during the night and would often be seen jumping and growling at something I couldn't see, at the cellar head.'

Other, stranger things began to be experienced by both Mrs Parker and her husband. One morning she was feeling a little out of sorts and stayed in bed rather later than usual. Suddenly she heard footsteps coming up the stairs. Thinking it was her husband coming to scold her for lying in, she turned her face to the wall and pretended to be asleep. The footsteps stopped beside the bed and she heard a pitying voice saying, 'Oh dear,' following which the footsteps went back down the stairs. Mrs Parker said, 'I shouted out "What time is it?" but there was no reply. I then thought to myself, "Funny, him pitying me." Anyway, I got up and went downstairs only to find the house empty.'

It had not been her husband. She discovered later that he had not been back to the house all morning as on that particular day he too had been late up and was behind with the milking. However the most amazing part of the story is yet to come. I will let Mrs Parker tell it in her own words, exactly as she told it to me.

'It was after that I felt some sort of affinity with the ghost. "He" had pity for me, something my husband never had. When I was upset I used to go to the staircase and cry on it and somehow seemed to draw comfort. So the footsteps continued outside my room and I felt safe. Then one day came the realization that I couldn't continue like this and I had to get away from the house as soon as possible. A friend came to the house some weeks later to tell me I had got another house and as he stood at the kitchen door telling me this, a coat hanger came flying through the room and hit him on the head. It was as if the ghosts or whatever didn't want me to go.'

The reader may find this story difficult to believe, but there are many witnesses to these happenings up at the old house, who are prepared to swear to the events described here.

Swinsty Hall, at Timble, is well over four hundred years old and looks, from the outside at least, like the background location for a horror movie. Its present owners, Mr and Mrs Cuckston, have lived here for the past thirteen years and during that time they have had several experiences of the paranormal, and although the ghosts have never been seen their presence is both heard and felt.

The first incident took place a year after the Cuckstons had moved into Swinsty Hall. Mrs Cuckston was in the basement kitchen, when she heard someone call, 'Hello.' She says she was quite alone in the house, except for her young daughter who was quietly eating her dinner. Mrs Cuckston shouted back, to let the person know where in this large house she could be found; and at the same time she started up the stairs to the door to see who was there. She was surprised to find no one.

Several weeks later, both she and her husband were in the kitchen when suddenly her husband shouted, 'Hello?' as though in reply to someone shouting to him. Mrs Cuckston had not heard the voice herself, but watched her husband going through the same motions that she herself had done earlier.

Later, more bizarre and disturbing events occurred. The main bedroom, used by Mr and Mrs Cuckston, is spacious and dignified, with a stone fireplace. Many people will have been born and will have died in this room over the centuries. Because of the layout of the room, the bed can only be placed in one of two positions and therefore, again, for over four hundred years previous occupiers will more than likely have sited their beds where the Cuckstons have theirs today.

One night, Mrs Cuckston had gone to bed some time before her husband, Alan, a music historian and harpsichord enthusiast, was listening to some music downstairs on the stereo. She was rather tired and ready for sleep. Some minutes later, whilst beginning to doze, she thought she heard her husband come upstairs and a few minutes later felt him climb into bed beside her, although, strangely, he didn't turn out the light. Mrs Cuckston fell asleep, but awoke after only a few minutes to find the bedroom light was still on and her husband was not in bed. In fact, he was still up and dressed and listening to his music downstairs.

In 1971, the Cuckstons' youngest daughter was born in the middle bedroom of the house, at 1 o'clock in the afternoon. During the remainder of the day, Mrs Cuckston slept quite a lot and the baby lay in the crib beside the bed. The room had been well prepared for the happy event and was warm and pleasant but, despite this, during the night Mrs Cuckston was awakened by a feeling of almost paralysing coldness. The bedclothes were still in place and she was unable to account for this eerie coldness. After a few moments she felt a warm blanket being placed over her. The sudden warmth was as comforting as the cold had been disturbing and she soon fell asleep again.

The following morning when Mrs Cuckston awoke, the room was warm and the baby was awake in the crib beside her. She later thanked her husband for bringing her an extra blanket during the night and was surprised when he told her that he had been exhausted and had slept soundly in the master bedroom, without once getting out of bed!

* * *

My final ghost in this chapter is that of a woman, described as being over six feet tall, who troubled a family in their corporation home at Meltham, Huddersfield, in 1961.

The ghost was first seen in the parents' bedroom on the night of Friday, 31 March. It was big and horrid, said the occupants. The figure was seen three more times during that Easter period, then again in the middle of August of the same year. Mrs Horn, the wife of the occupier, was sleeping alone because her husband was working the night shift. She was terrified, especially as the ghost reached out, touching her face with hands that were like cold mist.

Mrs Horn's husband, Arnold, saw the ghost one Sunday night in October. He hit out at it and it appeared to back through the bedroom wall into the room where his six-year-old daughter was sleeping. Suddenly she screamed and came rushing out of the bedroom.

About a week later the ghost was seen by a neighbour and a youth. The parents then learned from their eight-year-old son that night after night the ghost had sat on his bed and spent some time talking to him and massaging his legs; he was not afraid of it. The couple had often heard the boy talking aloud in the night about what he had been doing at school, but they thought he had been talking in his sleep. Now they were not so sure.

A medium was called in and while the children slept, a seance was held in the parents' bedroom where the figure had first manifested itself. The medium claimed afterwards to have seen the distinct form of a woman aged about sixty, with her hair tied in a bun. She also claimed to have heard a voice whisper the name 'Annie' and had been subjected to a strong desire to open one of the drawers in the dressing table behind her, in which she believed a photograph of the spirit could be found.

The description fitted that of Arnold Horn's Aunt Annie, who had died nine years previous to these events. It now appeared likely that the apparition of this relative had returned to help heal one of their children; for the boy to whom it constantly appeared had been stricken with meningitis when he was only two years old. Doctors had said he might never walk again. I understand that within two years of these events taking place, the boy managed to regain the full use of his legs and in a very short time, became a normal, healthy child.

Thanks to the healing spirit of Great Aunt Annie!

The Haunts of the Drinking Man

Until fairly recently the village pub, like the church, was the focal point of the community. On winter evenings the locals would gather round the roaring fire, telling and re-telling the stories and legends of generations, or listening to the tales told by passing travellers. Perhaps it was the travellers themselves who, as victims of a leg-pull, brought away with them terrifying tales of apparitions which are said to haunt some of our older watering places. No doubt some of the ghost stories told over a quiet drink were a mixture of fact and fantasy, but many of them were not, as some of these ghosts still rattle their chains from time to time, even today. The following stories are by no means exhaustive and whether or not the reader believes them, the establishments themselves are well worth a visit for the beverages alone.

The Bailey Club at Monk Bretton, near Barnsley, adjoins an old Quaker burial ground, which is thought to be the reason for some of the mysterious manifestations that have been witnessed in recent years. Members of staff have often seen the apparition of a man in an old Quaker-style hat, looking, as one told me, 'like yon chap on t'porridge packet'.

One manager working in his office late at night, looked up to see the figure swaying in the middle of the room, before disappearing. The temperature dropped rapidly and an icy blast swept the room. Another member of staff heard the concert-room door open and shivered as a gust of cold air preceded a dark figure, which glided past. However, the most amazing occurrence was when several members of staff together witnessed the club's organ being played by invisible hands, producing not 'punk rock' or the latest 'pop' tunes, but an old hymn!

* * *

The Crown Hotel at Askern, near Doncaster, has a room which is haunted and which frightened the life out of Mrs D. Banks of Pogmoor, Barnsley, some years ago.

She told me that when she was in her teens, her parents were the licensees of the Crown and she had a bedroom on the first floor, directly at the foot of the stairs leading to the second floor landing. The second floor consisted of bedrooms and a bathroom, and at the end of the corridor was what she describes as 'The Room'.

She said, 'Although the other rooms on the second floor were in constant use with bed-and-breakfast clientele and had been for many years before we moved in, the room in question had not been used and by the look of it, it had never been opened in years.' The room was full of junk and dust covered everything. As she had such a small room on the first floor, Mrs Banks asked her mother if it could be cleaned out and made into a room for herself. She continued: 'My mother agreed and we set to work cleaning it out and decorating. Pleased with the finished result I moved my belongings into my new room, a room, I might add, in which I was only to spend one night.'

That night, eagerly contemplating the delights of a larger, newly decorated bedroom, she went to bed happily and was soon asleep. Although she says she usually slept right through the night, and still does, on this particular night she was awakened by the strangest of feelings. Mrs Banks said, 'It may sound odd to say I was wakened by a feeling, as one is normally awakened by a sound. But there was no sound, only the strangest feeling of not being alone, of being watched. It was a most uneasy atmosphere.'

For some inexplicable reason she looked over towards the windows and the heavy drapes blocking out the light, when suddenly and without any warning the drapes began to open. She went on to say, 'I can see them now, slowly drawing across the window and flooding the room with moonlight. I can still hear them, the only sound in that strange atmosphere, the sound of the curtain runners on the rail, as they worked together to open the curtains.'

Who or what opened the curtains? Mrs Banks did not wait to find out. She fled in sheer panic, for as the room was filled with moonlight, she could see that she was still alone. In fact she spent the remainder of the night sitting on the bed in her old room, with the light on.

The following morning, her brother found her still sitting on the bed in her old room. She told him of her horrifying experience of the previous night and he asked whether, when she and her mother cleaned out the room, did they not consider it strange that the windows were barred, or that there was a large lock and several bolts on the *outside* of the door? He went on to say that many times, when using the bathroom next door to this particular bedroom, he had heard noises, rather like the sounds of furniture being moved about, although the room was, he knew, only full of junk.

The pub is over two hundred years old and although it has not been possible to find out who haunts it, one thing is certain: whoever or whatever was locked in that room, someone had tried to make sure it never got out.

Leaving Lancashire from Colne on the B6250 at Laneshaw Bridge, passing through what was once part of the forest of Trawden and over the Keighley Moors towards Haworth, one passes through the tiny village of Stanbury. Standing just outside the village on the right-hand side of the road, silent and lonely, is the Olde Silent Inn, a beautiful old inn, formerly known as The Eagle, but far better known as the place where, with a price on his head, Bonnie Prince Charlie was given shelter and food. One can still see the trapdoor through which the Young Pretender is said to have dropped on to the back of a conveniently placed horse to make good his escape, as his pursuers hammered at the door.

However, it is not the ghost of the young Charles Stuart who haunts this lovely old inn, but the soothing spectre of a previous landlady, a sweet and kindly old soul, who strokes the forehead of fitful sleepers. She was a lovely old dear who used to feed the many wild cats that once roamed these moors, calling them for their food by ringing a small bell. Folk in these parts say that she can still be heard at times, her little bell tinkling in the distance, soft and gentle like the sound of fairy bells being carried on a gentle breeze.

* * *

At Long Preston, the eighteenth-century coach house, the Boar's Head, has quite an interesting history. It was originally built as a stable for a local landowner, but was turned into a public house in 1752. In the great days of the stagecoach, the pub was a busy hostelry at the side of a toll road. It is interesting to note that the names of every landlord since 1752 are recorded on a plaque in the village.

Tradition has it that one of these men hanged himself in the hotel's beer cellar, and his ghost is said to haunt the building. There is an old photograph hanging in one corner of the bar. It shows an old woman, said to be the mother of the dead man. Legend says that providing the photograph hangs in the hotel 'for all time', it is believed the ghost will not return.

On 5 January, 1981, it was widely reported in the press that landlady Lynda Hall was leaving her husband, Derek – because of a ghost which pulls pints. Lynda said that the ghost also flushes toilets, jams doors and wanders around the bedrooms, and every morning it leaves a glass upside down on the bar of their pub, the Ship Inn at Swinton, near Mexborough.

The ghost is thought to be that of a former landlord who died behind the bar some years ago and Lynda wanted Derek to call a clergyman to exorcize it. She said, 'It's becoming more and more unnerving and it has scared me to death. I'm leaving and I'm not coming back until Derek has got rid of it.'

Over 150 years ago, a crowd of townsfolk stood around the gallows which had been erected in the yard of the Feathers. They had come from the surrounding districts to witness the demise of a highwayman, convicted not for highway robbery, but for the particularly nasty murder of a serving wench from the old inn. Since that day, the old pub at Pocklington, about sixteen miles from York, has been haunted by a ghost which the locals are convinced is that of the highwayman.

Room number 7 has an uncanny atmosphere about it and many residents have refused to sleep there after the first night. Sounds of heavy breathing are heard, as if someone is trying to pull a heavy object along the corridor. The atmosphere in the room becomes so frightening that, although nothing is seen, the unfortunate occupant is unable, through fear, to get out of bed to investigate.

Out on the Yorkshire Moors, about ten miles north of Pickering one will find a signpost showing the way to Saltergate. At the bottom of the Devil's Elbow stands the only building for miles, the Saltergate Inn, built around 1760 and known until recent years as the Waggon and Horses. The inn, well known for its cuisine as well as its associations with the old salt smugglers, is also famed for its ghostly legend, thanks to Brenda English's lively book set in Saltergate in the eighteenth century, *Crying in the Wilderness*.

No apparition has been seen at the inn, but there can often be heard, outside on the silent moors, the sound of a woman crying. When the inn was built, the very first landlord lit a peat fire, which right up to the present day has not been allowed to go out, for it is said that should this be allowed to happen, great misfortune would fall on the inn and its inhabitants. Local legend says that the fire keeps an evil spirit imprisoned beneath the hearth, the spirit of a witch who was buried on the spot where the inn now stands and whose malignant ghost is kept at bay by the smouldering peat.

Near the old harbour at Scarborough, tucked away up a narrow alleyway, stands a unique museum. This narrow building was, until earlier this century, an inn, the Three Mariners. This fascinating old inn, built in 1300, is riddled with bolt-holes, secret passages and concealed cupboards, which in the old days were used by smugglers and sailors wishing to avoid the authorities or the press gangs. Tradition has it that a tunnel runs from the old harbour to the inn, which was used to smuggle the American John Paul Jones to safety after his ship, *Le Bonhomme Richard*, was sunk by a superior British squadron off Flamborough Head.

However, of more interest to the ghost hunter is the room which is reputed to be haunted by the ghost of a headless woman, who is said to have appeared on several occasions to warn the local fishermen not to put to sea. One story tells of two fishermen who, setting off early to a day's work, saw the headless spectre as they approached the Three Mariners in the early morning mist. Seeing her, one of the fishermen refused to go any further and returned home for the rest of the day. His partner laughed and poured scorn on the unfortunate man, saying that he was more afraid of what his wife would say if he returned home empty-handed than he was of the headless ghost. He continued on his way down to the quay and took his boat out to sea, only to be drowned later in the day, when a sudden squall caught his boat and turned it over off Yons Nab.

I understand that when the building was still in use as an inn, many people reported seeing the headless ghost in the haunted room. One woman complained that an unseen hand had snatched the clothes from her bed in the early hours of the morning. No one knows who the headless woman is and today no one will admit to having seen her recently. However the fishermen still look for her as they make their way down to the quay for a day's fishing.

At Sutton, near Cleckheaton, there is an old pub said to be haunted by a phantom known locally as the 'dripping innkeeper'. It appears that many years ago when the old innkeeper lay dying, he called for his only son and requested that after his death his body should be placed in a watertight coffin filled with ale. The son promised he would carry out his father's wish and when at last the old man died, he spoke of it to all who came to pay their last respects.

Now, being Yorkshire men, the idea of all that good ale being wasted on a corpse instead of going down the throats of the mourners, was more than they could cope with and they threatened to boycott not only the funeral, but also the inn. The son, being the heir to the business, was also a practical man and he couldn't help but feel he would soon go bankrupt if he carried out his father's wish, so he compromised and filled the coffin with water.

Since that day, it is said the pub has been haunted by the ghost of the old innkeeper who, even today, materializes dripping wet and seeking to wreak vengeance on all those who deprived him of his last drink of ale.

* * *

Behind Selby Abbey stands one of the oldest pubs in the town, the Crown Hotel, where several unusual occurrences have taken place in the last few years.

The former licensees, Ronnie and Joyce Whitaker, told me that not long after they moved in, in January 1977, they were disturbed by heavy footsteps several times during the night. At first they thought they were coming from the premises next door, until they discovered they were empty. Nothing much was thought about it until lunchtime on Christmas Day, 1978, when both Ronnie and his wife, and a number of customers, saw a picture on the wall behind the bar detach itself and fly across the bar to smash on the floor. This was a picture of the pub, which had been taken around the turn of the century.

A barman was frightened one night by a grey figure of a woman, which materialized at one corner of the bar and just as suddenly evaporated. Ronnie explained that earlier this century a landlord murdered his wife in the bar, after a heavy drinking session one Christmas, and it is thought to be her ghost which now haunts this old riverside pub.

The Fleece Inn at Elland has a permanent reminder of a foul deed perpetrated there many years ago. An old beggar, known as 'Leathery Coit' because of his tanned, leathery skin caused through spending a lifetime on the moors, was brutally murdered in one of the upstairs rooms and his body dragged down a flight of wooden stairs, leaving a trail of blood which no amount of scrubbing could remove. Old 'Leathery Coit's' ghost has been seen in the pub and in nearby Dog Lane.

For a number of years, there were reports of a ghost, dressed like a Victorian gentleman, haunting the cellars of the old Golden Lion that used to stand in North Street, Leeds. The ghost of an old lady, her hair done in ringlets, was also seen in one of the bedrooms.

It is believed the two spectres were a husband and wife who lived on the premises in the early part of the century and who loved the old place so much they were loth to leave it, even in death. The pub has now been pulled down and I have been unable to locate its actual site, but I wouldn't mind betting that before long, someone in the glass and concrete jungle now built over the area will report seeing a lady whose hair is done in ringlets and a gentleman dressed in Victorian clothes.

Howley Hall Golf Club, near Batley, was once the farmhouse belonging to Howley Hall, the sixteenth-century home of Sir John Savile, first mayor of Leeds. In 1643, the Duke of Newcastle demanded the house be handed over to the King, a demand which was scorned by Sir John and which caused the deaths of several stout defenders when it was blasted to smithereens by cannon fire. What was left of the estates was let out to various families including the well-known Villiers. One of them, Lady Anne Villiers, was said to have accidentally drowned whilst bathing in a nearby spring.

One afternoon a few years ago, the figure of a woman wearing a long dress, with a dark top and veil over her head and shoulders, was seen near the ruins before suddenly fading from sight. Two men and a woman were seen one evening by a man walking his dog. These figures, dressed in seventeenth-century clothes, vanished when he approached them. Whether these are the ghosts of members of the Villiers family or whether they are the ghosts of the defenders of Howley Hall is not certain, but I think the latter would be most likely.

The Royal Hotel at Armley, Leeds, has a frightening ghost of a grey lady, who appears from time to time. One night in 1972, a young barman got the fright of his life when he went into the cellars to turn off the beer pumps and saw the dim figure of a woman slowly taking shape before his astonished eyes and staring fixedly at him for several seconds.

Stories have been told of this ghost for many years, but it was only recently that it was discovered that in 1858 the then landlord of the Royal Hotel had shot his mistress on the premises.

The Weaver's Restaurant, at Haworth, formerly The Toby Jug, boasts the one ghost I would most like to meet, that of the novelist Emily Brontë, who was brought up at the parsonage, less than a hundred yards away. Emily's ghost is said to appear each year on the anniversary of her death, 19 December. She was first reported as being seen in 1966, when the owner saw a small figure in a crinoline, carrying a wicker basket and smiling and giggling, cross the room to where the staircase used to be and begin to climb up to the bedroom above. He recognized her as Emily from her portrait which was painted by her brother Branwell and which still hangs in the parsonage museum.

However Colin and Jane Rushworth, the present owners, told me that, although they stayed up to see her on 19 December, 1978, she failed to materialize.

Also at Hawarth, the Sun Inn was said to be haunted for many years. The interior was altered somewhat during the early 1970s and when it was re-opened, the new landlord was told of the ghost by the locals. He was very sceptical, but just to be on the safe side, he had a good luck charm, in the shape of a gargoyle, placed over the door, but refuses to say whether this has been successful or not!

Just north of Easingwold stands a lovely old private house, known as the White House. During the seventeenth century, it was a coaching inn, run by a man called Ralph Reynard. The building has obviously changed quite a bit since those days, but it only needs a little imagination to visualize how it must have looked back in the 1620s when the events took place which gave rise to its ghost.

Ralph Reynard courted a flighty, buxom, dark-haired servant girl from Thornton Bridge. Seemingly all went well, until one day the two lovers quarrelled and the girl broke off their relationship. In due course she met and married a farmer called Fletcher, of Moor House. She had no real love for him and, as time went by, the young Mrs Fletcher began to realize her mistake in marrying him and wished instead that she had continued her romance with Ralph.

One day, she and Ralph met quite by accident and in the course of time they became reconciled, but of course it was too late and Reynard was left to brood alone at the inn. As time went by, the villagers began to notice that Mrs Fletcher's horse was often to be seen tethered outside the inn, and it wasn't long before the inevitable happened and Fletcher found out about the affair between his wife and Reynard.

Determined to put a stop to it once and for all, Fletcher made for the White House Inn, but on reaching Dauney Bridge, was set upon by Reynard and his ostler, Mark Duncan. He was knocked off his horse into the stream and his two assailants jumped in after him, holding his head under the water until he drowned. The two men and Mrs Fletcher, who had remained hidden during the killing, then made their way back to Easingwold with the body of the unfortunate Fletcher wrapped in sacking, and there, under cover of darkness, buried him in the garden of the inn.

Several times after this, Reynard was confronted by the ghost of Fletcher, who would point an accusing finger at him and intone in a deep voice, 'Oh Ralph, oh Ralph, repent. Vengeance is at hand!' After meeting the ghost again at Topcliffe Fair, Reynard was terrified for his life and galloped home. As he went, the spectre glided ahead of him, trailing a sack behind it, until on reaching the inn the apparition walked through the hedge and with a sigh dissolved into the ground where the body was buried.

Arriving at the inn, Reynard confessed all to his sister who, horrified at what her brother had told her, had no hesitation in notifying the local magistrate, who lived at nearby Raskelf Park.

On 28 July, 1623, Mrs Fletcher, Ralph Reynard and Mark Duncan were hanged at York and their bodies were suspended from the gibbet at Gallows Hill. The ghost of Fletcher, however, remained on at the White House Inn for many years afterwards. For a good number of years coach horses would show fear on approaching the place and today, as a private dwelling, 'White Walls' is still said to be influenced by the events which took place here all those years ago, although the ghost of Fletcher has not been seen for a good number of years.

The Wyke Non-Political Club at Bradford is haunted by a ghost known to all as 'Fred', who first made his presence known in 1972. Shortly before midnight a member of the staff decided to visit the ladies' room before leaving for home. As she opened the door she saw, standing a few feet from her, a grey-haired man in a dark suit, with staring eyes and bedraggled clothing, which gave him a sinister appearance. Turning to run from the room, the frightened woman felt a cold hand under hers on the door knob, a cold hand with four fingers, but no thumb. The poor woman fainted through sheer terror.

Other strange things have happened here. One morning a table with four chairs around it was found on the stage. No member of staff had put them there. Four wet rings were found on the table, but there were no glasses to be found nearby. A cleaner, having finished cleaning the dressing rooms, was returning to the main hall of the club, when she almost ran into the figure of a man sitting on some steps, with his head in his hands. The lights in the building have turned off and on by themselves and there is often an atmosphere and a feeling of being watched by unseen eyes.

Whose ghost is it? Well, it appears that the club was built on the site of a dyehouse and mill dam. Years ago a millwright, who had lost the thumb of one hand, was accidentally drowned in the dam. Why he is determined to scare the daylights out of the staff is a mystery, although some people think he might be resentful of the changes that have taken place since the dyehouse was pulled down.

Not far from Westgate, Wakefield, is the Grove Inn, where quite a number of extraordinary occurrences have taken place, as a result of a ghost taking up residence there in the latter part of the 1950s. There are also suggestions of poltergeist activities, for heavy furniture has been moved, mirrors smashed and things have been thrown about as if by a naughty child.

One lady complained of waking in terror and feeling as if she were being smothered by an invisible being. On another occasion three boys sleeping in the same room complained of a similar feeling. No one knows who or what this ghost is, or why he should suddenly become attached to the pub, but whenever anything untoward happens, 'Fred', as he is called, is sure to be blamed.

Just outside Sheffield at Kiverton Park stands the Saxon Hotel, built in the early 1960s and haunted by an unusual whistling ghost. Successive landlords have heard enough to convince them that the place is haunted.

The ghost is thought to be that of a monk who was murdered hereabouts many years ago, and it is believed he was connected with the chantry which at one time stood on the site of the hotel. 'He' is nearly always experienced in the cellars, when his presence is made known by a distinctive whistle, as if he is trying to attract attention. Sometimes his presence is so overpowering that anyone in the cellar quickly leaves it to seek reassurance in the comfort of the bar. Although 'The Whistler', as the ghost has become known locally, has never invaded the privacy of the landlord's quarters, he can often be heard padding down the cellar steps, seemingly as if wearing carpet slippers.

The Blue Ball Inn, at Soyland, is an isolated eighteenth-century inn with nineteenth-century additions, and stands on the ancient Blackstone Edge pack-horse road, near Ripponden. Here, in 1766, James Proctor wove shalloons, worsted cloth used chiefly for coat linings. Later the inn became known as 'Rudman's Place', a popular eating house. Fugitives from Halifax with Royalist troops in hot pursuit fled this way in 1643, as did Daniel Defoe in the 1700s.

The Blue Ball is said to be haunted by the ghost of a serving wench, who worked here for a notorious landlord known as 'Iron Will', some time in the eighteenth century. 'Iron Will' was a renowned lecher and he is said to have raped the girl and then drowned her on the moors. Faith, as she was called, can be heard on quiet nights during the winter, running across the floor of what some people say was 'Iron Will's' bedroom, presumably to escape from his amorous advances.

The Ribblesdale Arms at Gisburn, built in 1635 by Thomas Lister, boasts a bed with foot carvings which resemble small children dressed in shrouds and the ghost of a young girl. Needless to say, both can be found in room number thirteen.

Legend tells us that one Lord Ribblesdale, a rake and a waster, seduced a young local girl in this bedroom, who became pregnant as a result. The theory now is that although Lord Ribblesdale is long dead, and buried in a silver coffin, the ghost

of the girl returns seeking to avenge herself. Although the ghost
has not been seen in recent years, the proprietors take no chances
and don't let the room unless pressed to do so. Even then they
have taken the precaution of fitting a bell behind the bed so that,
in the event of any ghost hunter, or innocent guest for that
matter, finding themselves in difficulty, they can ring for
assistance.

Finally, for the last ghost in this chapter, we visit the Angel Inn
at old Catterick village, which was, in its time, the largest
coaching house in the area. Despite its size, it only catered for
two stagecoaches and its long row of stables was used by
breeders and racegoers. The Angel also had at one time a cockpit
and there are tales told of huge wagers being laid on rowdy
nights following a day's racing.

The Angel was haunted by the ghost of a nun, thought by
many to be connected with the name of the inn. According to
local legend, the nun was imprisoned below the church for being
over-familiar with a priest from St Martin's Church, nearby. I
am told there used to be a tunnel connecting the church with the
inn; and it was along this tunnel that the ghost of the nun was
said to walk.

The haunted inns of Yorkshire would fill several volumes, but
sadly there is no further room in this book for more than just a
small selection. However, should the reader happen to visit any
of them during a leisurely summer's drive, take a good look at
the person sitting quietly and alone at the next table ... After
all, it might only be me, but then, on the other hand ...!

Mary Queen of Scots and Turret House

There are many alleged hauntings by the unhappy Royal prisoner, Mary Queen of Scots. Like Elizabeth I, her ghost pops up wherever she is supposed to have stayed prior to her execution. Few hauntings can be authenticated but others, like the ghost that haunts the Turret House, attached to the old manor castle at Sheffield, can be authenticated by historical fact and eyewitness account.

By the fifteenth century, the Earls of Shrewsbury had acquired the castle and when the third Earl died in 1473, at the age of twenty-six, he left a son, George, who became the fourth Earl at the tender age of five. George married the daughter of his guardian, Lord Hastings, and took up residence at the castle, where he lived throughout the reign of Henry VII.

He was a man who liked his comforts and he felt the great castle was too spartan by far. We know the young Tudors liked comfortable living and George was no exception, preferring glass in his windows, large comfortable beds and chairs which conformed to the contours of the human anatomy. He therefore built himself a more comfortable residence in the castle park, which subsequently became known as Manor Lodge.

Manor Lodge was furnished magnificently throughout. Two hundred and forty 'Crowns of the sun' were spent on wall hangings alone. The forlorn remains which now stand in Manor Lane bear little comparison to the original, but the armorial overmantle and plaster ceilings of the Turret House give some indication of the ornamentation the house contained.

The Turret House was built as a porter's lodge by Earl Gilbert, although many people believe that it was built especially to house the unhappy prisoner, Mary Queen of Scots. There is evidence to show that Mary was indeed held captive here. She

was handed over to Earl George Talbot, grandson of the fourth
Earl of Shrewsbury, at Tutbury in 1569 and was incarcerated in
Sheffield Castle itself on 28 November, 1570. She had brought
numerous retainers with her, though their number was cut down
to thirty on the orders of Queen Elizabeth.

Now the castle became a prison, not only for the poor Scottish
Queen, but also for the young Earl and his wife, Bess of
Hardwick, whom he had married in 1568, because the slightest
relaxation of vigilance set the Royal prisoner plotting her escape.
As a result of this she was eventually moved into the Turret
House.

History records she spent nearly fourteen years a prisoner of
the Earl and by 1584 he had had enough and petitioned Queen
Elizabeth to release him from this intolerable duty. Elizabeth
agreed and, no doubt with great relief, Earl George transferred
Mary into the custody of Sir John Somers and Sir Ralph Sadler.

Mrs Ida Elliott, of Sheffield, spent quite some time at Turret
House with her late husband's relatives who during the 1930s
were retainers of the late Duke of Northumberland, having spent
many years in service to the Estate. She told me: 'As I remember
it, the place was very gruesome and my in-laws used to tell me
some hair-raising stories of unaccountable happenings. None of
them would stay in the place alone, day or night.'

Mrs Elliott went on to say that on the Sunday following the
Coronation of King George VI, she was at Turret House, having
been invited with her husband to have tea with his mother and
an old aunt who lived with her. During conversation the aunt
said, quite casually, that she had seen the ghost of Mary Queen
of Scots on the night of the Coronation. No one but Mrs Elliott
appeared the least bit surprised, but she sensed they felt a little
uneasy when she pressed the old lady to tell her more about it.
However, persistence won the day and she was told that the
aunt had been sitting up in bed drinking her cocoa when the
apparition appeared, dressed in a long black dress and looking
very beautiful, and glided across the room, evaporating into the
opposite wall. Mrs Elliott asked her mother-in-law, who shared
the room, whether she too had seen the ghost but, although she
did not deny it, she refused to discuss it further.

'As time went by and I got to know the family more, I asked if I could stay the night with them,' said Mrs Elliott, 'but I was always given a flat "no". When I asked them why not, the only reply I would get was that it was an evil house with very strange happenings and friends who had stayed there in the past had run out of the house in the early morning hours, refusing to go back, even in daylight.' Some years later, Mrs Elliott met one of these people and she was told that although they had not actually seen anything, each time they were dropping off to sleep, they had the sensation that someone was trying to smother them and they had to fight off an unseen intruder.

During the 1930s, Turret House was, unlike today, set more or less in open country and to reach it one had to walk along a long drive. Apart from one or two farms and their outbuildings, it was surrounded by fields. Mrs Elliott said, 'My mother-in-law used to tell me that at twilight, one could often glance at the window and see someone, dressed in what appeared to be a cape and a cowl, peering through at them. However, on going out to investigate, no person could be found. They soon learned to draw the curtains before lighting the oil lamps.'

At that time there used to be a stone coffin just outside the house which was said to have been made for the Earl of Shrewsbury who, it has been suggested, was the lover of the Scottish Queen during her period of imprisonment there. On certain days, the family dog would never go anywhere near the coffin and, if for any reason he was shut outside alone, he would howl and frantically scratch at the door, only to cower shivering with fright after being allowed into the house.

The house itself contained only six rooms. The two on the ground floor, partly oak-panelled with thick walls and iron-studded doors, had been the guard rooms during Mary's time, but were converted in later years into a kitchen and lounge. A stone, spiral staircase led to two rooms on the first floor. These were used by the family as bedrooms. Two further rooms, unoccupied, made up the second floor. These two rooms were said to have been the rooms where the Scottish Queen was held. The staircase continued up into the turret and led on to a flat roof, which was the only place where poor Mary could exercise in the open air. Mrs Elliott said, 'As I remember it, her sitting room was quite ornate with a magnificent fireplace. On the chimney breast was depicted her own coat of arms. The ceiling was of ornate plaster with various symbols and Latin phrases incorporated in it. The windows were diamond-leaded and heavily barred, but in each diamond-shaped glass there was a red Tudor rose. These windows made the room very dark and dismal and one could see little through them.'

In one of these rooms was a very old incense burner, which had probably been in use since long before Mary's time to keep away evil spirits. Made from stone, it was about two feet tall and cut in the shape of an imp. Smoke from the incense came out of gaping sockets where the eyes and mouth should have been. On a number of occasions everyone in the house was awakened by unaccountable noises coming from the rooms on the top floor. Fearing intruders, the men of the house hurriedly dressed and went to investigate, only to find nothing amiss.

One night, having been disturbed they went and checked and found as before that nothing was wrong, so they went back to bed. After a while the noises started up again, but louder and more persistent. Mrs Elliott continued: 'Up they went again. There was still no one there, but they were convinced that the old incense burner had been moved to a different part of the room.'

However, after a lengthy discussion they decided that perhaps they had imagined it after all, and to make absolutely sure they drew a chalk circle around it on the stone floor before once more going back to their warm beds. 'They were disturbed throughout the night,' said Mrs Elliott, 'but they decided to ignore it until the next morning, when on investigation they found the incense burner, which was too heavy for them to move, was completely outside the chalk circle.'

Turret House still stands, but it is now derelict and uninhabited, except by rats and mice. The Duke of Norfolk bequeathed it to the Sheffield Corporation, but the cost of restoration and maintenance was too much for them to be able to do anything with it. The farms and fields which once surrounded it are now gone and modern housing estates have replaced them. The twentieth century has at last caught up with it.

Does the sad Scottish Queen still wander about those upper-floor rooms seeking solace, or plotting escape? Or has she, too, succumbed to a modern way of life which seems to have no place in it for antiquity?

Ghostly Monks and Phantom Nuns

Phantom monks are ten-a-penny in the British Isles. Most ruined abbeys and monasteries claim one and several have been recorded on film. In the 'white rose' county, perhaps the best known and probably the best documented of all these phantom monks is the ghost of the Black Canon who haunts Bolton Priory in Wharfedale.

Each year many thousands of holidaymakers visit this beautiful ruin which stands alongside the Wharfe, in what is considered to be one of the most scenic parts of the county. The whole area is a delight to the eye and one can never leave without thinking how peaceful the priory must have been in days gone by. But visit the site as I have done after dark, when the moon casts shadows beneath archways and doorways, and even the most hardened and unimaginative will feel a cold shiver run down their spine, for on these occasions it doesn't need much encouragement for the imagination to run riot.

The Augustinian canons made a start on their priory at Embsay, a few miles away, on land bequeathed to them by Cecilly de Romille in about 1120. Round about 1160, the de Romille family provided new lands beside the River Wharfe and the canons decided that this was a far better site for their church. By moving there they provided work for many local craftsmen on and off for the next three or four hundred years.

Following the Battle of Bannockburn, the priory was plundered by the Scots and it was not until about 1330 that life was resumed here again and a new band of men-at-arms was trained to defend the priory and surrounding lands against all enemies. During the Dissolution of the Monasteries, the Brothers were sent packing, but the Prior managed to stay on and complete his work alone. Perhaps this is why a small part of the building was allowed to remain intact and became the parish church.

Among the many reports from people who have claimed to have seen a ghost at the priory, particularly in the years before the First World War, the eyewitness account of the late Marquis of Hartington remains the most detailed.

In 1912, the Marquis, who was only a small boy at the time, was on holiday from his school at Eton and, with others, was a guest at the Rectory during the grouse season. The Rectory is believed to stand on the site of the old priory guest house. One night on going to his bedroom, the Marquis was surprised to see a figure standing at the bedroom door. It was a man in his late sixties, dressed in nondescript clothing with a heavily lined and wrinkled face which seemed unusually round and which might have been the face of a woman, had it not been for several days' growth of grey stubble on the chin.

The Marquis was at the top of the staircase, looking towards his room at the end of the passage. He ran downstairs for another light, but by the time he had got back to the passage again, the figure had vanished. King George V showed much interest in this ghost and although he did not see it himself he heard, with the Duke of Devonshire and Lord Desborough, the Marquis of Hartington's account of what he saw.

In 1911, one Reverend MacNabb, Rector of Bolton, was standing looking out of the windows at the Rectory, when he felt compelled to turn around. On doing so, he saw the apparition watching him from the doorway. It was seen again in 1920 by Lord Cavendish and more recently in 1965, when a man entering the gatehouse saw a figure, dressed in a black cassock with a white overlay of what looked like wool, black cloak and flat black hat, walking towards him. The figure has also been seen in the ruined choir, in the priory grounds and in the precincts of the church and the sound of sandaled feet is often heard in the Rectory.

Most of the more recent sightings have been in broad daylight, usually in the month of July, but, although I went over every inch of the site in July 1979 and again in 1980, I'm afraid I must report being disappointed.

* * *

Fountains Abbey, near Harrogate, is also only a ruin now, albeit one of the most magnificent ruins to be found in Yorkshire. It was once the richest Cistercian abbey in the whole of England. There is no authentic record of any apparition being seen on the site, but the sound of monks chanting an old psalm has been heard quite often, on still, quiet evenings.

The ghost of the Abbess Hilda is said to haunt the remains of her old abbey at Whitby, a majestic ruin above the sea. In summer, if one stands in Whitby churchyard, one can see the north side of the abbey, just past the north end of the church. Here, if one is lucky, one might just catch a glimpse of the Abbess, dressed in a shroud and standing in one of the highest windows. The abbey site also gives rise to a nice little legend: Many years ago, a herdsman lay in the straw of the abbey stables feeling rather depressed. He could hear the layworkers singing and was sad because he could not join in their nightly revelries. Suddenly the stable glowed with an eerie light, which became brighter as a shining figure appeared before him and commanded him to stand up and 'sing of the beginning of created things'. The frightened herdsman ran to the abbey to report what he had seen to the Abbess. She told him the story of Genesis which he later recited in plainsong. So affected was the young herdsman by his experience, that he later became a monk. His name was Caedmon, the first English Christian poet.

Today, the sounds of a choir echo faintly in the ruins of Whitby Abbey at the hour of dawn on Christmas Day, singing the songs of Caedmon, the father of English song.

Kirkstall Abbey, near Leeds, is a fine example of Norman architecture and even though in ruins the layout of the monastic buildings is quite clearly defined.

The abbey was built in 1152 for Cistercian monks from Fountains Abbey. The church and accommodation were completed in 1182 and little is known of its history for the next four centuries. It was surrendered to the Crown in 1540 and was allowed to fall into decay until being bought by Colonel North and presented to the City of Leeds for restoration, back in the last century.

The former gate-house, which now houses the abbey museum, is said to be haunted by the ghost of an old Abbot. One lady who worked there for a number of years has told of strange noises which can be heard late at night, and she claims to have seen a ghost pacing the building in 1935.

All roads through Selby lead to the abbey, one of the finest in the country. It was built originally as a monastery by Hugh de Lacy and its origins are said to have been politically motivated. Work began in 1097 but was not finished until 1340.

In 1936, a curate was alone in the abbey after evensong and as he cleared away vestments in the sacristy, he heard voices, followed by the sound of groaning. The young man went into the main body of the church to see if someone had been taken ill and was in need of assistance. Not a soul remained in the building, although the groaning continued. The frightened curate ran to tell the Canon of his experience and on being asked whether he should not have looked more closely into the matter, apparently replied, 'No, sir, I ran like the Devil!' Other people have had uncanny experiences here, but no explanation can be given as to the cause of these rather unnerving occurrences.

York Minster is said to have several ghosts, but the most famous is that of Dean Gale who died in the Minster in 1702 and who is buried there in a lead coffin.

Shortly after the Dean had been buried, a preacher was taking evening service. He finished reading the sermon and, as he stepped from the pulpit, he saw the old Dean sitting in his usual place. The Dean's son on hearing of the apparition would not accept the story, which had by this time caused enough of a stir to interest Samuel Pepys. Over the years this ghost has been seen sitting silently in the pew which was always used by Dean Gale.

Of course the roads of Yorkshire abound with other spectres besides those of highwaymen. For instance, the A164 near Driffield has been the haunt of Elfrida, the headless nun, for centuries. She was said to be a beautiful young novice who fell foul of the jealous Abbess and fled the abbey with a young local blade, with whom she had fallen in love. She was said to have become pregnant and her lover, on learning this, suddenly lost his ardour and threw her out. She returned to the abbey where, despite her remorse and pleas for forgiveness, she was sentenced to death and beheaded.

Her ghost is seen drifting through the fields near the village of Watton and if the hardy dare approach her she will turn towards them, to reveal that the inside of her flowing head-dress is empty.

Of course, not all spectral clerics are to be met in abbeys and churches, many can be found in the old halls of Yorkshire, which, like the big houses of Lancashire and Cheshire, had their connections with the church and were riddled with bolt-holes and priests' hides.

Gawthorpe Hall, Bingley (not to be confused with Gawthorpe Hall at Burnley), is haunted by the ghost of a nun who is said to have been killed by her lover. She has been seen, dressed in black cloak and hood, walking along the driveway. Likewise Ripley Castle is haunted by a mysterious, yet well-mannered nun who knocks on bedroom doors during the night. Why well-mannered? Well, unless the bleary-eyed occupant says, 'Come in,' she will not enter the room.

A monk, described as a kindly old man 'with a funny haircut', is said to haunt the upper rooms of a sixteenth-century house in Beverley and the figure of a monk has been seen at Pickering Castle as recently as 1970. The ghost was first seen in 1951 by an attendant as he sat in his room by the drawbridge of the thirteenth-century castle, one wet and miserable evening. The figure was tall and dressed in a long grey robe and his hood was pulled up over his head, making it impossible to see his face. He held his arms out as if carrying something and moved swiftly across the lawn from the direction of the keep, only to disappear on the site of the old castle ovens.

The site of Donisthorpe Hall, in Leeds, was the scene of an unusual haunting in 1970, when a team of men from the Gas Board were laying a new pipe main to the synagogue which was being built on the site. While digging a trench in which to lay the pipes, the men found a number of bones, both human and animal. The old hall had been a home for aged Jews and at the side of it stood a mausoleum. When the workmen moved the laying-out slab from it, they appear to have disturbed the spirit of one of the former occupants, for very soon afterwards three workmen saw the figure of an old Rabbi, wearing a flat-topped hat and grey cloak, watching them dig the trench. The ghostly figure was seen twice, but since the completion of the synagogue has not been seen again.

While in the Leeds area, mention should be made of a school at Crossgates which is said to be haunted by a headless nun.

In the 1830s this large rambling old building was an orphanage run by nuns. One day, when two small children were locked in a small room at the top of the building as punishment for some misdemeanour, fire broke out on the floor beneath them, leaving the two children trapped.

Hearing their screams, a young nun raced upstairs to rescue them. Fighting her way through smoke and flames, she managed to reach the room. She forced open the door, and dragged the two children clear of the flames, which by now had surrounded them. Just as she pushed the children to safety, a heavy beam fell and struck the heroic nun with such force that she was decapitated.

In recent years, the room where the nun died was the school sick-bay, but it had to be sealed off after several girls reported seeing the headless nun come through the wall and others complained of shrieks and the appearance of flames licking the walls.

A more substantial ghostly cleric made himself known to Mr F. Berridge, a retired engineer, and his wife when in 1950 they bought a small thirty-acre farm above Sowerby.

According to the deeds, the house and farm buildings were erected during the seventeenth century, but in the eighteenth century the whole place was destroyed by fire. For a long time it remained a desolate ruin, until it was bought and rebuilt by a clergyman who lived in it until his death.

All this was unknown to Mr and Mrs Berridge at the time, because the deeds of the property were deposited with the bank as collateral and it was not until many years later, when they sold the farm, that they were able to see them and learn the history of the old place. Of course, in those early days they were not all that interested; they enjoyed the peaceful life of the farm and the fresh air and hard work, which ensured that they both slept soundly at night.

However, Mr Berridge says, 'On several occasions, we were both awakened from our deep slumbers by a strong smell of burning, which seemed to fill the house. Alarmed and thinking the whole place was ablaze, we would quickly investigate, but could never discover any fire.' On each occasion, after checking the house, they would go outside and check the outbuildings and, although they never found any trace of fire, they always found that one of the farm animals was in some sort of trouble. He continues: 'I recall that once it was a cow which had got its tethering chain entangled in the drinking bowl and was in danger of being strangled. Another time, it was one of the sows in difficulty over farrowing, or one of the cows having trouble in calving.' Mr Berridge is certain that had he and his wife not been roused, they would almost certainly have lost a valuable animal.

They have reached the conclusion that the spirit of the clergyman lives on at the farm, keeping a watchful and benevolent eye on the place and warning the occupants of any imminent danger. Mr Berridge concludes: 'We never once saw the shade of the reverend gentleman, but we know now that he was there.'

Clementhorpe is now a populous area of York, but before it was developed it was said to be visited at night by the ghost of Archbishop Scrope, who was beheaded in 1405 following his trial at Bishopsthorpe. His execution took place in a field at Clementhorpe and it was here that his remains were said to have been interred until they were moved in time to York Minster. Travellers over the centuries have claimed to have seen a coffin, covered with a black pall and fringed with white silk, slowly floating through the air. Behind it walked the robed figure of the Archbishop, reading from an open book but with no sound coming from his moving lips.

Perhaps the most persistent story of his appearance was told by Robert Johnson, a slaughterman. Robert, accompanied by a boy, was returning one night to York, after going to a farm near

Bishopsthorpe to collect some sheep. On approaching Clemen-thorpe, they saw, in the road ahead of them, a coffin suspended in the air, moving slowly in the same direction as themselves. It tilted occasionally, as if borne on the shoulders of men who had been thrown out of step by the roughness of the road. Behind the coffin, walking with measured tread, walked a Bishop in fine linen, bearing in his hands a large open book. On and on went the strange procession, with the steady tread usually reserved for such august occasions, while the sheep kept pace, refusing to be driven past the apparition.

Robert Johnson said in later years that he could not have been mistaken, 'for although the night was dark, it was too light to admit of mistake'.

Psychic Phenomena

Over the years I have met many people who are gifted with prevision or second sight; the ability to foretell future events and to discern occurrences at distant places; to perceive things not visible to ordinary sight. I suspect that all of us may have it to some degree as a latent faculty that can come to the forefront in some crisis. Although most of the people in this chapter have never seen a ghost, in the true sense of the word, all have experienced at one time or another, some form of 'psychic vision'.

A lady wrote to me from Liversedge and told me that she had visions, particularly in times of anxiety and distress. A few years ago she was posting a letter to a sick friend who lived over ninety miles away. As she popped the letter into the post box, she said she had a vivid picture of the letter bursting into flames. Several days later, she received a letter from the Post Office apologizing for the letter being damaged after a mail bag caught fire in transit. Only her address at the top of the charred letter remained recognizable.

An eighty-six-year-old gentleman wrote to me from Horsforth and told me of two experiences he had had, which have always remained in his memory.

During the First World War, he was working in a factory in Leeds when, he says, he heard a 'ping', as if a rifle bullet had ricocheted, although he doesn't recall hearing the bang as it left the rifle. Later in the day, his younger brother came to the factory to tell him that they had just received a telegram from the War Office to say that his other brother, Hugh, was missing somewhere in Flanders. It later transpired that their brother had been killed by a sniper's bullet and his body had sunk into the stinking Flanders mud.

The second incident happened many years later when, on driving through Aberford with a friend, he had a distinct vision of his sister through the windscreen of the car. He remarked to his friend that he was sure something had happened to her and it was no surprise when he got home, to learn that his sister had collapsed and died at exactly the time he had seen the vision.

Mr Norman Lancaster, of Huddersfield, told me his late wife had been psychic and had the ability to see things which were very strange indeed.

In the spring of 1963, both he and his wife had been to a cricket match and had arranged to go on to his wife's mother's home for tea. On their way there, they passed a wood which was full of bluebells, so they stopped to pick a bunch. They then continued on their way, when suddenly Mrs Lancaster stopped dead in her tracks and threw the flowers away. He told me: 'A strange look came into her eyes and she just said two words, "Mother's dead!"' When they finally arrived at her mother's home, a neighbour was waiting for them with the sad news that she had found Mrs Lancaster's mother dead on the floor earlier in the afternoon.

Mr Lancaster is sure his wife's spirit lives on at their home. One night he was sitting alone watching television, when he distinctly heard his wife's voice saying, 'Are you there, Norman?' He said, 'On several occasions since, I have felt a hand on my shoulder and can only think that it is my wife, God bless her.'

Miss Doreen Bennett, of Leeds, related an interesting experience she had while visiting an old lady who lived nearby and who was practically blind. Miss Bennett told me that she noticed the old lady's eyes seemed to be looking out of the window and moving as if she was watching some activity outside. She asked if she could see something and was surprised when the old lady told her she could see a courtyard and a stagecoach. People were getting out of it, wearing Georgian-style clothes. The men wore satin breeches and jackets with lace around the wrists, the ladies wore crinolines. Nothing unusual in this, one might think. But what the old lady didn't know, was that her back garden was on the site of the courtyard of one of the last coaching inns in this part of Yorkshire.

A blind lady called at a house in Huddersfield and asked to speak to a Mrs Shackleton. She had got the wrong house, as Mrs Shackleton lived next door. However, the neighbour, realizing the blind lady's difficulty, asked her in and offered to pop next door and bring Mrs Shackleton to her.

Mrs Shackleton told me: 'I thought I was having my leg pulled, but when I went back to my neighbour's house, I was surprised to find a very small and very old lady waiting for me. She told me she had a message from someone called Mary, who was now in the next world.' Mrs Shackleton knew without doubt that the old lady was talking about her late grandmother. 'She told me many things. Things she couldn't in any way have found out beforehand,' she said.

The old lady left, declining any assistance in finding her way home. Where she came from, who she was or how she knew of Mrs Shackleton, no one dared hazard a guess. About a week later, the mysterious old lady was under discussion and Mrs Shackleton asked if any of the company present knew of her. Someone said, 'Oh yes. She used to live down Whitestone Lane. She died a few days ago!' Mrs Shackleton said that while the old lady was talking to her she had said that she hadn't much time in which to give her the message and she must have died only a day or so later.

Mr Barry Wildsmith, of Batley, was for over ten years a clairvoyant medium and during this time he experienced hundreds of instances of psychic phenomena. Although he could not relate to me for obvious reasons cases involving individuals, he was very willing to talk about experiences concerning his own immediate family.

Some years ago his two-and-a-half-year-old daughter, Lynn, died following a long illness. A few months after her death, Mr Wildsmith was sitting in the kitchen when he distinctly felt someone grasp the back of his chair and shake it quite forcibly, almost enough to dislodge him on to the floor. Some minutes later, he went into the living room and saw, to his amazement, a small dark figure standing on the living-room table. His immediate reaction was to assume it was his young son, Stephen, and he called out, 'Get down off that table, before you fall off it!' But before he had finished the sentence, he realized with a shock that the figure he saw was not his son at all, but was that of his daughter. His son in fact was leaning on the same table, with his head and arms a few inches from her yet quite unaware of her presence!

Mr Wildsmith said, 'Around this time, I was again alone in the house listening to the record player and my wife, Christine, was outside in the garden. Suddenly, I lost my balance for some inexplicable reason and almost fell to the floor. On going outside I discovered that my wife too had fallen, having lost her balance at the top of the steps leading to the back door of the house.'

After the Second World War, the Camp Hill area of Leeds was nothing more than a derelict maze of back-to-back, mid-Victorian terraced houses. In 1945 many of them were pulled down and I remember as a youngster playing with my mates among the shells of these slum dwellings.

In November 1945, another group of youngsters was playing here, jumping from rafter to rafter of the upper floors, now bereft of floorboards. One of the boys, looking down through a gap where a window had been, was surprised to see, instead of the piles of rubble, bricks and half-burnt timbers, a well-kept garden about fifteen to twenty yards square, with roses in bloom and an old gentleman attending them.

As anyone who knew the Camp Hill area before and immediately after the war will tell you, the thought of flowers growing there would have been ludicrous, but at the time the fact that here was a garden full of roses in bloom in late November did not strike the boy as odd as the thought uppermost in his mind was to avoid being caught by the old man. Shouting to his mates he quickly made his way out of the house, before the old man could see him ... Later, thinking about it, reality suddenly dawned. He searched the area, but there was no break in the heaps of waste and debris and, try as he may, he could not imagine any of the obstinate scrub turning into bushes, let alone rose bushes in full bloom.

Was this a trick of the mind or a flashback into the past? The Merrion Centre now covers the area and even though I lived here in the old days I find it impossible to trace the exact location of the streets, let alone the site where a garden might have been long before the terraced houses were built in Victoria's day.

There are many stories just like these, told across the country. People claim to have predicted many things, from the sinking of the *Titanic* to the murder of Earl Mountbatten. Many claim to have found lost objects and missing persons by using their psychic powers and I can well imagine the sceptics among my readers thinking to themselves, 'Ah yes. Anyone can be wise after the event.'

That these stories are difficult to prove, I am the first to admit, for until recently I too tended to look upon second sight and prevision with a rather jaundiced eye. That is, until an incident occurred while I was researching for this book, an incident which not only left me more open-minded, but also stopped me in my tracks.

A remarkable lady phoned me from Bradford one evening. Verging on hysteria, she explained how during the day she had been into Bradford to do some shopping and at five o'clock that same afternoon had passed through a certain part of the city. Suddenly she had been overcome with a dreadful sense of fear and felt a numbing coldness surrounding her. It was obvious, even to me, that she was thoroughly distressed about the whole incident and she felt that something terrible was about to happen.

As a psychic researcher, one gets letters and telephone calls from all kinds of people, some seeking help, some seeking notoriety, some describing experiences or telling me of ghosts I had not previously come across. This lady didn't fall into any of those categories, and by her manner I was convinced she wasn't a crank either. Following our conversation, I pondered about it for a while, intending to contact her again after a couple of days to see whether anything had indeed happened.

In the event I didn't need to bother, for on the front page of my daily paper the following morning, I was shocked to discover that the so-called 'Yorkshire Ripper' had struck in Bradford overnight. A phone call confirmed that the victim had been killed within a few yards of where this lady had been standing at five o'clock the previous afternoon and where she had felt the overpowering feeling of coldness and fear!

If the reader finds that difficult to believe, then consider the experiences of the parents of an eleven-year-old girl living in Sheffield, a bright, pert child with dark hair and intelligent hazel eyes. Looking at her she appears very much like my own daughter did at her age, except that she is different. Uncannily different.

The girl, whom I will call Julie, has been psychic since she was eighteen months old, when, sitting on the floor one day, she suddenly looked up and said, 'Picture fall, Mummy.' She crawled across to her mother just in time to avoid being hit by a large picture which came crashing down off the wall seconds later. Coincidence? Perhaps.

Some time later, Julie was taken to the City Road Cemetery to visit her grandfather's grave. As they walked between the rows of gravestones, Julie suddenly said, 'My friend David's buried up there.' Her mother asked her to show her, so Julie took her mother's arm and led the way up a long slope and over to the other side of the graveyard, where she pointed to a worn gravestone. The legend on it read 'DAVID beloved son of Clara and Frank. Died 1903, aged 18 months.'

Julie's parents questioned her about David. How did she know about the gravestone beyond the hill? But all she would say was what she always says, 'I know,' and nothing more. Yet another coincidence?

Another time, Julie's mother went into the kitchen and found her daughter staring at a table mat with a picture of Westminster Abbey on it. The little girl, who had never been to the abbey, was talking aloud to herself . . . 'The King won't let us ring the church bells. The King's closing all our churches. If we want to partake of the Host we have to hide the priest. The King's taken all our goblets and treasures.' . . . Her dumbfounded mother realized that Julie, only eight years old at the time, was talking about the Reformation of 1517!

Still sceptical?

If Only It Could Talk

For a number of years, my wife and I have collected old furniture which we restore as a hobby. We are not alone in this, as the number of antique, and so-called antique, shops to be found in even the smallest village bears out. On obtaining a piece of furniture, we often wonder about the original owners and speculate on the tales it could tell if only it could talk, for furniture, like houses, absorbs the character and, sometimes, the spirit of the owner. The rocking-chair seems to be the favourite among the more comfort-seeking spectres . . .

A family living near Hull bought one such chair in an auction. On returning home, it was placed at the end of a long kitchen table, facing the door. The lady of the house, on going through the kitchen a few days later, saw to her surprise an old man with dark hair and white narrow trousers, sitting in the rocking-chair and looking at her with a kind of benign expression on his face. Shocked, she asked him what he wanted, but he didn't answer and shortly afterwards disappeared.

At the Busby Stoop Inn, eight miles from Northallerton, one will discover a similar chair positioned next to the piano. It is a brave or foolish man who will dare to sit on it, as it is said to be reserved for the ghost of Tom Busby who, as we saw on page 52, was hanged in 1702 for the murder of his father-in-law, Daniel Auty. It is said that whoever sits in this particular chair will be cursed by Busby's ghost and will die within a few weeks. I am told that so far, only one man has been foolish enough to challenge the curse and he died within a fortnight.

❊   ❊   ❊

Mr T. Dignam of Sheffield told me of a curious incident he once experienced which concerned an old wardrobe.

On retiring to bed one night, he was disturbed by curious rapping noises which appeared to be originating from the back of his wardrobe. He says, 'I checked the inside and the exterior of the wardrobe, finding nothing that could stimulate the rapping, neither could I attribute it to contraction of the wood, as that would create its own obvious sound.' Mr Dignam felt sure the noise was caused by someone tapping their fingers lightly on the inside of the wardrobe. He continued: 'I couldn't fathom it out and so I tapped back and, to my surprise, I received an answering tap.' He then asked a series of questions, using a simple code of two raps for 'yes' and one rap for 'no'.

'Surprisingly enough the raps answered,' he said. 'I asked if it was evil, to which it replied with two raps and I held quite a conversation using the simple code.' Eventually he got into bed, because the room had become increasingly cold during this time, but the raps continued for a further ten to fifteen minutes before they finally ceased.

Mrs Denise Branks told me of a friend who had a similar experience with a piece of furniture, but for which she has offered a possible explanation.

The gentleman in question was brought up in an old farm in Pogmoor, Barnsley. He was in bed one night when he became overcome with a feeling of not being alone, although there was enough light in the room to see that no one else was present.

On his dressing table was a low mirror, more or less standing on a level with his bed, and his attention was drawn to this. He said that a face appeared in the mirror that was so clear it was as if someone was looking into it, although he was the only person in the room. The face was of a beautiful young woman, with clear skin, large eyes and long dark hair. At first he experienced a stab of fear but almost as if sensing this, the young woman smiled at him and, as she did so, an overwhelming feeling of warmth crept over him, dispelling the fear which was replaced by a feeling of peace. He said, 'I just turned over, closed my eyes and went to sleep, although I felt the face was still looking at me.'

The dressing table has long been thrown out, but Mrs Branks tells me that it had been in the family for years. The solution? Well, her friend had lost his mother when only a boy and Mrs Branks thinks it could perhaps have been she who was watching over him, although I personally have some doubts because, even if he was not able to remember his mother, he must have seen photographs of her and, as he says, the face was so clear that 'I would recognize her at once if I was ever to meet her.'

All Brontë lovers know that when Anne Brontë spent three unhappy years at Blake Hall, Mirfield, her memory of it was such that she used the Hall as the setting for her novel *The Tenant of Wildfell Hall.*

About thirty years ago, Blake Hall was demolished, but the magnificent old staircase was saved from the hands of the demolition men by an American lady and shipped to New York State, where it was re-sited in her home. The lady now claims that she has seen the ghost of Anne, wearing a long Victorian skirt, gliding up the stairs. The ghost of a Brontë in America? Perish the thought.

Piercebridge, which stands astride the Yorkshire–Durham border on the B6275, about nine miles from Scotch Corner, boasts a seventeenth-century coaching house, The George. Hanging in the bar is an old clock which was the inspiration for the song 'My Grandfather's Clock'.

This old timepiece was made in Darlington for two brothers and was by all accounts a superb piece of craftsmanship and a perfect timekeeper. One of the brothers died and from that day on, the clock began to go wrong. The other brother lived well into his eighties but, on the day he died, the clock stopped and all efforts to make it go since have met with failure, hence the song:

The clock stopped, never to go again,
When the old man died.

Mr J. C. Kenyon of Harrogate related a rather interesting experience his father had which again involved a piece of furniture, a chest of drawers.

Many years ago his father, John Kenyon, served as coachman at Holgate Head, Kirkby Malham. One evening on entering his room, he was surprised to see a lady in period dress in the act of opening or closing a drawer in an old-fashioned chest of drawers at the foot of his bed. On his approach the apparition disappeared. Several times he returned to his room to discover the drawer open and it was subsequently discovered that this had at some time been a 'bottom drawer', which in the tradition of the old days was reserved as a repository by a girl who was anticipating marriage. Whether in this case the lady in question ever attained the state of matrimony, neither Mr Kenyon nor his father were able to say, but it seems logical to surmise that some human tragedy is associated with her reappearance as an apparition.

The story of the ghost seen in a mirror, though otherwise invisible, is fairly widely distributed. One old Whitby story tells how, about 200 years ago, after several bad fishing seasons, a group of desperate Whitby men turned to piracy, making their unfortunate victims walk the plank. On one of the unlucky ships that was attacked by the pirates, the Captain was sailing accompanied by his wife. She was wearing a beautiful silken shawl and as she walked the plank to her death one of the pirates snatched it from her slim shoulders. He took the shawl home as a present for his wife, neglecting to tell her how it came into his possession.

On the following Sunday, as the wife was dressing for church, she tried the silken shawl over her shoulders, admiring the lovely pattern and colours as it fell in graceful folds around her. Suddenly she saw in the mirror the pale and tragic face of the drowned woman looking at her over her shoulder, her white bony hand pointing an accusing finger at the shawl. We are told that the pirate's wife went mad with terror and died shortly afterwards. No one knows what happened to the shawl; perhaps it was burned, or perhaps given to some other unsuspecting fishwife.

Although poltergeist phenomena are not, strictly speaking, paranormal and apparitions are not usually encountered in poltergeist cases, there are the odd exceptions. Whichever way one looks at it, though, the activities of the poltergeist can be most distressing.

A lady from Sowerby Bridge, who wishes to remain anonymous, told me of some interesting poltergeist phenomena she encountered some years ago which concerned household furniture.

She described how, after the children's beds had been made, the next person to go upstairs would find them all untidy again. On another occasion, while everyone was watching television, the toilet roll from the bathroom unrolled itself all the way down the stairs, while still fastened to the holder on the wall in the bathroom.

As if this was not enough, all the rods came away from the staircarpet and when they were eventually replaced one was found to be missing. Although the whole house was searched, the stair-rod could not be found. Some three or four days later, the piano in the lounge was found to have been moved by some mysterious force and was at least three or four feet away from its usual place against the wall . . . the most amazing thing of all was that the missing stair-rod was discovered lying twisted behind it.

A gentleman from Sheffield experienced what he thought to be, at the time, a series of incidents caused by poltergeist activity, which began about four or five years ago.

He told me: 'The first incident occurred when I was staying with my son and concerns my wrist-watch which, when I go to bed, I always place under my pillow near my head.' On this particular occasion, when he woke the following morning, he could find no trace of the watch. It was not until he and his son had undertaken an intensive search that they found the watch inside the pillow slip and at the opposite side of the bed to where it had been placed the previous night.

Some time later, in his own home, my correspondent was awakened one night by what appeared to be the sound of rushing wind. Being half asleep he did not bother to get up to investigate, as he knew the windows were not open. He might have dismissed the whole thing as a dream if, on getting up the following morning, he had not discovered that a small wooden reading lamp which stood near the window had been overturned and the plug had been removed from the socket!

On another occasion he found a number of articles on the passenger seat of his car. These included a perfectly good Kodak camera already loaded with unused film, two different lipsticks and a 'charity' pencil which originated in the London area. Once, when he had put a clean handkerchief in his breast pocket, he found it torn to shreds when he came to use it, and on two separate occasions the lining of his jacket was also found to be badly torn.

These events were eventually put down to the mischievous spirit of an old friend who had lived in Rustington and who had died about six or seven years before these events took place. He was well known for his leg-pulling and for playing practical jokes on his friends. He was very fond of tinkering with watches and was renowned for his clumsiness in knocking anything over within his reach. The lipsticks and the camera? . . . Well, it appears that an amorous courting couple had broken into the car one evening and used it as a love nest, leaving some of their belongings behind. At least, that is what my correspondent likes to think!

There used to be a house in Mirfield, now long demolished, which rejoiced in the unusual name of 'The Elbow'. During the 1920s, a curious event occurred which was associated with a clock.

The youngest daughter of the family was lying in bed recovering from some childhood ailment, when her attention was caught by the loud ticking of a clock, except that there was no clock in the room. She looked across to the top of the staircase, which as in many of these old houses came directly into the room. The ticking grew louder, as if approaching the bedroom.

The frightened young girl now stared terrified at the stairs, the ticking grew louder and louder and then, as if from nowhere, a small man appeared. His features were indistinguishable, but on his head he wore a white hat, such as a plantation owner would wear, a white suit and white boots. In his hand he held what appeared to be a round clock which was ticking loudly.

The figure, appearing not to notice the terrified girl, turned, showing the creases in the back of his jacket as he did so, and disappeared through the wall, at which the child screamed out for her mother.

Who the figure was and what the ticking clock signified, she was never able to discover and never saw the figure nor heard the ticking again. As the house is no longer standing, indeed the area itself has altered so much since those days, it has not been possible for the author to pursue the mystery further.

Ghosts and Greasepaint

Many of the country's older theatres are haunted by ghosts more dramatic than anything which might have been acted out beneath the proscenium arch. The theatres of Yorkshire are no exception, although many managers seem reluctant to discuss the subject. Fortunately, the same cannot be said of touring actors and actresses.

It would seem reasonable to expect many of these ghosts to be of Thespians and this is certainly true of the ghost that haunts the Theatre Royal at Bradford.

The Theatre Royal is in fact haunted by the ghost of the legendary Sir Henry Irving, the son of a Somerset tradesman who, without doubt, became the best-loved actor of the Victorian theatre. After a performance of *Becket* he collapsed and died here on 13 October, 1905, but his ghost still walks the boards.

Fifty years after Sir Henry Irving's death the theatre had been converted to a cinema and, during the late 1960s, the manager was in the main body of the auditorium, after a well-attended show. The last of the audience were leaving the main foyer and the houselights were still on, cigarette smoke hanging above the stalls.

Suddenly he became aware of a figure, seemingly taking shape in the tobacco smoke above the front stalls, which, when quite solid, appeared to be bowing and scraping. Obviously, the manager was quite scared by his experience.

However, he later examined some old plans of the theatre and he discovered that when the alterations were carried out in 1921, the stage had been reduced by some considerable amount. In fact, where he had witnessed the figure was where, prior to 1921, the footlights would have been. He was left in no doubt that he had witnessed Sir Henry Irving taking his curtain call.

The old Theatre Royal has now closed down altogether and since the late 1970s it has been used by Bradford Metropolitan Council as a storage department. What a pity that they will not say whether Sir Henry Irving has put in any more appearances since.

Another Theatre Royal, this time in St Leonards Place, York, opened in 1740 and was built on the site of the old St Leonards Hospital, founded by King Stephen in the twelfth century. As was the custom in the Middle Ages it was run by nuns. The theatre's ghost is that of a young nun who broke her vows and was walled up alive as a punishment. (As a point of interest, this explanation, which is so common in accounts of this type of haunting, may be a distortion of the true facts. A spokesman for the Catholic Church told me that in the old days it was fairly common practice for nuns to show their commitment to the religious life and rejection of worldly goods by having their cell doors bricked up, leaving only a small window through which they received food and drink.) Whatever the reason for this haunting, there are several people who are prepared to testify that a ghostly nun does tread the boards here, still wearing her grey and white habit. She is most often seen in a small room near the dress circle.

Many occupants of this room have said that they were aware of a strange feeling, as if they were being watched. Others experienced an inexplicable chilling sensation. The manager told me that strange happenings still occur and some time ago a well-known actress was standing in the back of the dress circle and saw the figure of a nun, dressed in grey with a white coif, leaning over the edge of the stage box.

But the best-authenticated spectre at the theatre is that of an actor who died in a stage duelling accident during the last century. He was seen as recently as 1977, dressed in period costume and standing in the upper circle. He is said to wear a prominent ring with an awesomely large green stone and to have well-manicured hands. During the autumn of 1975 whilst rehearsals were in progress for *Dear Octopus*, the cast were assembled on stage to sing 'Kerry Dance Again'. They were puzzled to see a light slowly develop in the circle of the theatre. As they looked on fascinated, it increased in intensity and eventually took on the form of the head and shoulders of a man. This little incident only lasted for a few seconds, but it brought the rehearsal to a complete standstill until the cast had recovered their composure.

I have in front of me a photocopy of a letter sent to the *Daily Sketch* in 1965, from a Mr Harry Bennett of Hampstead, in which he says that while appearing at the Theatre Royal with his company, he managed to obtain permission to try to 'lay' the ghost. He says, 'Several of us occupied the dressing room and shortly we heard footsteps. The atmosphere became eerie and cold. To our absolute horror the figure of a tall woman appeared, hooded and gowned, having entered the dressing room through a closed door.'

Unfortunately, just at that time a female member of the company began to scream with fright and the apparition vanished.

The Palace Theatre, Halifax, was reputed to be haunted by the ghost of the comedian and playwright, Clarence Turner. 'Tubby' Turner, as he was known, collapsed and died on the stage in the early 1950s in the middle of his famous deckchair sketch. I have heard an unconfirmed story which relates how a local amateur dramatic society performed one of Turner's plays, *Summat For Nowt*, at the Palace. One young lady, who had difficulty in remembering her lines, spotted a strange man in the wings, mouthing the words to her. She later learned that her description fitted that of Turner.

Another star who died on stage was the much-loved character actor, Arthur Lucan who, together with his wife and partner, Kitty McShane, were a big draw at theatres and cinemas wherever they appeared throughout the north, as Old Mother Riley and her daughter Kitty.

Poor Arthur died on stage at the Tivoli, Hull, on 17 May, 1954, and I have it on good authority that his pathetic ghost has been seen on the site at least twice in the intervening years, dressed in his Old Mother Riley costume. Old Mother Riley was a great favourite with the kids of my generation, and Arthur Lucan's grave in the East Cemetery at Hull is nearly always covered with flowers, put there by children who never knew him but have seen his many films on television.

Alas, the Tivoli too has gone, closing down not many months after the death of Arthur Lucan. It was finally demolished in 1959 and a shop and office block was erected on the site.

The City Palace of Varieties in Leeds has had a chequered career. Like many music halls, it began life as the singing room of a public house, the White Swan, rebuilt in the 1790s on the site of a coaching inn. It was enlarged by Charles Thornton, best remembered for Thornton's Arcade in Briggate, to something like its present form and opened as 'Thornton's New Music Hall and Fashionable Lounge' on 7 June, 1865. The first chairman, in a long line of chairmen, was Harry Bowser, who wielded the gavel for many years before Leonard Sachs was born. It was closed in 1875 and was later bought by Mr Jack Stanfield and reopened as 'Stanfield's Varieties' round about 1877. More alterations were carried out in the next couple of decades as a number of managers came and went.

Nowadays, of course, the famous City Varieties Theatre is better known as the location for the successful BBC television series 'The Good Old Days'. It is also a centre of mystery. There are several underground passages which are said to extend for miles – even as far as Kirkstall Abbey. Mystery also surrounds a coat of arms over the proscenium arch which, local legend says, was bestowed by King Edward VII, who is reputed to have visited the old theatre incognito to see Lily Langtry when she appeared there with Bransby Williams in 1898. He, as Prince of Wales, was staying as a guest at Harewood House. By tradition he used Box D, to the right of the stage.

The City Varieties Theatre boasts at least two ghosts to my knowledge. One is the ghost of a female vocalist and the other that of an old-time pianist. Who they are, no one can be sure, but at least one night-watchman is on record as having seen them both on separate occasions.

Independent television producer Len Marten told me of his

experience, when he met one of the theatre ghosts during the time he worked for Thames Television as associate producer for the television series, 'Opportunity Knocks'.

He told me how one evening, whilst in Leeds doing the yearly round of auditions for the series, he took his production assistant to the theatre, as she had heard so much about it but had never actually seen it. Mr Marten said that at the time a revue was playing there and the manager, who knew him well, invited both him and his assistant up to the circle bar for a drink, where they and other members of the profession chatted until the bar closed.

He said, 'I went out to the cloakroom, which was in the bar area, and I had only been in there a minute or so when the lights went out. It was exceptionally dark and it took me a while to grope my way to the door and into the bar. Having got into the bar, I discovered that the lights in there were also out.'

He could hear his friends chatting as they descended the stairs to the exit and he managed to grope his way to the door, only to discover that it was locked. No one heard him shouting and he realized that he was locked in for the night or at least until the night-watchman came round and discovered him.

Mr Marten continued: 'So there I was, locked in for the night in complete darkness, except for the glow of a coal fire burning in the bar. I sat beside it and gradually became drowsy as the fire died down. I decided to lie down on a long seat, eventually dropping off to sleep.'

He had no idea of the time, but suddenly he woke up with a start. The room had become ice-cold and as he looked round he saw, standing by the fireplace, the ghostly figure of a woman in a crinoline dress, who appeared to be looking directly at him.

'I must have uttered a cry of sorts,' he said, 'because she faded away, seemingly through the fireplace. I was not dreaming, I saw her as plainly as if she were real flesh and blood and when she faded away, the room became warm again.'

It was not until some time the following morning that he was discovered by the night-watchman and released from his temporary prison.

The Georgian Theatre at Richmond is also reputed to be haunted, although the current manager, Mr Gregor MacGregor, is unable to throw any light on it. He told me in February 1981, 'To the best of my knowledge there would appear to be no record or evidence of any psychic phenomena in the Georgian Theatre, although in its 193-year history it would appear that it should have acquired something of the kind.'

A letter to the *Stage* brought a response from Mr James Patrick of Salisbury who told me that when, in 1966, he took part in the Stewart Headlam Company production of the eighteenth-century version of *King Lear* at the Georgian Theatre, a lot of publicity was given to the sighting by the company stage manager of the theatre ghost. Mr Patrick went on to say that at that particular time there was a strong ghost tradition at the theatre, although he did not feel or see anything unusual.

As Mr MacGregor says, the theatre ought to be haunted. Samuel Butler first brought the theatre to the town in the days when Richmond was the fashionable centre of Georgian Swaledale. He was a theatre producer from York who found enough people in the area interested in the theatre to support his new venture and to pay to populate his stage with such people as Sarah Siddons and Edmund Kean. It became, for a time at least, the social hub of the Dales and must have been patronized by many celebrities of the Georgian scene. However, in time interest in the theatre waned and the doors eventually closed, the building being put to various other uses.

When rediscovered, it was a furniture store, until restored to its former glory under the watchful eye of Dr Southern, an eminent authority on Georgian buildings.

Thanks to the dedicated staff of the *Yorkshire Post* I was able to track down a record of the incident Mr Patrick referred to and which was reported in the *Yorkshire Post* of 20 April, 1966.

Mr Jock Evans, a London schoolteacher, was acting as deputy stage manager for the Stewart Headlam Company, during the production already mentioned. Working alone in the theatre, he said everything suddenly went deathly quiet and he became aware of a presence. After a moment or two the feeling passed, the theatre appeared to come back to life again and he returned to his work. The paper reported that Mr Evans was not the first to have experienced the ghostliness, as other people had also felt it.

At that time, there were many who thought the presence to be the ghost of none other than the great bard himself, William Shakespeare, as the anniversary of his death occurred during the week of the play, and it was thought he may have disapproved of the eighteenth-century additions and subtractions in Tate's melodramatic and shortened version of the great tragedy. It's a lovely thought.

Perhaps the reader will allow me, out of interest, to digress here and mention two ghosts outside the borders of Yorkshire, but within easy reach.

A ghost has haunted the New Tyne Theatre at Newcastle for well over ninety years: the shade of a stage hand, Bob Crowther, who was killed whilst working there in 1887. Ever since his death, many actors, staff and patrons have experienced a strange and chilling presence and had the odd glimpse of a strange man in grey, walking about backstage. A couple of years or so ago, a producer took the advice of a psychic investigator, rather than have his company resign *en masse*, to try to put the spirit to rest. He was advised to make the ghost welcome, by allotting him a certain seat. Nowadays, to make sure that no one else takes this particular place, a shrouded dummy is always left in what has become known as Bob Crowther's seat, which is way up in the gods. Where else!

Sad to relate that since writing *Yorkshire's Ghosts and Legends*, it was reported in *Stage and Television Today* that the beautiful New Tyne theatre was severely damaged in a disastrous fire during the 1985–6 pantomime season.

The second ghost can be found barely a spit and a stride over the border, in the town of Ashton-Under-Lyne, at the Thameside Theatre. Here they have a ghost with the nickname of 'Ernie'. He always appears as a man in a raincoat, standing in the shadow of the upper balcony. The figure will beckon anyone fortunate enough to sight him, but once they begin to walk towards him he will vanish into thin air. Whose ghost this is I have never been able to discover, and the management seem rather reluctant to discuss it.

The audience has long since gone. The auditorium is empty.

The safety curtain is down. The lights are dimmed and the players, in some nearby public house, celebrate their evening's triumph . . . or drown the despair of disaster.

Yet the theatre is alive. Listen, you can hear it whispering in the corridors and stairways, watch its eyeless balconies gazing down, catch its breathing in the creaking of the scenery and rustling curtains . . . there is nothing more eerie, or more dramatic, than an empty theatre.

It is not surprising that actors are far more respectful of the unknown world of the supernatural than any other group of people. For in many theatres throughout the land it would be ill-advised to tempt the ever-present ghosts to make an appearance.

Dark, Mysterious Gentlemen

For every traditional grey or white lady in the county, there is a spectral male counterpart. The stories behind some of these ghosts may not be as romantic but they are equally as tragic in many instances. Some are doomed to haunt as a result of a foul deed committed in the course of some forgotten cause.

A sad ghost haunts Oakwell Hall, a lovely Tudor house at Birstall. A few days before Christmas 1684, the eldest son of the family, William Batt, was murdered while visiting relatives in London. The night he died, his family, knowing him to be in London until Christmas Eve, were surprised to see him enter the great hall and mount the stairs to the main bedroom without saying a word to anyone.

They noticed how pale and ill he looked and on the stairs saw a footprint in wet blood. Yet, when they looked in the bedroom they could find no trace of him. Not until the following day did they hear of his death and learn that he had been killed by a man called Graeme at Barnet. It's now believed that the ghost which roams the corridors of Oakwell Hall is that of William Batt.

As I write this chapter it is 5 November and I can hear children and their parents enjoying a huge bonfire in the fields behind my home. The periodic 'whoosh' of sky-rockets and the joyous 'oohs' and 'ahs' of parents and children alike, bring to mind a far happier and more carefree ghost which is said to haunt the lanes and footpaths of Nidderdale. This is the spectre of the young Guy Fawkes.

He has also been seen in the corridors of Scotton Old Hall, a place where he spent many of his teenage years with his mother and stepfather after his own father died when Guy was only eight. Young Guy Fawkes was very happy here and his teenage years were spent doing pretty much as he pleased, riding, walking, and often visiting family friends, the Ingilbys of Ripley Castle.

It is a funny thing, but although we always associate Guy Fawkes with gunpowder, treason and plot, the spirit he has left behind at Scotton Old Hall is that of a happy, aimless adolescent.

The ghost of William Constable haunts his old home, Burton Constable Hall, near Hull. This isn't surprising since in the mid-nineteenth century he did more than any other owner before him to turn the Elizabethan hall into a magnificent and comfortable home.

One night, a lady, sleeping in the Gold Room, awoke to see a figure in a velvet coat, standing at the foot of her bed. She recognized it from an oil painting kept at the hall as William Constable and was not in the least afraid, although she later claimed to have been more than a little startled when the figure allegedly spoke to her saying, 'I wished to see what you had done to my room!' Since that night, quite a lot of restoration work has been carried out at Burton Constable Hall, and where the ghost first materialized workmen discovered a spiral staircase leading to the hall below.

Who is the silent, shadowy figure said to haunt the ruins of Scarborough Castle? Most people seem to agree that it is the ghost of a Gascon immigrant by the name of Piers Gaveston, late Earl of Cornwall and one-time friend of Edward II.

History tells us that it was here that Gaveston surrendered the castle to the barons about six hundred years ago, on condition that his life be spared to stand trial. Gaveston had become increasingly unpopular with both peasant and noble alike, but when the Earl of Warwick laid siege to Scarborough Castle, he resisted valiantly for quite a time before hunger and thirst finally forced the garrison to surrender.

Warwick promised both Gaveston and his men safe conduct but, once the gates were opened, he treacherously broke his word and had Gaveston beheaded outside the castle walls. (Many historians argue that Gaveston was, in fact, allowed to ride away, but that Warwick had second thoughts and sent some of his soldiers after him, capturing him as he made his way south and taking him to the town of Warwick, where he was then beheaded as a public enemy.) Whichever way it happened, Gaveston's spirit, unable to rest because of the treachery of his enemy, now prowls the castle ruins. A fearsome headless apparition, he rushes towards those who are unlucky or brave enough to walk amongst the ruins after dark, and tries to chase them over the edge of the battlements.

Walter Calverley, of Calverley Hall, nearly succeeded in killing off all his family in a fit of insane frenzy. These deeds give rise to the belief that if a group of people join hands in a circle around his grave at Calverley churchyard and sing:

> Old Calverley, old Calverley, I'll have thee by thi'
> ears,
> I'll cut thi' into collops, unless tha' appears

then his spirit may be conjured up. Although why anyone should want to do so is beyond me, for Walter Calverley would revel in anything which had a touch of evil about it.

The Calverley family had been Lords of the Manor at Pudsey and Calverley for over five hundred years and, as the occupants of Calverley Hall, they were generally respected. However, every family has one and Walter was the degenerate of the seventeenth-century branch of the family; he drank and gambled to excess and invariably came face to face with financial ruin and all it entailed. Early in the 1600s, he turned on his long-suffering wife, a southerner, and accused her of being unfaithful. The more she protested her innocence, the graver his accusations became. Walter had, in fact, developed an unreasonable hatred towards the poor woman, just because she had been pleading with him to mend his miserable ways, even offering to sell her jewellery to help pay off his debts.

Now, Walter had a brother at university and one day a university friend came to Calverley Hall to seek some kind of financial help. He couldn't have come at a worse time, for this was to send Walter into a mad frenzy. He stormed off into a gallery alone and set about considering his financial state, for this was his moment of great crisis. He ranted to himself about how his prodigal course in life had wronged his brother, abused his wife and undone his children, and the abject misery he would leave his children in should he die.

Suddenly, one of his children, aged four, ran into the gallery and Walter, now quite insane, slew the child with his dagger. Lifting up the bleeding body, he carried it into the presence of his wife and the second child. Then he stabbed his wife in the shoulder and killed the second child. Now of his children only his youngest son, Henry, remained alive, but being 'at nurse' he was staying at Norton. Walter set off on horseback, intent on murdering again, but the horse, driven too hard, fell and rolled on him. Before he could free himself and resume his journey, he was overpowered and taken to Wakefield, where his faithful wife actually forgave him.

Walter Calverley paid the price for his misdeeds on the York Tyburn, but not before the journey from Wakefield had been delayed for several months, due to the plague. He did not plead at his trial so his estates were not confiscated. His body was buried at St Mary's Churchyard, in Castlegate, York, but his remains were moved secretly to Calverley, where his ghost was usually seen at night, mounted on a headless horse. He has also been seen striding along a corridor at Calverley Hall, but I understand that this particular corridor has recently been bricked up.

His ghost continued to be active at the Hall for many years. A local vicar, when staying there, had his night's sleep disturbed three times after being thrown out of his bed by an invisible being.

The last mad outburst of old Walter was the ringing of the bell in the church tower very early one morning. The bell tolled for a long time because no one could find the key to the tower. When it was eventually found, the bell stopped ringing.

Shakespeare was right when he wrote that, 'The evil that men do lives after them; the good is oft interred with their bones.' As we have seen, it is certainly true of unpleasant Yorkshire ghosts.

For instance, who was the saucy spectre who took a fancy to Sheila Broomhead?

Sheila lives in a ground-floor council flat in Cliff Street, Sheffield, and she was nodding off to sleep in September 1981, when the bed suddenly began to move from side to side. Then, something jumped on to the bed.

Now, Sheila may call an exorcist if the sexy spectre doesn't stop pestering her. She said, 'At first I thought the dog had jumped on the bed, but then I realized that was impossible, because she was locked outside in the hall.' She said that it was all over in a matter of a few seconds. She never saw anything or heard any noise whatsoever. It was all very spooky.

The Ingilbys of Ripley Castle were a proud family who produced one or two good ghosts in their time. One old Lord let his desires run away with him and although married had a mistress as well. He hid the latter, in the hope that his intensely jealous spouse would not find her, at Padside, a quiet spot between Pateley Bridge and Blubberhouses. Unfortunately the wife found out, tracked down her rival and cursed her husband, wishing him a quick death and an eternity of wandering in spectral form. Something he still does from time to time today.

A noisy ghost belonged to another black sheep, Thomas Preston of Low Hall, Appletreewick, about whom nobody has ever said a kind word. His spectre had terrorized Low Hall and Wharfedale for many years, making life intolerable with yells, bangs and groans. Eventually a priest had to be called to exorcize the noisy spirit, which he finally did by banishing it to a grave in Dibb Gill, in what is known today as Preston's Well.

Another ghost to be encountered around Appletreewick haunted a lane outside the village for many years. At last a hardy soul met the ghost one night when returning from a night out with the boys. Made braver no doubt by the local ale, he approached the ghost and asked him why he haunted the lane, scaring the villagers. The spectre replied in sombre hollow tones, saying that he had committed an unforgivable sin and moved his neighbour's landmarks, one by one, shifting boulders and stoops until he had gained an extra strip of land. Disaster after disaster followed his wicked deed. The neighbour hadn't noticed but the man had been struck by remorse and had committed suicide by taking poison.

The villager listened politely to the grieving spectre and promised to do whatever he could to help. He promised to see that the stoops were moved back to the right place and agreed to pay back the chemist, to whom payment was still owed for the poison. At this, a weird smile crossed the face of the ghost, who faded into the night, never to be seen again.

Standing back from the main road and almost hidden by trees, is a well-preserved and beautiful old house, with stone mullions and a magnificent rose window above the main entrance. This is Lumb Hall, once the home of Charles Darwin. Today it is the home of 'Charlie', the resident phantom. He appears to be quite harmless and has the odd habit of making a shuffling and scraping sound at the front door. On investigation, however, no one is ever found.

A few years ago, a lady staying at Lumb Hall underwent a strange and terrifying experience in the bedroom which she occupied. During the night she was awakened by an intense feeling of cold and was surprised to see a male figure in a fawn cloak rise from the floor and disappear through the ceiling. Some weeks later, part of an old staircase was discovered in the room above, evidently the stairs the ghost had known during its lifetime, the lower part of which had originally risen from the ground floor.

Lumb Hall is a large and interesting old house, with an equally interesting past. Within, there is a wealth of oak panelling, curious passages and an attractive staircase. The furniture is beautiful, having been made from period oak, which gives off an aura of olde worlde charm.

It has now been established that Charles Darwin, who was an ardent Royalist, lived here during the seventeenth century. Is he the 'Charlie' who scrapes and shuffles at the door? Or is he the figure seen wearing the fawn coat? Some historians believe the hall to have been in the hands of Cromwell's troops during the Civil War, when the house was occupied by the Brookes family, ardent Royalists. Is this the ghost of one of the Brookeses? No one knows.

During renovations in 1949, workmen, stripping off old panels, found a number of swords dating from this period, which were evidently hidden away and presumably forgotten. Unfortunately, the weapons were regarded as just useless junk at the time and the unforgivable happened – they were thrown away. Perhaps this is why 'Charlie' is unable to settle and still wanders the hall, seeking out his weapons.

During the 1920s, a psychic researcher spent a night at Bolling Hall, Bradford, hoping to spot one of the many spectres said to reside there, for apart from the mysterious manifestation the Earl of Newcastle was said to have seen back in 1643, mentioned on page 45, the ghost of Richard Oastler is also seen here from time to time.

Richard Oastler, the self-styled 'factory king', was a regular visitor to the Walker family, who were resident here in the middle of the nineteenth century. He had threatened to haunt the place after his death if the Walkers' son did not change his mind and believe in life after death. On the morning of 22 August, 1861, Richard Oastler died and his ghost was seen at exactly the same time by the son of the house. It has been recorded several more times since, usually on the anniversary of Oastler's death. It is not recorded, however, whether or not the psychic researcher was lucky enough to catch sight of him.

Hawkesworth Hall, near Guiseley, had a ghost of a Negro page-boy, who used to sneak into bedrooms and leave an imprint of his hand on the pillow. Also at Hawkesworth a cowled monk prowled through the corridors and galleries.

The Carnegie College at Leeds is host to the ghost of a former butler from the days before the building was taken over by the City of Leeds and was a manor house, known as 'The Grange'. He is said to have thrown himself off the top of the spiral staircase when his love for his mistress was unrequited.

Jeeves would never have approved!

Today this is the computer science centre of Leeds Polytechnic and it stands in the grounds of Beckett Park at Headingly.

It is still known by the students as 'The Grange' and it is claimed that there is more than one ghost on the site. The author has not been able to confirm this.

Ripon used to have an official called the Wakeman, whose job it was to protect the city at night. The last Wakeman was Hugh Ripley who, in 1604, became the first Lord Mayor. His old thirteenth-century house still stands in the market place.

By tradition, each evening a horn-blower blows a few blasts at the market cross and another blast or two outside the home of the current mayor. In the 1920s the mayor, who had married into the Precious family, who at one time had lived in the Wakeman's house, urged the corporation to buy it and preserve the building. He also suggested that the horn should be blown there as well as in the market square and outside the mayor's house. This was agreed to.

On the first occasion of the horn being blown outside the Wakeman's house, someone in the crowd shouted, 'Look up there at the top window!' As one, the crowd looked up and saw something white, with no distinguishable form, appear at the small window at the top of the house. Whatever the weird apparition, everyone in the square saw it.

People said that it was the ghost of old Hugh Ripley aroused by the sound of the horn outside his house. There were even those who were prepared to say that the ghost wore a smile at the honour bestowed on him by such a ceremony.

The Precious family lived at the house from about 1820 to 1910 and knew of the existence of a ghost. Many nights they had been awakened by a sense of some kind of presence in the room. Footsteps were heard, chairs which were in the way of the ghost as he walked the night hours were pushed away with a clatter, and once a ghostly form was seen moving about in one of the bedrooms.

Many years ago, an old porter at the original Darlington railway station, which in those days was not much more than a country station on the Yorkshire–Durham border, had a frightening experience when, one cold winter's night, some time near midnight, he felt chilly and decided to go and get himself a hot drink and something to eat. There was a porter's cellar where a fire was kept going and a coal house connected to it. He went down the steps, took off his heavy overcoat and had just settled himself on the bench opposite the fire and turned up the gas lamp, when a strange man came out of the coal house followed by a big black retriever. As soon as he entered, the porter's eyes were on him and likewise the man's eyes were on the porter. They watched each other intently as the stranger moved over to the front of the fire. The stranger stood looking at the porter and a curious smile spread over his face.

All at once he struck out at the frightened porter, who had the impression he had hit him. The porter, quite naturally, struck back at the figure, but his fist went straight through him, striking the stone above the fireplace, scraping the skin from his knuckles. The figure appeared to stagger back into the fire and uttered a strange and unearthly scream.

Immediately the black dog seized the porter by the calf of the leg, causing immense pain. The strange figure recovered and motioned the dog away. Then dog and figure backed slowly through the closed coal-house door. The frightened porter lit his lantern and nervously opened the door to the coal house and looked around inside, but there was no sight of either man or dog, nor was there any way in which they could have got out, except by the door itself.

Many weeks later, the porter discovered that, some years before, a man employed in the booking-office had committed suicide by jumping in front of a passing express train. His body had been carried into the cellar prior to its removal. He had owned a black retriever, just like the one that had attacked the porter. He later said, 'I ought to add that no mark or effect remained on the spot where I seemed to have been bitten by the dog!'

Another ghost associated with a railway station was reported by W.T. Stead in 1905.

The station stood just south of Middlesbrough on the old Middlesbrough–Whitby line. At the end of the platform stood what was known as 'the dead house', a small stone building often used as a temporary mortuary by the railway company, should any passenger expire on railway property. A young lad by the name of Archer was employed at the station as a telegraphist and, to him, the dead house seemed eerie and unpleasant. He was on night duty at the station and, when he left his office in the early hours of the morning, he was always very uneasy when passing the building alone.

One morning, at about 2 o'clock, he came out on to the station platform and was walking in the direction of the dead house, steeling himself to pass it alone, when to his delight he saw, standing on the platform ahead of him, the familiar figure of one of the signalmen from the box just off the end of the platform. Hoping that he would walk with him past the dead house, he stepped up to the signalman but to his utter amazement and horror, the figure vanished as if into thin air.

Feeling very frightened, and not knowing what to make of it, he went down to the signal box and told the signalman on duty what he had seen. The signalman looked at him in amazement and said, 'You have just seen Fred Nicholson? . . . It's impossible. Didn't you know that he was killed yesterday by a train? His body is lying in the dead house at this moment.'

It was now young Archer's turn to be dismayed; he was perfectly sure in his own mind that he had seen the man . . . And yet the man was dead.

Finally, a much more recent and mundane sighting. Mrs Barbara Yates of Hull saw a rather interesting ghost not so long ago. She told me: 'I was fast asleep and was suddenly wakened by a rustling sound, rather as if someone was rustling paper, although I knew there was no paper anywhere in the room and certainly not near the bed.' Wide awake now, she looked up to see what she could only describe as a beautiful little boy, dressed in Edwardian clothes and the typical white collar which youngsters wore in those days. She said he had a lovely face and blond hair. The child smiled at her before fading away.

Mrs Yates saw the apparition on two other occasions, each time standing beside the bed and smiling down at her.

Later she had another uncanny experience, quite unrelated, which occurred three weeks after the death of her brother-in-law. She said, 'One night I was unable to sleep, so I went downstairs without putting on the lights, so as not to disturb the rest of the family. I sat in the living room, and as I did so, my dead brother-in-law appeared and sat on the edge of the settee.' She told me she was not in the least frightened. The figure stayed there for a few moments, looking so real and unghostlike that Mrs Yates began to speak to him, which caused him to disappear suddenly, much to her disappointment.

Some Classic, Authenticated Ghosts

There are a number of ghost stories, which do not seem to fit neatly into any particular category, but which are far too interesting to omit. Therefore, before we turn from the subject of ghosts and look at the other supernatural aspects of Yorkshire, perhaps they should be mentioned here. Most are very old authenticated accounts of hauntings, several of which have remained unexplained for many years, which to my mind makes them all the more interesting.

To begin with I should like to describe one of the rarest cases of psychic phenomena that one will ever come across, the case of ghosts in law!

Only very occasionally has a ghost's evidence been accepted in a court of law. Records show that this did indeed happen in Yorkshire in the seventeenth century. The only case to gain notoriety happened in Scotland in 1750 and earned some celebrity from the fact that Sir Walter Scott edited the trial transcripts for the Bannatyre Club of Edinburgh, in 1830. The ghost in the Scottish trial was said to have influenced the jury, so that they found the prisoners in the case 'Not guilty'. However, in the case of Rex v Barwick, heard at York Assizes, the ghost did just the opposite and Barwick paid with his life.

On 14 April, 1690, William Barwick of Cawood pushed his pregnant wife, Mary, into a pond, holding her under the water until she drowned. Pulling the body out of the water, he buried it under some nearby bushes. He then walked to Rushworth and the home of his brother-in-law, a man by the name of Lofthouse, and told him that he had taken Mary to an uncle's home at Selby, where she was to be cared for until after the birth of their child.

A few days later, Lofthouse went to his well to draw some water and saw a woman sitting on a nearby hillock. He didn't take much notice of her but later when he returned for another pailful he saw the woman again, wearing 'on her cap something like a white bag hanging from it'. In his statement to the Assize at York in September 1690, Lofthouse said, 'Her face looked pale, her teeth in sight with no gums showing. Her looks being like my wife's sister, the wife of William Barwick.'

Lofthouse didn't tell his wife about the woman at first, but later, when he did finally tell her, she made him go to Selby and seek out the uncle to see if Mary was staying there or not. Discovering she was not, and never had been, Lofthouse went straight to the Mayor of York and told him what he knew. Shortly afterwards Barwick was arrested and he at once confessed to killing Mary. Her remains were discovered where he had buried them and not surprisingly he was found guilty of murder. He was executed at York and his body hung from the gibbet. Documents held at York give details of the trial and of Lofthouse's evidence which, surprisingly enough, does not appear to have been ridiculed by learned counsel.

That story brings to mind a recent case, when a man was brought before a local magistrates' court for refusing to pay his rent, because his council-owned house had a ghost. Unfortunately for him, the magistrates ruled that ghosts could not be admitted to exist and, therefore, he could not refuse to pay rent on the grounds that his house was already tenanted. He lost his case.

In 1904, Mr E. D. Walker, a former mayor of Darlington, told of an incident which had occurred when he was a child and living with his parents and younger brother in the village of Goldsborough, five miles north of Whitby. His father was a coastguard and was posted to Goldsborough in the 1860s. When the family reached the place, with all their belongings on the back of a cart, they found that there was no accommodation reserved for them. After staying at a local inn for several days while their furniture was stored in a barn, they were eventually able to rent the wing of a farmhouse, which had been unoccupied for several years.

They had not been in the house for more than three weeks, when one night the father came home some time between 12.30 and 1 A.M. He was sitting in the small kitchen and was about to make himself some supper, when the fender around the fireplace suddenly lifted up from the hearthstone three times and fell again with a loud bang. At the same time, one half of a double-doored closet opened three times and slammed shut with a crash. His wife, asleep in a downstairs bedroom, woke with a start and rushed to the kitchen to see what all the noise was about, only to find her husband sitting in bewilderment, trying to fathom out what was happening. They heard no more on that particular night.

A month or so later the coastguard's wife was in bed asleep, with her baby son in her arms, when she woke to feel the bed lift into the air three times and bang down again with a loud crashing sound. The poor woman screamed out in terror and lay, hardly daring to move, until her husband came home an hour or so later. While she was telling him of her ordeal, they both heard quite distinctly outside the window, what seemed to them like two dogs fighting in deadly combat, tearing each other to pieces. The coastguard took up his cutlass and dashed outside but discovered nothing. He now made up his mind to look into the house and its previous occupants more thoroughly.

The old widow who lived in the other part of the farmhouse told him that previous tenants had moved out after only a short time, saying there was something wrong. But, although she herself was only separated from them by a wall, she knew nothing of the odd happenings.

Two days later, a window cord snapped in the boy's bedroom and it was found necessary to call a joiner to repair it. He knew nothing of the house but, while working on the window, he was astonished to see a male figure draped in white appear as if from nowhere. The figure crossed the room and vanished. So did the joiner. He threw down his tools and rushed screaming in terror from the house. The coastguard dashed after him to see what was wrong and, when he finally caught up with him, the breathless joiner explained what had happened, refusing to go back inside the house even for his tools.

About a year passed and the widow who occupied the

remainder of the house died. The coastguard and his family were now in a position to buy the house in its entirety and set about having it modernized. (The Victorians spoilt a great deal of old property and furniture by their 'modernizations'!) One of the things they did, was to dig up the old flagstones in the kitchen and along with them the old hearthstone, and under this they discovered the reason for their haunting – a human skeleton.

Who the unfortunate victim was or how long he had lain there, it was not possible to discover, but once the skeleton had been given a decent Christian burial, the hauntings ceased and the family lived there happily for many years.

In 1979 I met a lovely old lady called Mrs Woodcock, who was ninety-three years of age and living in an old people's home in the West Riding. Alas, Mrs Woodcock died whilst this book was in preparation, but the story she told me is included here as a token of my respect.

She told me: 'My grandmother died in June 1880 at Driffield. Her death was a slow and painful one and a great blow to the family, especially my mother who, as the youngest of the family of eight, was particularly close to her.' The same month in which she died Mrs Woodcock's mother and father were married and went to live in Hull. In October of that year, her mother, who was now expecting her first child, was suddenly wakened by a feeling of someone kissing her full on the mouth. Thinking it was her husband, she sat up and was surprised to see her mother looking down at her and smiling as sweetly as she did in life. She was even more surprised when the apparition spoke to her and said, 'Time to get up, Sophia.' Mrs Woodcock continued: 'It was all so very natural that it was a few seconds before my mother realized that my grandmother had been dead for four months. As soon as she had spoken those words, she turned to go into the bedroom which she would have used whenever she came to the house.'

Mrs Woodcock's mother sat up in bed and watched as the apparition went out of the room. Through the open door, she saw her cross the landing, open the spare-bedroom door and then close it behind her; all done so naturally and deliberately. She had on her nightgown and a wrap had been thrown over her shoulders, just as a mother would have done in those early days when popping into her children's rooms in the early morning.

Mrs Woodcock said that when her mother herself died, she was living over a hundred miles away, but she was conscious of her presence with her; she felt as if she had taken her in her arms as she used to when she was a little girl and a feeling of irrepressible joy filled her heart.

There are so many instances of apparitions being recorded at, or after, the moment of a person's death, that they almost become tedious! They seem to crop up everywhere. One of the most famous and best authenticated cases of this kind which occurred in Yorkshire is what has become known as the 'Birkbeck Ghost'.

In 1789, Mrs Birkbeck, wife of William Birkbeck, a banker living in Settle and a member of the Society of Friends, was taken ill and died at Cockermouth, whilst returning from a visit to relatives in Scotland, a journey she had undertaken alone, leaving her husband and three young children at Settle. Fortunately for us, the friends at whose home the death occurred, made notes of every circumstance attending Mrs Birkbeck's last hours, so that the accuracy of the several statements as to time, as well as place, was beyond doubt. Better still, this foiled any unconscious attempt to bring the statements into agreement with each other later.

One morning, just before eight o'clock, a relative, who was caring for the children while Mrs Birkbeck was away, went into their bedroom and found them all sitting up in bed chattering excitedly. The eldest daughter said, 'Mamma has been here. She said, "Come, Esther".' Nothing could make the youngsters doubt the fact that their mother had come home, and the relative made a careful note of this fact, with the intention of mentioning it to Mrs Birkbeck on her return to Settle.

The same morning, unknown to the children, their mother lay dying at Cockermouth. It is recorded that she weakly told her friends, 'I should be ready to die, if I could but see my children.' She then closed her eyes, and her friends thought she had passed away. However, after about ten minutes of perfect stillness, she opened her eyes again, looked up brightly and said, 'I am ready now. I have been with my children.' She then passed peacefully away. The time – a few minutes before eight o'clock.

Apparently these events were investigated and subsequently reported in the *Proceedings of the Society for Psychical Research* and the notes taken both at Cockermouth and at Settle were in the possession of the Society for many years.

One of the problems with digging out old accounts of hauntings, particularly those written in the last century or the early part of this century, is that the writers very rarely give the name of the person they are discussing when talking about ghosts. Regular readers on this subject will no doubt have discovered this and, like me, will find it annoying. One cannot help but wonder why Mr P—— of S—— Street, in the town of M—— was afraid to make himself known, or was it just that the author wished to spare the blushes of the townsfolk, yet at the same time, assure his readers that the person really existed?

Recently I was fortunate enough to come into possession of an account of an occurrence which took place in Middlesbrough in 1867. It is hand-written and dated 1879, but the writer has followed the annoying habit of calling his source, Mr R—— of N—— S—— (North Shields?). Fortunately, he has told us that these events took place in Middlesbrough. The story is of interest because of similarities with that of the 'Birkbeck Ghost' and I make no apologies for reproducing it in its entirety:

During the cholera epidemic in the north of England in 1867, Mr R—— of N—— S—— had an experience which had a great effect upon his boyish mind at the time. He lived in M—— St, Middlesbrough and was the favourite of his great-grandmother, with whom he often stayed. The old lady was rather a (recluse?) in her habits, and occupied two rooms in her daughter's home. She was known to have some (paper?) money about her, which, however, she carefully concealed from her relatives. At the same time, it was known she had a particular partiality for one certain cupboard which she used as a wardrobe in her bedroom. I mention these particulars as possibly explaining what follows.

At three o'clock one morning, while sleeping in his own home, Mr R—— awoke to find the old lady standing at the foot of his bed, calling to him and beckoning him to follow her. He sat up in bed, terrified at the sight, but of course, manifested no desire to move. The old lady became impatient, and saying that she could remain no longer, begged of him to be sure and go to 'the cupboard', this being her usual phrase when referring to the small wardrobe I have alluded to. On the old lady's departure, he was so frightened that he felt he (dare?) not stay in the room, and yet, strange to say, he had sufficient courage to get out of bed in the dark and hurry off to his mother's room, crossing a dark landing on the way. He awoke his mother and told her what had happened. She (calmed?) him as much as possible and saw him off to bed again, but in the morning was so much impressed by his story that she accompanied him to school, and they called to see if there was anything wrong with the old lady. Imagine their surprise on reaching the house to learn that she had been found dead in bed, but a short time before their visit. The body was cold (proving?) that she had been dead for some hours, the doctor declaring that she had died of cholera. The inference (formed?) was that she must have died about the hour she visited Mr R——. Suffice it to say, an inspection of the cupboard revealed the fact that other hands had done duty there before theirs had a chance, but with what result will never be known.

It is a moot question as to whether the apparition seen at death is the ghost of the person who has died, or whether it is the double of a living person on the point of death. Could it be that in most cases it *is* the double of the dying and not the ghost of the dead that is manifested to the living? These two cases seem to point in that direction.

The final story in this chapter is another one of Victorian origin, the story of a ghost which kept a promise made in life to appear to those dear to it. It was recorded in 1883. Many instances have been recorded since, but this one stands out as a minor classic amongst psychic investigators. Robert D'Onston recorded this as having happened to him personally.

The date was 26 August, 1867. The time, midnight. Robert D'Onston, then residing in Hull, had been for some time engaged to be married to a young North Country heiress, it being understood that on their marriage, he would take her name and stand as prospective Liberal candidate at the next General Election. However, for the sake of his bride-to-be, he had to finish an affair with a Hull girl called Louise. Louise was young, beautiful and devoted to D'Onston.

On the night of 26 August, they took their last walk together and, a few minutes before midnight, paused on a wooden bridge running across a kind of canal, known in Hull as a 'drain'. They stood listening to the swirling of the water against the wooden piles and waited for the stroke of midnight, before Louise and he should part forever. In the few minutes before the clock struck, she quietly repeated Longfellow's 'Bridge', the words of which, 'I stood on the bridge at midnight', seemed quite appropriate.

Midnight struck and with a final kiss the lovers made as if to part; but Louise said just before he pulled away from her, 'Grant me one last favour, the only one I will ever ask you on this earth. Promise to meet me here twelve months from tonight at this same hour.' D'Onston, thinking it would be bad for both of them to re-open partially healed wounds, would not agree at first, but at last consented saying, 'Well, I will come if I am alive,' to which the girl replied, 'Say alive or dead!' D'Onston said, 'Very well then. We will meet, dead or alive!'

The following year, 26 August saw him at that very same spot a few minutes before midnight; and on the stroke of midnight, Louise arrived. By this time D'Onston, now married, had begun to regret the arrangement he had made, but considered it was 'of too solemn a nature to put aside'. He therefore kept the appointment, but said that he did not care to renew their affair. Louise, however, persuaded him to agree to meet her one more time, twelve months hence and, much against his will, D'Onston did so and again they left each other, repeating the same strange words, 'Dead or alive.'

1869 passed quickly enough, but in the first week in July, D'Onston was involved in a shooting accident. A party of four, including D'Onston, had hired the ten-ton yawl belonging to Thomas Piles of Hull, a fisherman and a reputed smuggler, to go yachting around the Yorkshire coast. For a reason I was unable to discover, on the fourth day out D'Onston was shot in the thigh by Piles and, on the same afternoon, 1¼ ounces of No 2 shot was cut from his leg by a doctor in a room at the Black Lion Hotel in Bridlington.

As soon as he was able to be moved, D'Onston was taken home again and is on record as having been treated by his own doctor, Dr Kelburne King of Hull. 26 August came and D'Onston was unable to walk without the aid of crutches and then only for a short distance, so he had to be wheeled about in an enormous Bath chair. The distance to the meeting place being quite lengthy and in view of his present situation, he felt he might have to disappoint the girl unless he obtained some assistance from an old retainer of the family into which he had married and who frequently carried out 'delicate' missions on his behalf. He also knew Louise.

Quietly D'Onston and his faithful retainer set out and arrived at the bridge about twenty minutes or so before the agreed time. It was a brilliant starlit night with a lovers' moon. Old Bob, the retainer, wheeled D'Onston to the bridge, helped him out of the Bath chair and gave him his crutches. D'Onston then walked shakily on to the bridge and stood, leaning his back against the top rail. He lit his pipe and had a comfortable smoke while he waited. He was annoyed at allowing himself to be persuaded to meet Louise a second time and determined to tell her that this was positively their last meeting. Besides, he didn't think it was fair to his wife. So, if anything, it was in a rather sulky frame of mind that he waited for his former lover. Just as the clock began to chime a quarter to midnight, D'Onston heard the distinct, click, click of the little brass heels that Louise always wore, sounding on the long flagged footpath which led for about 200 yards up to the bridge. As she got nearer, he could see her pass gas lamp after gas lamp in rapid succession, while the chimes of the large clock at Hull resounded across the still night air.

At last the footsteps sounded on the wooden bridge and he saw Louise pass under the lamp at the farthest end – the bridge was about twenty yards wide – and he stood under the lamp at his side and waited. When she got closer to him, D'Onston noticed that she wore neither cape nor hat and he thought that perhaps she had taken a cab to the farther end of the flagged footpath, and because it was a very warm night had left her wrap in the cab, coming the short distance in evening dress.

Click, click went the brass heels and she seemed about to pass D'Onston when, suddenly overcome with affection, he stretched out his arms to embrace her. She passed *through* them and as she looked at him he saw her lips move and form the words, 'Dead or alive.' He said, many years later, 'I even *heard* the words, but not with my outward ears, with something else, some other sense – what, I do not know. I felt startled, surprised, but not afraid, until a moment afterwards, when I felt but could not see, some other presence following her. I could feel, though I could not hear, the heavy clumsy thud of the feet following her; and my blood turned to ice!'

Recovering himself with some effort, D'Onston shouted out to old Bob, who was safely seated in the Bath chair in a nook, out of sight, 'Bob. Who passed you just now?' In an instant the old Yorkshireman was by his side. 'Ne'er a one passed me, Sir!' D'Onston replied that this was nonsense and that Louise had just passed him on the bridge. So she must have passed old Bob, because there was nowhere else she could go. The old man replied there was something uncanny going on. He heard her come on to the bridge and off it, but he was damned if she had passed him!

The following day, D'Onston, feeling unsettled, went to see members of Louise's family and was horrified to learn that she had died in Liverpool, three months before. Apparently she had been delirious for a few hours before her death and their parting compact evidently weighed on her mind, for she kept repeating, 'Dead or alive. Shall I be there?', to the utter bewilderment of her friends, who were, of course, unaware of her agreement with D'Onston.

Fairies, Trolls and Spectral Hounds

I understand that there was, and for all I know might still be, a society in the south of England, founded in 1936 and called 'The Fairy Investigation Society'. It had over three hundred members who were pledged to spread the fairy faith, collect records of sightings and carry out research and field work into fairy phenomena. So devoted were they that when, in 1973, the Maplin Airport project was first mooted, they, like the conservationists and local residents, were worried, not because of the possible effects on the flora and fauna or on the environment, but because the fairies would have nowhere to go. For according to them, this part of Essex was a great place for observing fairies.

Many explanations have been put forward to account for the belief in fairies. Some chroniclers have said that a fairy is a special creation and exists in its own right. Others suggest that fairies, like ghosts, are the spirits of certain types of dead people, for example those who died before the dawn of Christianity or babies who were unbaptized at their death or were stillborn. Another popular tradition gives rise to the belief that fairies are fallen angels, not quite so wicked as to warrant going to Hell, but not quite good enough to be allowed to pass through the Pearly Gates either.

In many legends it is difficult to know where to draw the line between ghost and fairy. In fairyland, as in the land of the dead, the passage of time is miraculous and both fairies and the dead are said to haunt prehistoric burial grounds.

Are there really fairies at the bottom of the garden? Fairies have always inhabited the more remote parts of the Yorkshire Dales, keeping well away from the marshy bogs and exposed areas, preferring the middle reaches of the valleys, where at a reasonable distance from farms and villages, they could dance until the first light of dawn showed on the horizon, to the sweet sound of the pipes.

The Craven fairies were often accused of kidnapping children and leaving one of their own fairy children in its place. But on the whole, Craven folk were on reasonably good terms with them, often entering into business transactions for fairy gold. Like the time a little grey man led his pony between the stalls of Keighley market. He was invisible to the crowd, unseen by all except one stallholder's wife. She was seen to leave the crowd, talking animatedly as if to herself, as she followed the invisible little man to the place where his wife lay in labour, for humans often acted as midwives to the fairy folk. Soon in the limestone caves near Settle, the stallholder's wife delivered a beautiful fairy baby, for which duty she received a bag of fairy gold.

At Burnsall, between Grassington and Bolton Bridge, the local drunk saw fairies dancing in the moonlight as he staggered home one night after a heavy session at the pub. For a while he kept a low profile, knowing it was unwise to disturb the fairies at play. However, in his excitement he forgot himself and called out, 'Nah then, lads. Ah'll sing thi a song if tha likes.' Now the drunken rendering of 'Ilkla Moor Bah't 'at' at that late hour was more than even the fairies were prepared to put up with and they set about him, kicking and pinching him. As he staggered away from the onslaught, he managed to catch one of the fairies and pop him into his jacket pocket but, unfortunately for the poor man, the fairy escaped and it took a lot of explaining to his sceptical wife, when she saw the state in which he arrived home.

A similar tale is told of how, some years ago, a farmer living at Kinsey was walking home over the fields one moonlit night, when he saw fairies dancing in the pasture. Being well versed in fairy lore and not wishing to disturb them, he skirted around the pasture quietly. The next day, returning to the field, he saw to his delight, hundreds of mushrooms, left, he was told, by the fairies as a gift for not disturbing their dance.

The fairies of Teesdale are more aquatic than their Craven cousins. Even today they are feared by Teesdale farm folk, for they demand a human life every year, usually through drowning in the Tees. Teesdale mothers still place knives in their babies' cots as a deterrent and it is claimed that by placing one's ear to the ground on Tower Hill at Middleton-on-Teesdale, the sound of fairies dancing to the accompaniment of pipes can be heard quite plainly. One Middleton woman claimed to have seen a fairy on this spot, with bright red eyes and a dress of green. Leck Fell has a pothole known as 'The Fairies' Workshop' where, if one listens quietly at the neck of the hole, the rumbling of the fairy lathes can be heard.

Perfectly sensible, rational people insist that they have encountered fairies at least once in their lives; and even in this century there have been some remarkable fairy reports, notably the case of the Cottingly Fairies.

31, Lynwood Terrace, Cottingly, was the home of the Wright family. Behind the house was a small glen where thirteen-year-old Elsie Wright liked to play with her South African cousin, ten-year-old Frances Griffiths. They also shared the glen with its tiny inhabitants, a number of fairies, which they set out to show to their sceptical family. Elsie asked her father if she could borrow the family camera and be shown how to operate it. For the sake of peace and quiet, her father agreed to loan it to her and showed her how it worked before loading it with film, expecting the resulting photographs to be bereft of fairies and thus close the subject and stop the girls' incessant chatter, once and for all. However, far from closing the subject, that first photograph taken early in 1917 was to set off a storm of controversy that still rages today.

When developed the negative showed Frances, posing with a band of dancing, winged figures, which the girls insisted were the little friends they had been playing with all spring and which Frances said were coloured in shades of green, mauve and lavender. They insisted they were the fairies that lived in the glen and denied that they had faked the photographs in any way.

A month later, the sceptical Mr and Mrs Wright were surprised when the girls produced another photograph, this time taken by Frances and slightly underexposed, showing a gnome with a pointed face, about to step lightly on to Elsie's hand. Elsie claimed he was dressed in a red jersey, scarlet cap and black trousers. The Wrights felt that somehow the girls had faked these photographs and they were put away.

They would have been forgotten, had not Mrs Wright attended a lecture on fairies at the local village hall, about three years later. As a result of doing so, she passed the photographs and negatives over to Edward Gardner, a psychic researcher.

At first Mr Gardner thought the photographs must have been faked, but experts said that they were genuine and showed movement of the fairy figures, consistent with single exposure. They could find no trace of studio work or re-touching and said that if they were fakes, they must have been done by a first-class photographer, and certainly not by two young girls. As always, other experts disagreed and said they were frauds, because since fairies don't exist, no camera could possibly take a picture of them.

As quite often happens in cases like this, the press, in this case the *Westminster Gazette*, sent the most cynical reporter they could find to Cottingly with instructions to track down the two girls and expose them. He retired baffled. Edward Gardner also went, with a loaded camera and marked plates and asked the girls to take more photographs with it in the glen. The girls obeyed, producing three photographs. One showed Frances with a leaping fairy captured in flight from the leaves of a bush. The fairy had hovered and then came so close to the girl's face she drew her head back. Another showed a fairy offering Elsie a posy of tiny flowers. Elsie said her wings were shot with brilliant streaks of yellow. The plates were checked again after development and the most stringent examination of both photographers and photographs failed to support any other conclusion but that they were genuine.

Mr Gardner and Sir Arthur Conan Doyle published the pictures with an article in the *Strand Magazine* for the 1920 Christmas issue. Scores of people wrote in later to say that they too had seen fairies like those in the pictures. Sir Arthur called it 'an event so sensational as to mark an epoch in human thought'.

Not long after this, Elsie and her cousin separated and no more photographs were taken. They always maintained the photographs were genuine.

As recently as 1971 the photographs were re-examined by Mr Brian Coe, curator of the Kodak museum in London. He really put his life on the line by pronouncing them fakes, saying they were just cutout fairies on cardboard. Were they? Were they perhaps projected thought forms or are there perhaps fairies at the bottom of the garden after all?

If there are no fairies at the bottom of the garden, then what about the other, domestic form of fairy – the boggart, or as he is known in the Dales, the hob or hobgoblin?

The moorlands of the north-east of the county are said to be true hob country. Up at Glaisdale End, Hart Hall had a hob which would always turn up at harvest time and help in the hayfields, or with the corn threshing, often carrying on into the night, long after the farmer and his family had retired wearily to bed. One day, someone actually caught sight of the hob and noticed how worn and shabby its clothes were. It was agreed that a new suit of clothes be made and presented to the hob as thanks for his help around the farm. This was a mistake, however, for it is well known that hobs and witches cannot harm anyone until he or she has received a gift from that person. Still, the people at Hart Hall were lucky, as the hob only disappeared, never to return.

Similarly, the hob who lived at Close House near Skipton, threshed the corn and helped with the haymaking. He cleared off after being presented with a red hood. The owners of Sturfitt Hall, near Reeth, gave a hob a new suit of clothes and never saw it again, thus proving that this is the most effective way of getting the hob to leave.

A small cavern known as the 'Hob Hole', near Runswick Bay, is said to have been the home of one of these creatures. Local people believed the hob could cure their children of whooping cough or 't'kink cough' as it's known in Yorkshire. So, those children that were suffering from the malady were taken to the cave where the parents then sought the hob's help by reciting:

Hob-Hole Hob,
My bairne's getten t'kink cough,
Tak't off, Tak't off.

It was a hob, disguised as a beggar, which is said to have caused the disappearance of a once proud town. Beneath the lake at Seamer Water, there is said to be the remains of a town. Tradition has it that a beggar once asked for shelter there, but was turned away by everyone except a poor couple in a hillside cottage. The next morning the beggar had vanished and when the couple looked out of the doorway, they discovered that the town too had disappeared under the lake. It is said today that the rooftops of the town can sometimes be seen below the surface.

The many potholes and caves in Yorkshire are a natural haunt for hobs, boggarts and trolls, who often emerge at night to threaten mankind. There are tales of shepherds who claim to have seen little dwarf-like creatures, just before a storm, or at lambing time. Little creatures with bow-legs and hollow eyes, cautiously leaving their holes in the ground. One such creature lived in Hurtle Pot at Chapel-le-Dale, near Ingleton. He was said to have been responsible for drowning people in the pool at the bottom of the Pot; and a boggart living in Clayshaw Level at Nidderdale was said to have pushed the wagons about. Trollers Gill, near Appletreewick, is the home of those shaggy-haired creatures, the trolls. A local story, recorded in 1881, tells how one man was riding near the gorge at midnight. His body was found by shepherds the following morning and marks were 'impressed on the dead man's breast, but they seemed not by mortal hand'. A similar accident befell a farmer who, returning from market under the influence, drove his horse towards Trollers Gill and fell into the chasm. It was whispered that the farmer had been lured by the trolls and had attempted the impossible feat of jumping across the Gill.

Kit Crewbucket is a female boggart who haunts the canal tunnels. She is reputed to have been seen quite often in Harcastle Tunnel, near Kidsgrove. Another female hob lived at Threshfield School at Linton-in-Craven. This boggart, called Pam, used to play in school during the night. Often the rector would write his sermon at the school and one Saturday he left his manuscript on the desk. Realizing what he had done, the rector returned to the school to pick it up. Pam resented the intrusion and beat the poor man about the head before bolting. The rector determined to rid the school of the tiresome hob. He knew that Pam was partial to a drop of strong drink and so one night he left a full bottle of brandy on the schoolmaster's desk. The hob became so drunk as to be incapable of moving, thus the rector was able to kill the inebriated imp and bury the body behind the school. Or so he thought. Whoever heard of anyone actually killing a boggart? Not long afterwards Pam returned, as mean and vicious as ever, to plague the poor rector for the rest of his life.

Not all boggarts take on a human form. What about those other denizens of the netherworld – the Hounds of Hell? Less pleasant than some of the phantoms one might meet in the houses of Yorkshire, these strange beasts roam by night, sometimes fore-telling the death of a person they meet. It was a creature such as this that inspired Sir Arthur Conan Doyle to write *The Hound of the Baskervilles*.

These beasts are not exclusively British: similar 'Hell Hounds' abound throughout Europe and are linked either with stories that date back to the dogs of pagan Nature Gods or with the old Norse mythology of the 'Wolf of Hell', who is said to symbolize the death that springs from sin. Be that as it may, the mere thought of these animals was enough to terrify our ancestors. Branwell Brontë once wrote of them: 'The Gytrash is a spectre ... mostly appears in the form of some animal – a black dog dragging a chain, a dusky calf, nay even a rolling stone.'

As I have said, the sighting of one of these dogs, hounds, Shuck, Gytrash, call them what you will, usually foretells misfortune or even death to the beholder, such as the black dog which is seen running and then falling from a ledge on the Corpse Way in Swaledale. A similar hound was reported at both Otley and on Ilkley Moor.

Kirkby Overblow, Cowling and Haworth also bring reports and on All-Hallows Eve in the countryside around Todmorden, where the reservoirs supply the industrial towns of the north, it is said the Hell Hounds rush across the water as easily as over the land, only to fade away as they approach the youth hostel at Mankinholes.

Appletreewick had a fearsome ghost dog with huge saucer eyes, shaggy hair and dragging a clanking chain. Flixton, on the A1039 west of Filey, goes one better and boasts, of all things, a werewolf, equipped with abnormally large teeth which glow in the dark and exuding a terrible stench like rotting corpses. Its eyes are crimson and dart fire, while its tail is almost as long as its body. It is said to be capable of felling any nocturnal wayfarer it might meet.

History books tell us that in about 940 A.D. a hostel was built at the village of Flixton, specifically to shelter wayfarers in winter time from attacks from wolves. In those days, it was not uncommon for packs of wolves to roam these parts and they were regarded with a certain amount of loathing, because in times of very severe weather they scavenged the graveyards. Their cunning in discovering unprotected cattle, their boldness in attacking travellers, plus their habit of suddenly descending in large numbers on an area where they had previously been unknown, all helped to give rise to the belief that the animals were not ordinary wolves, but human beings who adopted a wolf shape by night. A more modern theory is that at one time there could have been a member of the community who suffered from lycanthropy, a rare but real disease. The afflicted person behaves exactly like a wolf, even to the extent of moving about on all fours and gnawing raw meat. However, back to the wolves.

Their nocturnal visits and exploits were said to have been organized by an old wizard, whose innocent appearance enabled him to gather information about cattle, sheep and human wayfarers in taverns and market places. It wouldn't have needed much for travellers' tales of attacks by wolves to become distorted by repetition, and thus acquire some supernatural touches.

The Washburn Valley boasted a spectral dog that was able to hold a conversation in a broad Yorkshire accent. The story goes that, in the 1850s, a man living at Dob Park Lodge found a secret passage which led him to a brightly lit room. In the room he discovered a padlocked chest and a huge two-handed sword. On the lid of the chest was a glass containing a golden coloured liquid. The room itself was guarded by an enormous black mastiff, with eyes as big as saucers and bright as fire. As the man entered the room, the dog rose and said, 'Now tha's come lad, tha mun either sup yon cup, draw yon sword, or open yon kist.'

The man drank from the glass, at which the sword withdrew

and the chest began to open of its own accord. A loud clap of thunder reverberated around the room and the dog set up an unearthly howl that could be heard many miles away and all the candles blew out. There is no record of what the chest contained, but when the man eventually stumbled from the room and found his way back to the lodge, he was a gibbering idiot and his hair had turned snowy white!

At Kirkby Overblow, near Harrogate, a farmer left his dog guarding the sheep one bitterly cold winter's night and completely forgot about it. During the night the dog wandered back to the farmhouse and scratched at the door to be let into the warm kitchen. Unaware of the howling and scratching, the family slept on and the poor dog wandered off again and froze to death; not long after that, a phantom dog, which resembled the farmer's sheepdog, was reported to be roaming the district.

Not far from Whitby there stands a large old house, used today as a nursing home. Over a hundred years ago, a girl was found dead in one of the bedrooms, having been murdered. Her black and white collie dog lay across her body, refusing to let anyone near her and refusing both food and drink. Eventually the dog died and the girl was allowed to be buried. Is this the dog which nowadays creeps into that bedroom each night, lying on top of the sleeping occupant?

Some years ago, a new member of staff was informed on being given the room, that a ghost had caused two nurses to leave. She laughed at this and said that she didn't believe in ghosts. She was to change her mind quite soon, for on two successive nights she woke up feeling as if she was suffocating – as though a large and heavy dog was lying across her chest.

In the late 1890s, a Wesleyan preacher was returning home after making a charitable collection in a rather lonely part of Wensleydale. As night fell, he found that his route led him through a wood, a mile wide. Knowing there was nowhere in the area that he could shelter for the night, he steeled himself and trusted the Almighty to protect him from the dangers of the sinister woods. As he approached the edge of the wood and found a pathway that would lead him through, a large black dog joined him and padded silently ahead of his horse. He could not make out where the animal had come from, but it never left him and when the wood grew so dark that he was unable to see it, he knew by instinct that it was still padding silently in front of his horse. When he emerged safely at the other side of the wood, the dog disappeared.

Just then, the preacher realized that he had lost his purse containing all the money he had collected. It must have fallen from his pocket as he made his way through the woods. So, turning his horse around, he set off back into the sinister woods to search for it. At the entrance to the wood, he was again joined by the strange black dog, which padded along beside him; it never touched him and he never spoke to it, but having found the purse he made his way to the edge of the wood again and as he emerged the dog ceased to be there.

Years later, two condemned prisoners in York Jail told the chaplain that they had intended to rob and murder a Wesleyan preacher on that night in the wood, but he had a large black dog with him and when they saw that, they felt that the preacher and the dog together would be too much for them. A useful ghostly apparition indeed.

Mrs Rita Dixon of Dewsbury had an interesting experience when, in 1972, she was asked to take care of a friend's West Highland Terrier for about ten days, while her friends were on holiday in Switzerland.

'Two days after our friends left, Jamie, the dog, caught a kidney infection,' Mrs Dixon told me. 'We took him to the vet, who gave him injections and tablets, but that same night, the poor thing was so sick and looked so ill that we were worried he might not survive the night.' Mrs Dixon and her husband decided to take turns sitting up with the dog. She continued, 'I decided to stay up first while my husband went off to bed. After reading for a while, I noticed that Jamie had stopped being sick, but was rather fretful and needed comforting from time to time.'

By about 4.30 in the morning, she felt that the dog was settled enough for her to be able to leave him and try to get some sleep herself. Leaving him in his basket in the dining room, Mrs Dixon gave Jamie a fondle and then left, closing the door behind her as she went into the hall. She says, 'I made sure the door was fastened properly.' Then she climbed wearily into bed, making sure the bedroom door, too, was fastened, as the window was open and the door would keep banging otherwise. She knew that if the dog began to howl during the remainder of the night she would hear him as, since it was a fairly modern house, the walls were not very thick.

A few hours later, Mrs Dixon woke up suddenly to find the dog licking her hand, which was outside the bedclothes. His tail was wagging, and he seemed more like the old Jamie she knew. She turned to wake her husband to tell him Jamie had come upstairs, but when she turned back, the dog was nowhere to be seen. Getting out of bed, Mrs Dixon went to go downstairs, pausing to wonder how the dog had got in, as the bedroom door was still closed. In the hall she also noticed there was no dog and the dining-room door was still fastened.

Opening it and going into the dining room, there was Jamie, tail wagging and making a great fuss. It was then she realized that her hand was still wet from the licking he had given her upstairs. She said, 'I wondered about the closed doors and thought back to when I saw Jamie in the bedroom licking my hand. He looked real. He felt real. I had fondled his ears and stroked his back and he had given me a really wet lick in return.'

Mrs Dixon is convinced that, although she didn't feel an unnatural presence, it was Jamie's earthly spirit that had visited her bedroom. The dog died a few years ago, but Mrs Dixon says she will never forget that particular experience and will never be able to explain it to her own satisfaction.

Finally, as a cat lover, I couldn't end this chapter without the mention of a phantom pussy cat or two. Cats, as we know, are supposed to be blessed with nine lives. But I am one of many people who think they may have a tenth. A great many people have been convinced they have seen the ghost of a cat. I think that both my wife and I have, and from all accounts they nearly all seem friendly.

Bella was a cat of this nature, a beautiful and well-marked ginger. Crossing a busy road near her home in Tadcaster, she was hit by a passing brewery wagon and died instantly. Some time later, her distressed owner was sitting quietly by the living-room fire sewing. She happened to look up and saw Bella basking in front of the warm fire, contentedly licking her paws. It all seemed so natural that it was a few seconds before she realized that Bella was dead and buried at the bottom of the garden!

Another pet cat was found dead beside the garage of the house, by an elderly lady living in an isolated house above Hebden Bridge. It was her well-loved black and white cat, Thomas. She and her husband had thought the world of Thomas and were naturally upset at his sudden demise. She called her husband, who gently wrapped him in cloth and, although it was beginning to snow quite hard, he took him into the garden and buried him under a small tree, where for hours at a time during the summer months the cat had used to sit or sleep.

One of his endearing habits had been to jump on to the window ledge beside the back door and, reaching out with his paw, rattle the door latch when he wanted to come in. A couple of evenings after the cat's death, the woman was alone in the house and was surprised to hear the latch rattling on the back door. On checking she was amazed to see it gently moving up and down – just as it used to when Thomas was alive. She told her husband about the incident when he returned home later that evening, but he didn't believe her, and said she was imagining things.

The same thing happened a few nights later and she told me that she thought it was her husband, who was not known for his sensitivity, playing a cruel trick on her. She told me, 'I had the last laugh though, for the next night we were both at home when the same thing happened again and my husband, too, saw the latch move. He dashed to the door and opened it, but there was no one there, except for the imprints of a cat's paws on the window sill in the fresh snow. No other prints were found, either on the step or on the path, just on the window sill.' Her husband, who has since died, never laughed at her again and she herself found consolation in the belief that pets, too, can live on after death.

A note of comfort for those who mourn the loss of a beloved and faithful pet perhaps? I hope so.

Although most phantom cats seem to be friendly, as a child Mrs E. Nelson of Cleethorpes had a real scare when her cat, Tiddles, returned from the dead.

She said that one night she was awakened by a loud purring and something pulling at her bedclothes. She sat up, thinking that her cat, which had vanished several months before, had come home, but she was unable to find him, although she felt all over the bed. Thinking she had been dreaming, she lay down again and immediately the purring and clawing started again. Thoroughly frightened, she pulled the bedclothes over her head, but the cat, purring loudly, pulled so fiercely at them that she had to hold on tight to the sheets.

She reported, 'I shouted for my mother, but she couldn't hear me, as I was under the bedclothes.' Shortly the cat stopped, but she was too afraid to look and just lay terrified until morning, waiting for her mother to wake up. When her mother finally did wake, the girl called her to come in as there was a cat in the bedroom. Her mother came running, but there was no cat, nor any way one could have got into the room. Nor were there any paw marks on the sheets.

Yorkshire Witches

There are still several timber-framed houses in Yorkshire and Lancashire which preserve curiously carved beams that were once thought to be a defence against witches. The beams were planted upright to support the lintel over the hearth in the main room. A St Andrew's cross was usually inscribed at the top and horizontal bands were carved beneath it. Sometimes the date of the carving was added. Such was the superstition of the times, that it was believed a witch could not enter beyond the post; nor, while it stood, could a spell be laid on the house or occupants.

Witchcraft in England was almost invariably a crime of the poor. According to trial records, most witches were old women who got very little out of their alleged pacts with the Prince of Darkness. In fact, the most they asked for was a roof over their heads and a full belly – not much in exchange for one's mortal soul. Still, this doesn't mean that all witches were innocent of at least attempting the crime for which they were charged, as many witches were convinced of their own powers and their ability to curse their victim.

The curse was the ultimate deterrent; always providing, of course, that the victim knew about it. Autosuggestion could, and still can, do a great deal of damage. Supposed proof of a witch's ability to hurt her enemies by supernatural means was produced at hundreds of trials. The making of clay and wax images was the common rite for inflicting sickness and death, and it was thought that whatever damage was inflicted upon the image would then be transferred to the intended victim.

Possibly the two most famous witches of all times were Lancashire's Mother Demdike and Yorkshire's Ursula Southeil or Sontheil, also known as Mother Shipton. The latter was a grotesque woman who was destined to become our own Nostradamus.

She was born in July 1488, fifteen years before Nostradamus, to Agatha Southeil, a woman who herself had been tried and acquitted on a charge of witchcraft. She was born in a cave at Knaresborough, her mother dying while giving birth to her. It is recorded that Agatha's death was accompanied by strange and terrible noises.

Ursula was placed in the care of a local woman, who one day left the baby unattended in her cottage. When she returned with several neighbours, they were attacked by supernatural forces, finding themselves yoked by a floating staff from which one woman hung by her toes, whilst the others were compelled to dance in circles. When they tried to stop, they were pricked with a pin by an imp, in the form of a monkey. Ursula and her cradle were missing and later found to be suspended in the chimney, nine feet from the ground.

During her childhood mysterious events surrounded the cottage. Furniture moved up and down the stairs of its own accord and, at mealtimes, food would suddenly disappear from the table and the plates of startled guests.

In 1512, Ursula married one Toby Shipton of York and very soon showed an aptitude for prophecy which was to acquire her a national reputation. At first her prophecies concerned purely local affairs – whether or not someone would recover from an illness etc. – but soon they extended to natural and historical prophecy, often couched in subtle verse, one of the best known being:

> 'Carriages without horses shall go
> And accidents fill the world with woe
> Around the world thoughts shall fly
> In the twinkling of an eye . . .
> The world then to an end shall come
> In eighteen hundred and eighty one.'

The verses go on to apparently predict such things as the Crimean War, the building of the Crystal Palace, steamships and the end of the world, although thankfully perhaps, she was off beam there.

Ursula was called Mother Shipton by the local people and, by virtue of her appearance, was well suited to play the role of a witch. It is said that she was of very big build, with a crooked body and frightening features, but that her understanding was extraordinary. She naturally aroused local curiosity and neighbours were forever prying into her private life. Mother Shipton got her own back by bewitching a breakfast party at which many of her nosey neighbours were present, causing them to suddenly break out into uncontrollable laughter before fleeing the house, pursued by a hideous imp.

They, in turn, informed the local magistrates who summoned Mother Shipton to appear before the court, where she is said to have told them that far worse things would follow, unless she was left alone. Then she shouted out, 'Updraxi, call Stygician Helluei!' and was carried off by a winged dragon, according to the magistrates' report.

Many of Mother Shipton's prophecies, such as the invention of radio, submarines, cars and metal ships etc., are now known to have been the work, not in the sixteenth century, but in the late 1820s, of a man named Charles Hindley. Yet despite this, she still continues to be Yorkshire's most famous witch and the cave at Knaresborough remains as a memorial to her.

I understand that the cave has recently been bought by the television illusionist, Paul Daniels, who plans to run it as a commercial venture of some kind.

A ghostly drum which rises out of the waters of the well at Harpham and which is said to warn of impending doom, can be ascribed to the curse of a witch. The haunting of Drummer's Well is connected with the St Quintin family, which was the most powerful family in the district and hereditary Lords of the Manor.

Legend tells us that William the Conqueror, after winning a nearby battle, promised Harpham and all the lands surrounding it, to the first person to reach the well from the battlefield. A drummer boy won the race, but one of the Norman knights, the greedy Sir Quintin, was close on his heels and he murdered the boy, before the others could catch up with them, throwing his body down the well. Unfortunately for Sir Quintin, the murder was witnessed by a local witch, who happened to be related to the boy and he put a spell on the St Quintin family, prophesying that the drummer boy's ghost would return to beat a death roll on his drum, whenever a member of that family was about to die. Which he still does to this day.

The ghost of an alleged witch haunts the A170, Sutton Bank to Helmsley road, where over the past few years a number of motorists have reported being stopped at night by a woman at the side of the road, apparently in need of a lift. However on pulling up, the motorists have been surprised at her sudden disappearance.

This is thought to be the wraithe of Abigail Glaister, mentioned in Edmund Bogg's *Vale of Mowbray*, published in 1904. Abigail was pursued by hounds late one night, during the reign of James I, because she was thought by many to be a witch. To escape the fearsome dogs, she jumped over Whitestone Cliffs into Lake Gormire and was drowned. According to Edmund Bogg, the ghost of Abigail was seen several times in the district soon after these events and a number of motorists in recent years have written to the *Darlington and Stockton Times* to say that they have been stopped near Sutton Bank by this ghost.

A skeleton preserved at the Leeds Medical School is said to be that of another well-known Yorkshire witch, Mary Bateman of Leeds, who made her living by skilful confidence tricks. The most famous of these was to show a hen, apparently laying a magic egg on which the words 'Christ is coming' were inscribed. In 1809, she was found guilty of poisoning Rebecca Perigo, one of her gullible clients, and was hanged at York and later gibbeted at Leeds.

It is said that souvenir hunters stripped the body and then the flesh from the bones, to be used as tokens of good luck, leaving the skeleton to be claimed by the medical school.

Near Hardshaw, in Wensleydale, there used to stand two cottages known as Rigg House and Rigg Cottage. Originally they comprised a single dwelling and local legend tells us that the division of the property took place for the specific purpose of laying the troublesome ghost of a witch.

Many years ago, the house was occupied by a man by the name of Metcalfe, a man of surly and forbidding temperament, who was disliked by everyone who came into contact with him. He had formerly been a slave owner in the West Indies and was known locally as the 'Black Whipper'. There lived with him for many years, an ugly old crone who was reputed to be a witch, who one day disappeared under mysterious circumstances. It was not long after that stories were told of her headless ghost appearing around her old home, scaring the daylights out of all who had the misfortune to come across her.

Metcalfe, much to everyone's relief, eventually left the area, perhaps because of the ghost, or perhaps because of the gossip and dark suspicion on the part of his neighbours. Where he went, no one knew or even cared, but the headless witch continued her haunting, much to the distress and fear of later occupants of the house. In time a subsequent owner hit on the idea of demolishing the central portion of the house where the ghost was usually seen, as a means of removing the unwanted guest. This action produced the desired effect and the ghost was seen no more, once the property was reduced to two smaller dwellings.

A man living at Broughton, in the North Riding, felt that he had had a spell cast on him, so he went to consult the local wise man, who asked him who it was he suspected of having cast the spell. The man said he thought there were two possible suspects, the witch Nancy Newgill and a poor village tinker, known to be possessed of the 'evil eye'. The wise man suggested that the only possible answer to his problem was to put a counter-spell on both the witch and the tinker. However, should one of them be innocent, it would recoil on the victim and thus further add to his sufferings; so he suggested the man should go and see them both and accuse them openly.

This he did, convincing himself almost at once that Nancy Newgill was innocent of this particular bit of chicanery. She looked at him, straight in the eye, swore a fearful oath and beat him about the head. The tinker, however, was so shifty-eyed and non-committal that the man felt quite sure that he was the culprit.

Just before dawn the following day, he and the wise man lit a fire and, while it was burning, they took a ball of clay, beat it flat by hammering it with the back of a bible, and then scooped out of it a rough figure in the shape of a man. Into this rough cast they next poured a vile mixture, consisting of pitch, boar's lard and bullock's blood; and the whole lot was then melted and stirred over the fire. What remained after filling the mould was divided into two parts and one part thrown into water, worked into a ball and thrown away. The other was thrown into the fire where it flared up into a bright blaze, throwing sparks in all directions. When this had died down, the ashes were taken and buried in the local churchyard.

The figure was then taken out of the mould and two holes inserted in it, to represent eyes. A pin was inserted into one of these, a charm incanted and the spell was complete.

As the man was returning to his home later that morning, the pain caused by the spell suddenly left him, and it is recorded that at the same moment the evil-eyed tinker was struck by a seizure, which caused him to go blind for the rest of his life!

Another well-known Yorkshire witch was Molly Cass, who lived for many years in Leeming Mill. One night the miller and three of his pals were playing cards at the mill, and eight times in succession one of the players, a man called George Winterfield, had the nine of hearts dealt to him. At the ninth deal, one of the group laid a wager of a guinea that Winterfield would not receive the nine of hearts again.

Just then, Molly Cass put her head round the door and told him to put his money back in his purse as it was not for Winterfield. The man was terrified of getting on the wrong side of Molly and he at once put his guinea back into his purse. Molly then said to Winterfield, 'Tha's gotten it again; tak' thi hand up and see!' The man looked and, sure enough, he had again been dealt the nine of hearts.

Molly continued, 'Tha's gotten it hard enough; tha's had it eight times already. T'Old un's in thee nah, and he'll not leave thi 'til he's gotten thi. T'Swale's waiting for thee, lad. Waiting to be thi bridal bed; the longer tha waits, the longer tha'll be astopping.' Winterfield turned white as he stood up, saying, 'I'll wed her, Molly. Give me another chance. Ah've rued all ah've done.' But Molly was adamant and Winterfield left the mill, saying he would go at once to wed his jilted sweetheart.

Now, whether he lost his way in the darkness, or whether there was a more sinister reason behind it, is not known, but his body and the body of his sweetheart were found the next day, floating side by side in the River Swale . . . The strange thing was, he had not seen the girl alive that day, for she had drowned herself several hours before he set out.

Just south of Blubberhouses stands the small hamlet of Fewston, a scattering of farms, some of which were once part of prosperous family houses. Here too stands New Hall, the home of the Fairfax family, and it is from Edward Fairfax's *A Discourse on Witchcraft*, written in 1621, that we learn of evil doings towards members of his family by local witches.

He tells of spells and black magic being used on his daughters Ellen, Ann and Elizabeth, by a group of local women believed to be witches, which caused the death of all three young girls. Edward Fairfax made allegations against them and they were brought to trial at York. Twice they came to court and on both occasions the women were acquitted through lack of suitable evidence. What exactly happened to convince such a man as this that his neighbours were practising the evil arts and directing them towards his family?

According to the chronicles, the three Fairfax children became victims of the women, in whose company they spent much of their time. When Elizabeth Fairfax fell off a haystack and fatally injured herself, the blame was put on Bess Foster. Margaret Waite was accused of taking a pennyworth of corn without paying, to use in making spells. Margaret Thorpe was accused of throwing pictures of the children into water, triumphant when they sank.

It is also said that several women had carried the three children to the fell top, to witness the Midsummer Eve bonfire. When, a little later, Ann Fairfax died, this was attributed to witchcraft and, as we have seen, the women were hauled off to court, and were acquitted. On their release they returned to Fewston and celebrated their freedom with a feast, to which they invited many of their friends and sympathizers. The Prince of Darkness himself was said to have been sitting at the head of the table. It was said that the feast was so lavish, the food lasted right through until Good Friday.

Think of witches and one inevitably thinks of the Devil. Should the reader visit the churchyard at Kirkby Malham at midnight, you might find a banquet which has been specially prepared for you by the Devil himself.

The story goes that about 150 years ago, a boy and the vicar of Kirkby Malham were invited by the Devil to his banquet, which was all nicely laid out on a large family tombstone. The Devil said grace and chose a 'De Profundis', saying to the vicar, 'Don't you agree, my dear vicar, that a "De Profundis" is the most fitting for a banquet of the dead?'

The vicar, who never could resist a good meal, agreed and looked greedily over the outspread feast. Reaching out for a delicious looking leg of mutton, he asked for salt, at which all the food – and the Devil – disappeared. So, the moral appears to be, if you do wish to take up the invitation to a midnight feast in the churchyard, remember not to ask for salt!

People believed that witches could turn themselves into any animal they wished, but the commonest one was the hare, possibly because it was an animal difficult to capture on account of its tremendous speed over the most difficult terrain.

A story is told of a woman who lived in North Craven who was suspected of being a witch and was subject to a lot of gossip. The poor woman knew no peace. One day a group of men were out hunting when they saw a large hare sitting in the middle of a field. They gave chase and the animal bolted across the field, barely evading the huntsmen. Their dogs kept up with the horses, but one dog forged ahead of the rest of the party and as the hare jumped over a wall, the dog was able to snap at it and managed to bite out some of the fur.

However, the wall was too high for the dog to jump over and there the chase ended. One of the huntsmen who had witnessed the near miss rode up to the wall, thinking that perhaps the hare might still be in sight and possibly injured. He dismounted, climbed the wall, and there on the other side, squatting on her haunches, was an old woman rubbing her head from which a substantial clump of hair was missing!

Three rather merry revellers were returning from Boroughbridge races, late one crisp moonlit night, when they encountered a ghost on a white steed at the crossroads just outside Norton. The phantom horseman pointed to a spot on the ground and then faded from view. Then, a stoat with a dead rabbit in its mouth crossed the road and stood in the place at which the phantom had pointed. Suddenly, an arrow from an unseen bow struck the stoat in the heart and, at the same time, someone hiding in the undergrowth was heard to laugh out loudly. Each element of this macabre scene was to represent a future occurrence.

These strange events were blamed on a witch named Liza Horngill. One of the revellers, Owen Metcalfe, urged a crowd to drag Liza from her bed and duck her in the village pond. Liza screamed and cursed Metcalfe as, covered in slime, she crawled from the water, promising that two people in particular would be sorry. Because of the cruelty he had shown to Liza, Metcalfe's girlfriend, Alice, told him she would have nothing further to do with him and broke off their engagement.

That night, Gabriel's ratchets (barn owls) howled and cried, which was taken by the villagers to mean that someone had died. It was Metcalfe's ex-girlfriend, Alice. Her body was later found in the pond and it was accepted by all that she had been depressed about breaking off the engagement and had taken her own life.

Then someone remembered the ghostly happenings at the crossroads and demanded an explanation from Liza. She told them that the dead rabbit represented Alice, killed by the stoat before the crossroads were reached. The stoat died when the arrow pierced it and the arrow represented a stake. Liza said the villagers must tell Metcalfe to take the stake meant for Alice, who as a suicide would have it thrust through her heart, throw it into the air and catch it, three times.

Metcalfe thought it wise to do as was suggested, but as he caught the stake for the third time, a splinter lodged in his hand, causing some pain and in the end, tetanus. Before lockjaw set in, Metcalfe, in a deathbed confession, said that Alice had not committed suicide but that he had drowned her in the pond. Alice, then, was buried in consecrated ground; her place in a grave at the crossroads was taken by the body of Metcalfe. It was laid at the spot which the phantom horseman had indicated many nights before!

What about today? Is witchcraft still practised in twentieth-century Yorkshire? Many people believe so, although today's witchcraft is not so much magic as a serious form of religious worship.

The story of witchcraft and diabolism, from ancient times to the present, is a long and often complicated one. Things were much more simple in the old days, when everyone knew that witches existed, had supernatural powers and could be fought in known and definite ways by people with equal powers.

York – City of a Thousand Ghosts

York is arguably the most beautiful city in the county of Yorkshire. To a Yorkshireman such as the author, it is the most beautiful city in England. It is certainly one of the most interesting, for behind the busy life of the city lie many treasures waiting to tell the story of its history. Many of these treasures have alarming and sad tales to tell, which make York the haunted city it is today.

It is said that York is a city of a thousand ghosts and for every ghost story there are a hundred differing versions. In the words of Brendan Foley, 'Finding a ghost is a rare and tricky pastime. But if, on your travels, you discover the most beautiful city in England, then seeing a ghost is simply a bonus.'

One place which was not on the Victorian visitor's itinerary of York was the workhouse – or to give it its correct title 'The York Industrial Ragged School' – which still stands in Bedern, a few hundred yards from the Minster.

This forbidding building, just off Deangate, was a chilling blend of workhouse and orphanage which fell under the evil influence of a greedy and cruel workhouse-master, said to have been directly responsible through his neglect for much suffering and the deaths of a number of children in his care.

The workhouse-master was so cruel and evil that he even neglected the task of giving the dead children a decent Christian burial, particularly during the winter months when the ground became hard or snow-covered. He left the pathetic little corpses in a workhouse cupboard, where they would putrefy until such time as he could be bothered to carry out the grisly task of burying them.

It is said that during the long winter nights that followed, strange, eerie noises came from the locked cupboard which struck terror into the hearts of those unfortunate enough to hear them.

Even today, there are people who claim to have heard the eerie laughter of those long-dead children echoing through the old archway of Bedern, laughter which gradually changes into the unearthly and terrifying screams of the neglected orphans.

Marmaduke Buckle was a crippled boy who lived with his family in a house in Goodramgate (known today as Marmaduke's Restaurant) in the seventeenth century; a time still plagued by superstition, a time when physical disabilities were looked upon as a punishment sent by God.

He was born into a wealthy family, but he was isolated by his disability, mounting ignorance and superstition, and he took to living in his own room at the top of the house, where he would sadly sit for hours on end at his upstairs window and watch the lively goings-on in Goodramgate below.

It is generally thought that Marmaduke hanged himself in 1715, when the torment of his disability, coupled with his loneliness and depression, became too much to bear. Just before he hanged himself from the beam in his room, he scratched his name in the plaster wall, along with the details of his birth and death:

MARMADUKE BUCKLE
1715
1697
17

This can still be seen to this day and the presence of the poor crippled Marmaduke is still felt. He is not an unpleasant ghost and to my knowledge he has never been seen, but he will open doors and turn on lights and in general get up to mischief. On rare occasions it is said that people have the feeling of being watched – watched by those same eyes that gazed wistfully down at the hurly-burly of life in Goodramgate over two and a half centuries ago.

* * *

At about eight o'clock each night during the summer months, Mr Harry Mercer and his son David leave the Anglers Arms in Goodramgate with a party of tourists for a ghost walk of York. It is no coincidence that they leave from the Anglers Arms – which incidentally stands immediately next door to Marmaduke Buckle's house – because this cosy old pub contains three ghosts, all of which have been vouched for by several witnesses over the years.

The top floor of the pub is haunted by the distinctive smell of lavender, which wafts through the rooms, only to disappear as quickly and as mysteriously as it came. No figure is ever seen, nor is there ever any change in the temperature, just the presence of the fragrant smell of lavender.

On the stairs of the first floor, one can sometimes spot the petite ghost of a Victorian child. The story goes that the figure is that of the young, lively daughter of a former landlord, who once ran down the stairs and out of the front door, right into the path of a passing horse-drawn dray, which killed her instantly.

Her little ghost is said to be friendly and playful. The pub cat often seems to enjoy playing with her, purring round the feet of an invisible figure. She has often been seen sitting on the stairs, looking down at the more solid inhabitants imbibing in the bar below.

But it is the third ghost which lurks in the cellars that is the most interesting: a ghost that is neither playful nor friendly, being described as 'something of great age, intelligence and utter evil'!

I am told that the only entrance to the cellar is through a trap-door behind the bar itself. Yet suddenly and frequently, the beer pumps are turned off, and turned off with such force the landlady has great trouble in turning them back on again. Neither the playful cat nor the pub dog will ever venture into the cellar – and when the pub is empty and dark, wild horses would not drag the landlady down there either!

Another ghostly child can be encountered in the Raffles Tea Room, a tall, narrow building in Stonegate, which was once the home of a distinguished Victorian doctor.

His youngest daughter, who was about six or seven years old, had her bedroom at the top of the house. She was described as being of a friendly disposition, with beautiful long blonde hair, and she was very much loved by her father and the servants.

Being a celebrated doctor, the child's father often entertained influential friends at dinner parties given in the house. On one such occasion, the young girl was introduced to the guests before being packed off to bed. Disappointed at being sent off in the midst of all the excitement, the child obediently went up the three flights of stairs to her attic bedroom, where she lay awake, wishing she could join in the laughter which carried up from the party below.

Eventually, she crept out of her room and on to the attic landing, leaning forward over the banister inquisitively, to hear what was being said. Unfortunately, she slipped on the polished banister rail and tumbled forward screaming to fall to her death three storeys below.

Over a century later, the child's delicate footsteps are still heard as she obediently climbs the stairs to her former attic bedroom. I understand that she has only been seen on one occasion, sitting on the shop counter, a pretty Victorian child with the most remarkable blonde hair.

York was a Roman garrison, so it is only natural that perhaps its most famous ghosts – and certainly its oldest – should be those of the Romans.

Back in the 1950s, an apprentice plumber was working in the cellars of the Treasurer's House, which stands in the Minster Yard, when the mysterious blast of a trumpet, growing louder and louder, drifted through the thick cellar walls. Slowly, through the seemingly solid wall, there emerged a big, shaggy and muscular horse. On its back rode a Roman soldier.

The frightened apprentice fell off his ladder with shock and stared open-mouthed as more and more figures, this time on foot, emerged behind the rider. These figures, wearing rough sandals and green tunics, stumbled dejectedly after their leader. At which point the terrified apprentice took to his heels and fled.

Over the years, several similar sightings of these Roman ghosts have been reported and it is now known that at the time when the city was the Roman garrison of Eboracum, the site on which the Treasurer's House was later built was in fact a major Roman road.

A few yards from the Treasurer's House stands the old St William's College where, in the sixteenth century, two brothers, prompted by greed and jealousy, lay in wait for a well-to-do clergyman. As the priest made his way from the Minster, the boys emerged from the shadows and brutally slew him, stripping the body of whatever valuables it carried, before seeking the safety of their upstairs room in the college.

It appears that the younger of the two brothers had been a reluctant partner in the crime and the thought of the retribution which must surely follow terrified him. He therefore locked himself and the valuables in an ornate oak cabinet. The elder brother had no such scruples, however. Fearing that his young accomplice might confess to the authorities, he decided to waste no time in betraying him, in the hope of gaining pardon for himself.

When he returned from reporting his younger brother, he paced the corridors of St William's College, unable to face the youngster, who was eventually found in the oak cabinet, arrested, and in due course found guilty and hanged before a large crowd at York Castle, whilst his smooth-talking older brother walked free.

However, guilt soon came upon him and, following the hanging, he paced the corridors and rooms of the college day and night, haunted by his betrayal of his own brother. His death a few years later, whilst he was still a young man, failed to eradicate the guilt, and today his footsteps can still be heard as he paces the corridors in St William's College, just as he has done for over four centuries.

The story of Margaret Clitherow is so well known, it is not my intention to repeat it here in any detail. Suffice to say she was the wife of a wealthy butcher who lived in the Shambles during the sixteenth century. She was converted to Catholicism and began to lead a brave and dangerous underground life, sheltering priests in her own home at a time when religious persecution was at its height.

In 1586 she was caught and sentenced to the particularly horrible fate of being crushed to death. A large wooden door was laid on her spread-eagled body and slowly covered with heavy weights. Despite this cruel torture, she refused to renounce her faith or to implicate others, and eventually she died.

Her old home in the Shambles is now a shrine and although Margaret Clitherow has never, to my knowledge, appeared as a ghost, she has left behind her a spiritual peace. Numerous visitors to the shrine have remarked on the uncanny peace and stillness that surrounds her former home, despite the fact that the front door opens on to one of the busiest and noisiest streets in the city.

Like all self-respecting cities of any age, York has more than its fair share of haunted pubs and inns, one of which I have already referred to.

The Cock and Bottle Inn stands on the site of the much older Plumbers Arms, demolished some time ago. Who built the original pub isn't known, but it is known to have stood in the grounds of the former mansion of the Duke of Buckingham, on Skeldergate.

History tells us that the infamous George Villiers, second Duke of Buckingham, used this as a centre for alchemy in his efforts to turn the base metals into gold. The odds are that he also practised a bit of black magic here on the side, for he certainly appears to have left some evil influences behind him.

Despite being a favourite at the Court of Charles II, Villiers died a disgraced pauper. He spent his last years in York but it was actually at Kirkbymoorside that he died, his body being taken to Westminster for burial in a pauper's grave, while his shade returned to the York that he loved.

Some very frightening events have taken place at the Cock and Bottle, beside the more mundane opening and closing of doors, bangs, thumps, footsteps and the inevitable cold draughts. A man wearing a wide-brimmed hat has been seen quite often who suddenly evaporates, and anyone wearing a crucifix on the premises is quite likely to have it roughly snatched from them by unseen hands. I was told that one man was seized by an invisible force in an upstairs passage and pinned to the spot for several minutes, during which time he saw the apparition of a milkmaid carrying a yoke and buckets.

At some time in 1972 a skeleton was found nearby on the site of the Duke of Buckingham's library, which might possibly have some connection with the hauntings. More recently it was reported that a stone at the back of the fireplace occasionally glows more brightly than the fire itself and some customers reported seeing the shadowy figure of a man sitting alone at a table, who suddenly dissolved into thin air.

Poltergeist activity has been frequent over recent years, with small articles being moved around the bar by unseen hands, and unnatural cold spells when the temperature drops dramatically leaving an atmosphere of gloom over this normally lively pub.

The York Arms in High Petergate has an industrious and shy ghost who, in the past thirty years or so, has made several appearances, but who seems happiest when she is invisible.

The figure, when it deigns to show itself, forms a whitish-grey blur, which many people say resembles an old woman or a nun. No one knows who she really is, but she seems to be fond of rearranging objects around the pub and on one memorable occasion, in front of eye-witnesses, an old pair of fire bellows unhooked themselves from the wall, rose upwards, avoiding an ornamental plate, and glided slowly down to land on the floor some eight to ten feet away.

Over the years cutlery, tape cassettes, records, ashtrays and other small objects have flown across the bar, whilst doors have opened and have been politely closed again by unseen hands. One recent manifestation happened in an upstairs bedroom, where a small ornament on a window sill fascinated the ghost. The window was firmly shut, but this did not prevent the ornament from sliding up and down the length of the sill of its own accord and for some considerable time. A family portrait then crashed from the wall.

Despite the ghost – or perhaps it is because of it – this is one of the most thriving pubs in York.

* * *

Another thriving ghostly pub is the Black Swan, off Stonebow, a medieval building where ghosts have been putting in appearances in numerous rooms since time immemorial.

One spectre is that of a small man who wears an Edwardian suit and a bowler hat. Some people who have seen him say he has a look of irritation on his face, as if waiting impatiently for someone, whilst others say he is a miserable little man. Whatever his features, after about ten minutes the disgruntled ghost appears to become fed up with waiting and slowly dissolves back into thin air.

But the most famous and most frequently seen ghost at the Black Swan is that of a wistful young woman with beautiful hair and a long, light-coloured dress who fascinates those fortunate enough to glimpse her. Yet, despite her frequent appearances, no one has ever seen her face, since she is always either gazing thoughtfully out of the window with her back to the witness, or staring down into the glowing coals of the pub fire.

It is because of this that the pub's beautiful ghost has remained unidentified for so long.

Finally, let us take a look at just a few of York's old and beautiful haunted churches; churches such as All Saints in Low Ousegate, which claims to possess the most beautiful ghost in the whole county.

Before entering, just as a matter of interest, take a look at the fearsome creature cast in dark metal that forms the handle to the heavy wooden door. No one knows its true origin, but over the centuries many thousands of souls – both living and departed – have passed it on their way into and out of the church.

But it is another soul that we are interested in, one whose spirit is prompted to put in an appearance whenever there is a funeral. This beautiful ghost always appears as the funeral procession reaches the church, always in front of a crowd of witnesses and always in the daytime. Her beautiful and serene face is framed by long shining locks of hair, and her dress appears to be made of shimmering white material which reaches down to the ground. For years, people have argued amongst themselves as to whether this is in fact a dress or a shroud; no one seems to be able to make up their mind.

She then beckons the mourners into the sanctity of the church before she vanishes as quickly and as mysteriously as she arrived, leaving behind her an atmosphere of peace and tranquillity.

How different this ghost is to the one which is said to haunt Holy Trinity Church in Goodramgate.

Thomas Percy, seventh Earl of Northumberland, was your original 'Action Man'. He lived in the sixteenth century, a time of political turmoil, and his dissatisfaction with the way Queen Elizabeth I ruled the country, as well as his desire to see a religious counter-reformation, led him into open rebellion against the Crown.

The Percys had always been hotheads and Thomas was no exception. His rebellion crumbled after a short series of battles and sieges and he was forced to flee to Scotland where he was eventually betrayed and captured. King Philip II of Spain and Pope Pius V both attempted to arrange a ransom for his release, but Elizabeth was not impressed and Thomas Percy was brought back to York in chains under heavy armed guard to be executed for high treason.

At the block he stood defiant, declaring that he would renounce neither his religion nor his deeds and it is said that he went bravely to his death wearing a precious relic given to him by Mary Queen of Scots – a thorn from the crown of Christ, set in a gold cross. His last words before the axe fell were 'I am a Percy, in life and in death.'

After his execution, Percy's head was stuck on a pole above Micklegate Bar, where it remained for some time until a family sympathizer stole it and reputedly buried it in secret in the grounds of Holy Trinity Church in Goodramgate.

Today it is said that the headless body of Thomas Percy, seventh Earl of Northumberland, can be seen on certain nights, lurching between the tombstones in the churchyard in search of his head; something which gives a chilling significance to his famous last words!

Another Holy Trinity Church stands near the Bar in Micklegate. This was once part of a Benedictine priory attached to the Abbey of Marmoutier in France. This old church is renowned for its three ghosts, that of its last abbess, a woman and a child.

History records how the abbess came to haunt the church: she defied the soldiers sent by King Henry VIII to carry out his policy of dissolution, saying that they would only enter her convent over her dead body. The soldiers attacked her and, as she lay dying, she promised she would haunt the place until another sacred building rose on the spot, a promise she kept until the convent was demolished completely, when she then moved into the church. She is often seen on Trinity Sunday and often in the company of a woman and child.

Not far from the church there lived, in medieval times, a small family. The couple were young and had just one child. They lived quietly and happily until a series of disasters overtook them. First the father died suddenly and his grieving wife watched as he was interred near the organ window of Holy Trinity Church.

Quite soon afterwards the child began to develop the symptoms of the Black Plague and, despite the desperate young mother's care and attention, the child died. In accordance with regulations to prevent the spread of the disease, the little body was buried in the great plague pit still to be seen outside the city walls near High Petergate. This was too much for the young mother to bear and she too died of a broken heart within a very short time.

She was buried with her late husband near the organ window in Holy Trinity Church, but although united with him in burial, the family were separated even in death by the child's burial in unconsecrated ground.

And this is where the abbess again comes into the story, for it is said that the spirit of the young mother could not rest without the child and that the spirit of the abbess now brings the child from the grave outside the city walls to the grave of its mother and father at Holy Trinity Church.

They were seen in the mid-nineteenth century and again in 1876, when a worshipper recorded having seen a bright light, formed like a robed and hooded woman, glide rapidly from north to south at some distance outside the east window. The figure returned some time later accompanied by the figure of a child. The child was not seen again, but the woman returned and hurriedly completed a final trip across the window.

And finally, a lovely little story attached to the Church of St Mary, which has stood in Bishophill for over a thousand years. For centuries the surrounding land and the buildings on it were part of the living of the church and on the site of what is now a dancing school there once stood a building connected with the upkeep of St Mary's Church. Today an invisible scene from the past slowly unfolds, breaking the silence of the empty hall.

Somewhere, from far beyond the mists of time, comes the sound of someone counting money. An invisible box of coins is heard being emptied noisily on to an invisible table. The sounds of the coins tipping out are followed by silence. Then, slowly and methodically, each coin is heard to slide across the table as it is counted, before falling into a metal box, presumably resting on the ghostly counter's lap.

The click, click of coin into box grows louder, until, after the last coin has fallen into it, the lid is shut with a loud bang. Even in death a Yorkshireman cannot stand to be parted from his money!

Lancashire's Ghosts & Legends

'Nay, it's never a ghost.
But whatever it is,
I wish it'd go away!'

Attributed to a Colne
farmer

Unexplained Phenomena

Ghosts, as innumerable studies have shown, are a worldwide phenomenon which has been recorded for almost 2,000 years. In my experience many people who see ghosts are often reluctant to advertise the fact. Usually they go to great lengths to find some rational explanation for their experience, rather than put it down to the supernatural. In time, however, even the most hardened sceptic can become convinced if the explanations lack credence.

One such person is Mr Charles Nelson of Barrow-in-Furness. Mr Nelson related to me a fascinating story of a sexless figure seen in the bedroom of his home about ten years ago which, like many hauntings, appears to have no logical explanation.

He told me: 'My parents bought the semi-detached house in Roose Road in 1934. Roose Road is one of Barrow's main highways. Having carried tramcars in the past, it is quite wide. I was fifteen years old at the time, and I remember we had not been in the house very long before strange noises were heard during the night.' He said he well remembers lying awake, listening to the mysterious taps and rustling sounds which seemed to come at one minute from the ceiling and at the next from under the floorboards. A noise, as if someone were rubbing two pieces of paper together, was also heard on several occasions. Yet despite investigation, nothing could be found to account for it or provide a logical explanation.

A young girl living in the house next door was afraid to go to bed at night, as it appears that this house too was badly affected. Often, Mr Nelson's parents and the next-door neighbours would ask each other, 'Did you hear that lot again last night?'

These noises usually occurred round about 1 A.M. Sometimes they would be accompanied by what sounded like the noise of someone chopping wood in the back garden, but whenever anyone got out of bed to see who it was, the gardens were empty and the chopping noise would suddenly cease. Noises were also heard in the roof space, but again, investigation amongst the rafters would reveal nothing – not even a bird or a mouse.

'One night,' said Mr Nelson, 'we all distinctly heard someone come in through the front door, wipe their feet on the doormat and then come upstairs. Dad and I rushed out of our rooms together to see who it was, but again the noise stopped and there was no one there.'

Mr Nelson lived in that house for forty years. His father died in 1973 and his mother died several years ago, leaving him alone in the house. A bachelor who neither drinks nor smokes, Mr Nelson worked until well after ten o'clock each night and, rather than go to the trouble of cooking himself a meal at that time of night, it was his custom to eat out at a small café in Barrow town centre.

One particular night, having made his way home to the house, which was some distance from the town centre, he unlocked the door as usual, picking up the evening paper from the doormat as he let himself in. He went into the living room and after he had removed his coat, settled down to read the paper before going to bed. He said, 'I had not been sat down for more than a few minutes when I heard a terrifying thud which sounded to come from the roof of the house. It seemed to be a signal, for the house lights became dimmer and then went out altogether, leaving me in total darkness.'

Taking a torch, Mr Nelson went out into the hallway, to a cupboard under the stairs which contained the electricity meter and fuse boxes. At first he thought there was a mains failure, but as the street lights were still on, he realized it must be a fault which was confined to the house. The house next door was now empty and up for sale, so he couldn't check on them. Search as he did, he could not find any fuse which might have blown and caused the blackout. He said, 'I hadn't long had the house re-wired and as I never had experienced any previous trouble with the electricity, I felt more than a little uneasy.'

There was nothing for it but to go to bed. So, picking his way up two flights of stairs by the beam of his torch, he managed to undress and climb into bed in the dark, putting the torch on the chair which stood next to his bed. It was summer time, and the room seemed hot and stuffy. That, plus the strange behaviour of the lights, unsettled him and he found some difficulty in going off to sleep.

Suddenly, he heard a fumbling outside his bedroom door on the outer landing. Living alone, he was not in the habit of fastening the door, which he now saw to his horror was slowly opening. He went on, 'I could feel my heart palpitating and even though it was quite dark in the room, I was able to make out a figure quite clearly. It was as clear as if it had been daylight. It seemed to attract light to it; the face was quite clearly visible, although I could not see the lower part of its body, nor determine its sex. It looked, in fact, like a coat with a head and arms, but no hands or trunk.'

The figure stopped, standing sideways at the foot of the bed. It totally ignored the terrified Mr Nelson, seemingly staring at the wall which divided the house from the one next door. No sound came from the figure, which seemed to stand quite motionless for several minutes. 'It' didn't move and Mr Nelson was unable, through sheer fright, to move himself.

The figure looked normal enough in the sense that it was not in any way transparent and it did not seem to be menacing in any way. Because of the blackout, Mr Nelson was unable to switch on the bedside light, but as his thoughts began to clear, he remembered the torch at the side of the bed. Trembling, he fumbled for it and switched it on, pointing the beam at the figure. 'The figure held the beam of light,' he said. 'It didn't, as I expected, go right through it. For a further three or four minutes it didn't move, then, without once looking in my direction, it began to move slowly back towards the door. Suddenly gathering speed, it went backwards through the door on to the landing. The door appeared to have been pulled shut, as it closed with a terrific rush of cold air.'

Mr Nelson jumped out of bed and, pulling open the door, he dashed out on to the landing where he hoped to catch sight of the figure again, but the landing and staircase were silent and empty. He searched the whole house, only to find the doors firmly locked and bolted, and there was no trace whatsoever of the strange, sexless figure. He was alone, although he knew he had not imagined it – he still held the torch in his trembling hand.

Shuddering, he went back to bed, this time locking the door behind him. 'Whatever it was didn't appear to have come through the solid door. I felt a little more secure in this and lay on the bed facing the door for the rest of the night, although I didn't get a wink of sleep,' he said. 'I didn't fancy seeing the thing again. I was fifty-four years of age, not at the age when one ought to be given the fright of one's life. What it was, where it came from or what it wanted, I honestly have not the slightest idea.'

My own investigation into these remarkable events has drawn a complete blank on why the house should have been haunted, or what the figure was. All I have been able to discover about the house is that it was built in 1933 by a local builder and during the preparation of the site some old foundations were uncovered, although no one can throw any light on what might have been there prior to this. The only theory I can come up with – based on the description Mr Nelson gave of the figure – is that perhaps the earlier foundations may have been connected to some form of annexe to Furness Abbey, and that the figure may have been that of a monk. However, that is only guesswork.

Ask Mr Hubert Rigg, the curator of Burnley's Towneley Hall, if it, or its grounds, are haunted and you will receive an emphatic 'no'. Ask the locals and many will tell you that it probably is. Ask Brian Watson and he will tell you that it most certainly is; particularly the grounds.

The story of the remarkable Towneley dynasty has been written many times by well-qualified people, so let me just say that the family were staunch to both Crown and Catholic Church, and no family ever suffered more for the sake of loyalty than this one.

Generations of Towneleys distinguished themselves in warfare; a Richard Towneley fought at Agincourt with a band of local men in 1415; Charles Towneley – born in 1600 – was a staunch supporter of Charles I and bled to death at the Battle of Marston Moor; his son Richard engaged in a plot to restore

James II; his grandson, another Richard, joined the Jacobite cause in 1715, was caught and tried at Preston, but was acquitted; the second Richard's brother Francis joined a company supporting Bonnie Prince Charlie in the '45 rebellion and was executed after the Battle of Carlisle in 1746; Sir John Towneley escaped from Culloden, serving the same cause, managing to reach France where he sought refuge.

With a history like this, no wonder people claim the Hall is haunted; that whispering conspiratorial voices can often be heard in the long gallery; mysterious lights have been seen in the windows long after the Hall has been closed for the night; many have complained of an inexplicable cold chill on the stone steps leading to the kitchens; and phantom footsteps have been heard in the grounds outside.

Mr Watson said recently, 'Many years ago, when I was about sixteen years old, I remember climbing over the wall into Towneley Park, near the gate which leads to the golf house and the main pathway to the Hall. It was midnight and the trees that border the pathway made the dark night quite eerie.' He and a friend had dared each other to walk round the Hall and park, looking for a ghost. They had heard that the grounds were haunted by a white lady, who was reputed to appear in the woods and wander across the small bridge. They both explored the grounds, passing the bowling greens and turning right to wend their way through the trees and bushes to the bandstand. They saw nothing, so they decided to make their way through the woods to the spot where the ghost was supposed to haunt the bridge.

Mr Watson said, 'About halfway from the gate we were startled by the sound of marching jackboots. I suggested to my pal that he went to investigate, but he was too scared and suggested that as the whole thing was my idea, I should investigate, which, with the bravado of youth, I did.'

He edged his way slowly towards the safest spot to observe the pathway without being seen. 'The marching sound became gradually louder, but just as I peered round a bush to get a better view – it stopped! I stepped out from my cover, determined to face whatever I might see, but there was nothing to *be* seen! Now I lost all my bravado. Whatever it was couldn't have

Margaret Clitherow's house, York. This delightful building, tucked away in The Shambles, is not haunted by the ghost of Margaret Clitherow, yet it is remarkable for its uncanny peace and stillness

York: the Minster towers above the medieval Bootham Bar. York Minster is the home of many ghosts, the most famous being that of Dean Gale

Marmaduke's Restaurant, York: formerly the home of a crippled boy, Marmaduke Buckle, who took his own life and whose spirit has remained behind

Treasurers House, York. It was here, during the 1950s, that a young apprentice plumber witnessed a group of ghostly Roman soldiers, apparently lost, who walked through the thick cellar walls

Holy Trinity Church, Goodramgate, York. The grounds of this old church are said to be haunted by the headless apparition of Thomas Percy, Seventh Earl of Cumberland. His head is thought to be buried somewhere near the tree to the right of the path, and his ghost is said to be seen searching for it

St William's College, York: the courtyard of the college where a terrible murder took place over four hundred years ago. The ghost of one of the perpetrators still paces the corridors today, his death failing to ease his guilt

Bedern, York: the remains of the old Ragged Industrial School, where today it is claimed that the laughter and screams of long-dead orphans can be heard, echoing through the old archway

ABOVE: The Merrion Centre, Leeds, built on the site of the Camp Hill area of the city, a derelict maze of mid-Victorian back-to-back terraces. Here the ghost of an old man was seen, tending roses amidst the ruins, in mid-November 1945. *(Chris Wall)*

LEFT: The Grange, Beckett Park, Leeds, today the Computer Science Centre of Leeds Polytechnic. It is said to be haunted by a former butler who threw himself down the stairs

ABOVE: The studios of BBC Radio Leeds, where for years staff have worked alongside a ghost, flying kettle lids and eerie footsteps. *(Chris Wall)*

RIGHT: Leeds Library, founded in 1768. Here, at the turn of the century, the ghost of a former librarian was seen on several occasions. *(Chris Wall)*

LEFT: The reception area, Old Silent Inn at Stanbury in Yorkshire. This lonely old inn is famous for its associations with Bonnie Prince Charlie and its soothing spectre

BELOW: Watton Abbey, near Driffield, haunted by a headless woman, said by many to be the ghost of Elfrida, but more likely to be that of a Civil War victim searching for her child

RIGHT: Weaver's Restaurant, Haworth. This former hand-loom weaver's cottage is thought to be haunted by the giggling ghost of Emily Bronte

BELOW: East Riddlesden Hall, Keighley: recording an edition of 'Ghosthunt' for BBC local radio. *(Left to right)* author; Mrs A. Townsend; Judith Roberts (producer); and Major Morris-Barker (Curator). Behind us is the old coach house where Mrs Townsend and her daughter had their frightening experience. *(Mrs A. Townsend)*

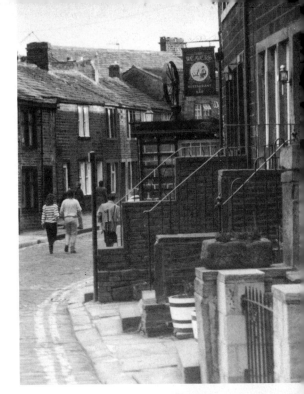

LEFT: Mr Charles Nelson in 1934, at the age of 16, standing outside the house in Roose Road, Barrow, the scene of some mysterious events over the past 40 years. *(Charles Nelson)*

BELOW: Peter and Marilyn Auty, of Rastrick, who have shared their lovely cottage with the ghost of an unidentified woman for a number of years

RIGHT: Towneley Hall, Burnley. It was near this point that Brian Watson heard phantom goose-stepping footsteps

BELOW: The Dunkenhalgh Hotel at Clayton-le-Moors. The spectre of a young woman has been sighted crossing the ballroom floor and in one of the guest rooms

Unit 4 Cinema, Accrington: formerly the 'Classic Cinema', where the cinema cat was said to have been chased by mysterious blue lights

Wycoller, Colne: the old packhorse bridge and, in the background, the ruins of Wycoller Hall. A woman in black has been seen on the bridge, and a courting couple were terrified by a phantom coach and four when they were parked on the green sward, in front of the ruins

The author, broadcasting from the haunted Studio 2, at BBC Radio Lancashire's studios at Blackburn. *(Joe Wilson)*

LEFT: This boulder stone in the churchyard at Woodplumpton marks the grave of the Fylde witch, Megs Shelton. She was buried upside-down to stop her from scratching her way out!

BELOW: Accrington: the Black Abbey area of the town. Once this was a green and tranquil place. It is said to be the haunt of the screaming ghost of a beautiful young woman who fell in love with one of the Black Abbots from an abbey which once stood here

ABOVE: Chipping. Perhaps the most beautiful village in the whole of the Ribble Valley, 'Chilling Chipping' has more ghosts than inhabitants. Hollins Lane is the scene of some strange encounters

LEFT: Clitheroe Castle. The keep is now 800 years old, and the hole in the thick walls shares the distinction of being caused by the Devil and improved by Cromwell

ABOVE: Melling Hall Hotel, near Lancaster. Once the home of the Darlington family, this beautiful old hall has three ghosts, the best known being that of Lady Darlington herself

RIGHT: Studio Arts, Lancaster. The people who work here are afraid that their friendly ghost might be scared off by an evil presence which has recently taken over

ABOVE: Chingle Hall: priest's hide in the old chapel fireplace

LEFT: Chingle Hall. A ghostly figure has been seen several times looking out of this window in the room where St John Wall was born and where most of the ghostly activities take place

Chingle Hall, Lancashire: the cross discovered behind the plaster work, after two ghostly monks were seen here, kneeling in prayer

Entertainer Ronne Coyles, who has had a number of experiences of theatre ghosts, but who was most frightened by a ghost he couldn't see. *(reproduced by permission of Mr Ronne Coyles)*

LEFT: Grand Theatre, Lancaster, haunted by the ghost of Sarah Siddons. This ghost was seen by the late Miss Pat Phoenix. *(Gordon Harrison)*

BELOW: Television actress Miss Pat Phoenix, who shared her home with the ghost of a 19th-century actress; and who saw the ghost of the actress Sarah Siddons, whilst sitting in the Grand Theatre at Lancaster. *(reproduced by kind permission of the late Miss Pat Phoenix)*

possibly hidden, and to this day, I often wonder what it was I heard, marching in jackboots up that path.'

Could it have been Roundheads from the days of the Civil War, sent by Cromwell to arrest Charles Towneley, only to discover he was already at the Royalists' side at Marston Moor? Could it have been a stray Royalist soldier seeking sanctuary from the Civil War? Or was it perhaps the shade of a faithful retainer, returning with the sad news that his master was dead, killed in the frightful slaughter of 2 July, 1644?

'Whatever it was,' said Mr Watson, 'to this day, if ever I walk at night along that pathway, I can still sense the eeriness of the place and think back to that particular night.'

The mere mention of the name 'Hobstones Farm' was once enough to send shivers down the spines of the good people of the village of Foulridge, near Colne. Once demons wailed against its withered walls, in the cobbled courtyard a wizened monk brandished his own amputated arm, windows were smashed and objects thrown about. The present occupiers, Mr and Mrs Berry and their family, lived through some terrifying experiences, until one wild September night in 1974 an exorcist invoked 'the blood of Christ and the power of Michael and his archangels' and the evil spirits fled! Or did they?

Nowadays the ancient farmhouse appears silent, the very stillness disturbed only by the murmuring breeze rising from the silver waters of Lake Burwain, which seems to surround Hobstones and its violent past in a soporific haze. But it was not always so. Even the name of the farm, which dates back beyond recorded human memory, points to a sinister association.

'Hob' is an old Saxon word for hobgoblin, an evil dwarf or elf. There are accounts which tell of children in medieval times, singing of the elves and fairies in the 'stones'. Did their own little ancestors in Saxon times have a similar ritual? For many centuries, the land on which Hobstones Farm is built was considered by the locals to be the home of fairies, elves and hobgoblins. There is thought to be an ancient burial ground somewhere on the land, and even Lake Burwain – a man-made reservoir – takes its name from the old English, and means 'burial ground'.

The farmhouse dates back to the fifteenth and sixteenth centuries, but was totally rebuilt in the eighteenth century. The land on which it stands belonged for many generations to the Parker family of Alkincoats Hall at Colne. It is known that during the Civil War Colonel Parker supported the King and it is thought that a skirmish was fought on Hobstones land, between Colonel Parker's supporters and Parliamentarians.

Many locals argue that it was through this skirmish that the village of Foulridge took its name. According to local legend, a Roundhead officer was looking across the site just before the short but bloody fight. It was a wet and dismal day, with a cold wind sweeping across the valley. He is said to have turned to a fellow officer and remarked sourly, 'This is a foul ridge on which to stand and fight.' Thereafter the name stuck. However romantic that legend might be, the village actually gets its name from something much more down to earth and means nothing more than the 'ridge where foals graze' and comes from the old English, going back many centuries before the Civil War.

However, records suggest that a skirmish did take place on or near the farm and events over the past few years do tend to bear this out. On a couple of occasions in recent years, there have been reports of a phantom troop of Roundheads seen crossing one of the fields, heading in the direction of Colne. Some were riding, others were walking and carrying pikes. Mrs Pat Berry told me that on at least three occasions she has gone into her youngest daughter's bedroom and has been confronted by a ghostly Cavalier in various states of undress, something which ties in with the theory that this was once a Royalist household. (This same ghostly Cavalier is thought to haunt the New Inn, about a mile away.)

The remarkable but foreboding entrance to the cobblestone courtyard consists of a stone archway surmounted by three pitted stone globes and a headstone carrying the legend '1770 E.S.'. This rather imposing edifice seems too important for what would once have been a large but humble farmhouse. Is there some deeper significance?

Perhaps there is, for back in the 1950s one tenant farmer claimed that he was sitting in the outside lavatory early one morning when the door suddenly burst open and he saw the figure of a dwarfish man, dressed as a monk, with a weather-beaten and twisted face, holding out a bleeding arm, from which the lower part had been severed just below the elbow. This took place in broad daylight and the poor man was so startled that he just sat and stared open-mouthed at the motionless figure for several minutes, until it suddenly vanished into thin air.

Nothing else happened for several weeks, and the farmer decided that someone must have been playing some cruel practical joke on him. Then suddenly, out of the blue, the figure appeared again, this time in front of the farmer and his wife. It stood looking at them for several seconds, before slowly moving towards them. When it was about an arm's length away, it disappeared again, but from that day, the ghostly little monk with his horrible wound appeared more frequently, both in the house and out on the surrounding lands. As a result of this, the couple shortly afterwards left the farm.

Mrs Berry told me that they themselves had never seen the monk, but she has a theory that he may have been connected in some way with the archway entrance. She said, 'I think the stone which was used in the rebuilding of the farmhouse and the later building of the archway, back in the eighteenth century, may have come from the ruins of Sawley Abbey.'

After the little monk appeared, Hobstones became the scene of some strange and violent happenings, which culminated in the service of exorcism in September 1974. At the beginning of 1970, the Berry family began to experience strange noises, and thumpings against walls and floors. Objects inexplicably moved around the house. One day the washing machine was flung across the kitchen, a tray of eggs with it. When the family went to investigate, they discovered that all the white eggs were smashed – the brown ones were still unbroken, and lay in the tray in the shape of a cross.

On another occasion, twenty-six diamond-shaped panes of glass from the small leaded mullioned windows were smashed, and forced outwards into the yard. When Mr Berry went to have a look, the glass, which he expected to find broken into pieces, appeared to have been ground to a fine powder.

One morning, having seen her husband off to work and the children off to school, Mrs Berry opened the door at the bottom of the stairs, intending to go up and make the beds. As she opened the door, a pile of rocks and stones rolled down the stairs towards her. Where they had come from, no one knows to this day. On another occasion a loud thumping on the front door brought everyone rushing to the window. They could see no one – all they saw was a giant fist pounding the door with such force, they felt sure it was going to break it down.

These incidents reached a climax on the night of 29 September, 1974 when, according to local newspaper reports, 'Demons besieged the walls and the ceilings began to shake as though the house was about to collapse.' Mr and Mrs Berry, out of sheer desperation, contacted the rector of Colne Parish Church, the Rev. Noel Hawthorne, who in turn brought an exorcist from the Fylde coast. The strange exorcizing ritual was performed and holy water was sprinkled throughout the house, and although the hauntings did not cease altogether, things certainly became much more bearable.

I went to the house with a BBC Television crew in 1983. I had met Mr and Mrs Berry some two years before and had interviewed them at length about their experiences, for radio. Now I was returning with the intention of telling their amazing story for the regional magazine programme, *Northwest Tonight*. The crew took shots of the lake, the surrounding lands and animals, and the exterior of the house. Next we went indoors and filmed inside the living room, the staircase and the kitchen, and returned to Manchester, convinced we had some spectacular material.

Filming had been done with a 16mm Arriflex camera, which was lighter and easier to handle than the electronic video cameras normally used, so we didn't know exactly what our visuals were like until the film was processed at the studios. On viewing it, we saw we had some lovely shots of the lake, the surrounding lands and animals, and the exterior of the house. Of the interior we got nothing but several hundred feet of completely blank film.

Today, Hobstones Farm has been converted into three pleasant cottages. The old barns are run down, but the globes on the old archway still loom over the cobbled courtyard, and the memories of old still linger. Many people are convinced that the hauntings have now ceased, but the animals are not, for even as

I write, cows graze in all the fields around Hobstones Farm, but for one – the large stretch of green that sweeps up to Colne Edge. The site of the ancient burial ground? The site of the Civil War skirmish? Who knows, but there the animals steadfastly refuse to go!

'Has tha seen t'ghost?' This was a question which greeted nearly everybody in the shipbuilding town of Barrow, on the morning of 9 January, 1926. The stories which were circulating had certainly caused great interest and speculation, as well as fear in the more timid residents of the area, according to the Barrow *Evening Mail*.

It seems that reports were received concerning a ghostly figure in the neighbourhood of St Luke's Street – reports which were various and obscure and which several intrepid reporters failed to clarify. It was said that the ghost of a man had been seen on several nights in the Roose district; policemen came across it on their night beats and more than one member of the force chased after the enigmatic phantom; others fled in terror. A tram-driver narrowly missed 'running the ghost down', and innumerable inhabitants appear to have seen the strange apparition on his nightly perambulations.

Recent investigation into this particular spectre reveals an interesting story and has also come up with a likely explanation.

It appears that the ghost was first seen by a policeman sometime between 1 and 2 A.M. on 7 January, 1926, when he sat on the windowsill of a shop to rest his feet and have a sly cigarette. He was actually in Cambridge Street, looking towards St Luke's Street, and was astonished to see a white apparition rise from the grating of a house cellar. The figure drifted across the road and down the opposite side, towards where the astonished officer was standing.

As it drew nearer, the policeman called out, at which the apparition suddenly vanished. Not long afterwards, another policeman patrolling Roose Road reported having seen the strange apparition and he threw his baton at it. Again the figure suddenly vanished. The author has seen a standard police report which was made out by both police officers and it is still on file.

A correspondent, referring to this ghost, told me: 'I was only about eight years old at the time, but I remember most parents kept their children indoors, once the story got out. A friend of my own age had come to play with me and although he only lived in the next street, I remember him being so afraid to go home by himself, my father had to take him.'

Another correspondent told me: 'My father was an engine-driver and he had to clock on at the railway depot in the early hours of the morning when on the day shift. He was asked by a friend whether he had seen the phantom as he walked down St Luke's street to work. Dad replied, "No, it must have been some bloody fool dressed up and trying to scare people."'

Despite the mammoth hue and cry and a police hunt which went on for several weeks, the phantom was never seen again, but the file still remains open.

There are various theories about the identity of the ghost, but the general consensus of opinion seems to agree on the spirit of a man who had resided in the district and who had a violent argument with his family. Before quitting this mortal coil, he threatened to haunt them to their dying day. Years passed, and whether the disagreements were healed or not it is now impossible to say, although it is thought that the man's spirit did come back for a short time at least, and certainly terrorized the neighbourhood, if not his own family!

Leagram Hall, the ancestral home of the Weld family, stood on the edge of the village of Chipping, a beautiful moorland village about halfway between Clitheroe and Longridge. By 1963, the Hall had fallen into such a state of decay and dereliction that it was thought to be dangerous and uneconomic to repair. So it was demolished.

The coffins from the family vault in the old Hall chapel were removed to the nearby Roman Catholic churchyard and rein-terred. The locals claimed that it would 'upset 'em no end to be amongst ordinary folk'. It was not surprising, given this expectation and the centuries-old tradition of hauntings at the Hall, that strange events soon began to take place. Cars were said to have stopped inexplicably in the lane which skirted the old Leagram estate and wouldn't restart; figures leapt from the bank into the path of moving vehicles, which, unable to stop in time, went right through them; sounds, mists and the whole range of paranormal phenomena were experienced.

A few days before Christmas 1966, Mrs Kenyon, whose family had been at Leagram Hall for several generations, set out with her teenage daughter along the deserted lane that leads from the village, past the site of the old Hall, towards the moors. They were taking their dog for its usual walk. It was late in the afternoon, dusk was just starting to settle and a misty nip was in the silent air. About thirty minutes later, when they were about half a mile from the village, they decided to turn back, and were just about to do so when they both saw three figures approaching them from the direction of the moor.

Because the light was fading, the figures appeared at first to be little more than silhouettes, but soon they became distinguishable as a woman and two boys, who looked to be about ten or eleven years old. Mrs Kenyon thought they were members of a local farming family whom she knew slightly, and they would certainly want to stop for a chat. Then she began to realize that things were perhaps not as they should be, for despite the quietness of the countryside, neither Mrs Kenyon nor her daughter heard a single footstep on the gravelled road.

As they drew nearer, she noticed that the oncoming party were complete strangers, which was strange enough, but what frightened her most was not that, nor the uncanny silence of their approach, but the fact that her normally amiable dog was crouched on his stomach, teeth bared, hair bristling, as he fixed his eyes on the approaching figures, snarling savagely. Having tried to quieten the dog, Mrs Kenyon then looked back at the strangers – only to discover they had completely vanished. The family who, only seconds before, had been no more than two or three yards away had disappeared completely. There was no possibility they could have gone past because it was still possible to see a fair distance up the road, and in any case, their movement would have been noticed.

The disappearance of these three figures had a dramatic effect on the dog. Suddenly he leaped forward, as if he were fighting with some invisible enemy, snarling and snapping at the air, ducking and weaving as he attacked and then retreated from the invisible foe. Then, abruptly, in what seemed to be a particularly vicious phase in the battle, the dog was utterly defeated. Turning in ignominious flight with his tail tucked between his legs, he made a frantic swerve as if to avoid some force attacking his flank. Then he broke away, rushing headlong down the lane, howling pitifully.

Bewildered, Mrs Kenyon and her daughter stared at the dog as it raced towards the village, obviously terrified. Then, as they peered into the dusk where seconds before there had been nothing but the empty lane, the three figures suddenly materialized again about thirty feet away, waving their arms threateningly as they appeared to chase after the fleeing dog! Mother and daughter watched horrified as dog and apparitions disappeared round a bend in the lane. It was only then that they spoke confirming that they had both witnessed the same nightmarish scene.

For a long time afterwards Mrs Kenyon refused to use the lane, fearful that the terrible phantom family might still be stalking it. Eventually, however, as the months passed and there were no more reported sightings, they resumed their usual walks, although it seems the dog would never go that way again.

Another strange thing occurred in Hollins Lane and involved four men who had been playing cards at a farm one night and were returning home by car. They assured everyone that they had not been drinking. It was 3 in the morning. Suddenly, a man appeared in the road in front of them and there was a sickening thud as the car hit him, knocking him to the ground. Yet when the men got out of the car, they looked around but could find nothing, not even a dent in the vehicle's bodywork!

No wonder the village has acquired the title Chilling Chipping.

Spectral cats seem to be among the more familiar phantoms. Just why this should be no one seems to know, but they are one of the more common phenomena. The tradition of ghostly moggies goes back to the time of the ancient Egyptians who worshipped them as gods, and across the centuries tradition has asserted that the Devil himself can assume the guise of a friendly cat. It was Christina Hole who said, 'No one who has ever loved a cat can possibly believe that faithful friend to be a mere soulless creature that lives for a few years and then dies for ever.'

Perhaps the fact that there are manifestations of deceased people means there is some kind of life after death for human beings. Happily the same proof is available with regard to a future life for animals. According to the late Elliott O'Donnell, the most prolific writer on ghosts and hauntings in this century, there do seem to be as many animal phantoms as human. Perhaps more.

All this, of course, was unknown to Mrs Gladys Golden, when she and her family moved from Birmingham to Barrow, some time in 1975. Even if she had been aware of the various theories and arguments surrounding animal ghosts, it is doubtful whether it would have explained the mysterious cat which kept appearing in her home over a period of several weeks. She told me, 'One day I was making my daughter's bed, when I thought I saw a black and white cat run into the bedroom, and under the bed. Thinking it was our cat, who was not allowed upstairs, I shouted and shooed, and when I looked under the bed, it seemed to have gone. However, to be on the safe side, I checked the bathroom and the other bedroom. There was no sign of it.'

Following this, Mrs Golden went downstairs and was surprised to find her own cat fast asleep on the hearth-rug. She was even more surprised when she realized that the living-room door had been shut all the time and there was no possible way for her own cat to have got upstairs.

Some time later, Mrs Golden's daughter, Linda, came from Birmingham to stay for a week. Linda and her sister, Christine, who was still living at home, decided they would sleep together downstairs on the bed-settee. As they were making it up, Linda and her mother became aware of the loud purring of a contented cat, although Christine, the youngest, heard nothing. Mrs Golden continued: 'I went through into the kitchen where I discovered my own cat was asleep on his bed. The purring Linda and I heard appeared to have been coming from the rug in front of the fire.'

The following morning, Linda said that she had been unable to sleep for most of the previous night, on account of the loud purring of the mysterious phantom cat. Later that same day, the milkman called for his money. Mrs Golden said, 'As I paid him, this big black and white cat ran up the stairs. I said to the milkman, "Did you see that cat run upstairs?" He said he hadn't seen it, but Linda, who had followed me out into the hall said, "I saw it, Mum!"'

Just a little to the north of Carnforth stands Carex Farm. According to old directories, it was originally known as Jabez House – Jabez being an old Hebrew word meaning 'perhaps he will cause pain'. This old farm is well over three hundred years old and was said to have been built originally as a priest's house. Over the years Jabez House became known as Dairy Farm and latterly Carex Farm.

It was as Dairy Farm that Mr Alan Clegg of Hoghton knew it, when he lived there as a teenager, and he has related a number of extremely fascinating incidents which took place there several years ago. He told me, 'One of the astonishing facts is that the house has never appeared on old maps of the area. The older part of the house was partitioned off with oak panelling to form rooms downstairs and three bedrooms above. The exterior construction is of stone and lime plaster, with two of the ground-floor windows being of the old mullion type. At a later stage two additional rooms were added, together with a new staircase. This part was quite old and above it were two attic rooms with fully boarded floors and real Georgian windows.'

When he was quite small, Mr Clegg always refused to go upstairs on his own, whether during the day or after dark, and he would never go to bed unless he was accompanied by an older brother. He said that this uncomfortable feeling was always with him, though at the time he didn't know precisely what he was afraid of. He said, 'I remember when I was about ten years old I walked through one of the bedrooms, which led into a corridor, where I saw an elderly woman dressed in black, seemingly coming out of another door at the far end of the corridor. She did not, however, open the bedroom door nor the door which led up to the attic rooms. She stared at me and then disappeared through the attic door access.'

Being a farmhouse, the kitchen was large, measuring something like twenty feet square, and shaped like an inverted letter

T. To the left of the fireplace was the door to the scullery and to the right, the door to the pantry and the back door. On the wall immediately facing the fireplace were two doors, one at either side, which fastened with the old-fashioned sneck, familiar to older readers. On many occasions first one of these doors would open, and then shortly afterwards the second one, as if someone had entered, crossed the back of the room and had gone out again through the other door, leaving both of them swinging wide open. Mr Clegg said, 'No one cared to be left in this house on their own of an evening. I've often sat in a chair with the old farm sheepdog as my only companion, when these doors have opened and I've literally frozen. The dog has stood up, fur standing on end, incapable of further movement.'

On one occasion Mr Clegg's parents, sleeping in a bedroom in what was known as the 'newer' part of the house, were awakened by footsteps, as if someone were going up the stairs. His father immediately jumped out of bed and opened the bedroom door, which was at the top of the stairs. He couldn't see anyone, but he decided to investigate further, looking into each of the other three bedrooms, which were all occupied, though there was no sign of anyone having moved, let alone jumped out of bed. The following evening an identical occurrence was experienced, but again investigation revealed nothing.

Odd tappings would often be heard on the small window beside the fireplace in the living room. As the window did not rattle and was easy to open, it was possible to quickly check to see who was there, yet at no time was anyone ever seen. Mr Clegg said, 'It would have been quite impossible for anyone to play tricks, particularly during the daylight hours, because someone would immediately go to the window whilst others would rush out of the back door. On other occasions, especially on still winter nights, there would be simultaneous tappings on both the living-room windows!'

Late one evening, Mr Clegg's mother and father had occasion to go to the washhouse, which was at the far end of the main block of the building. They went to check some eggs in a chicken brooder and discovered it was short of fuel. The washhouse was illuminated only by a candle carried by Mrs Clegg. Mr Clegg's father returned to the house for something and, whilst he was away, she felt a chilling sensation about the neck and face, whilst at the same time the candle flame seemed to burn over at an angle, as if there was a slight draught coming from one side of her, yet there wasn't. 'Once again, my mother felt the presence of some other being,' said Mr Clegg, 'but on my father's return, the candle immediately resumed its previous angle of burning and the chill feeling disappeared.'

To this day, no one knows why the house should be haunted or by whom.

Spectral Workmates

Over the years, as a freelance broadcaster, I have spent many hours in Studio 2 at BBC Radio Lancashire at Blackburn editing tapes and mixing programmes for my 'Ghosthunt' series, blissfully unaware that the studio is haunted. Admittedly, when I have been there it has usually been during the daytime when the building is bustling with activity, although I once had occasion to go into the building at 3 o'clock one morning. Even then, apart from hearing the odd creaks and clicks which one associates with a building of this nature, I never suspected the place had a ghost. Other colleagues have not been quite so lucky and at least one producer ran out of the building late one night, absolutely terrified.

Station assistant Chris Yates told me: 'I was fairly sceptical when I was first told there was a ghost here, until one night deep in the depths of winter when I had to spend some time in Studio 2 editing for the early morning magazine programme. It was getting on for about 2 o'clock in the morning and all sorts of strange things started to happen. A building like this, of course, does tend to rattle and make noises, and as it's an oldish building I put it down at first to natural causes, structural movement and so forth.'

But then the noises began to get louder. It seemed as if someone were banging and kicking on the outer walls of the studio. This went on for a good five or ten minutes, and as Chris was the only person in the building, he said it started to get quite frightening. He left the studio to have a wander round the building, just to make sure no one had somehow managed to get inside. He said, 'One thing I did notice. I had switched the lights off in the main office before going into the studio and when I came out to see if there was anyone there, the lights had miraculously turned themselves on again.'

News reporter Vicky Whitfield was a little more sceptical. She told me: 'I've heard noises behind me, bumps and clicks, and one gets the feeling sometimes that someone is watching you. But I don't think it is anything other than my own over-active imagination.' She went on to say that everyone at the radio station has heard that Studio 2 is supposed to be haunted and that it certainly does feel a 'bit funny' at times. She continued: 'Thinking back, somebody had told me about the ghost, because I said I thought that particular studio felt a bit creepy and I didn't like being in there late at night. I certainly won't work in there at night unless all the lights in both parts are on. But again, I think there is some logical explanation for it.'

Basil Barker certainly knows from experience that there is an explanation for it – it's haunted. Basil, who worked at the studios some years ago prior to moving to BBC Radio Manchester, had the biggest fright of all, for he actually saw something and was terrified. When I interviewed him in the plush surroundings of New Broadcasting House, he told me of the night he ran out of the building, leaving every light on in the place and driving home several miles out of his way, so as not to have to leave the well-lit built-up areas. Basil isn't given to over-dramatizing and is a level-headed producer – something which makes his account all the more important.

He said: 'About 1970–71, I was doing a series of programmes about local dialect and was sitting in Studio 2 editing and mixing the programmes. Whether I was tired or not, I don't know. In front of me there was a glass screen and behind that was the studio proper. Now, as you know, there is only one door into that studio and in order for anyone to get in there, they have to come in through the control room where I was editing and where I could see them.'

It was a Sunday night and Basil was busy trying to put two or three programmes together. There was nobody else in the building, something which didn't usually bother him at all; like most of his colleagues he was used to working in the studios alone and late at night. But he said: 'You know, sometimes you get a feeling and look around to see who's looking at you. I kept looking up at the little glass porthole in the door, but there was never anyone there. So I carried on working. Yet this same feeling came over me two or three times and I began to think it was my own imagination which was playing tricks.'

Just to clear the air, Basil tuned the console to VHF to listen to Radio 2, before switching back to his own programme to try and settle down again. He continued: 'I hadn't been going very long, when I suddenly began to feel very cold and I looked up at the glass screen. Well, as you know, if you look through to the studio, because there are two pieces of plate glass in the window for soundproofing, you can see a double image of yourself. There were no lights on in the studio itself and from my chair in the control room I could see myself reflected very clearly in the window. Then I thought I caught some movement and, although I knew it was impossible for anyone to have got through, I put the lights on and went in and, of course, there was no one there.'

Basil sat down at the tape decks again and about five minutes later he looked up again, but this time, instead of seeing a double image of himself in the window, he said it looked as though there were several layers of glass between him and the studio, reflecting several images back at him. He suddenly realized there was another person standing behind him – a definite dark shape. 'I turned round to look behind me and there was a figure standing there,' Basil said. 'I can't describe it, other than to say it was the shape of a person. Definitely a person! I didn't look up at his face, I just went icy cold. Swinging round to the console again, I switched the VHF transmission on again and started singing. But this time I really was scared, I can tell you.'

He took the tapes he was editing off the tape decks and, putting them in his briefcase, hurriedly left the studio and the overpowering atmosphere which now pervaded it, leaving the lights on and the power still switched on in the console, and came out into the hallway. He said: 'You can imagine being in this long hallway with no lights on and everything black. I was terrified by now, expecting someone to jump out into the corridor. I don't know why, but I left every light burning behind me, as I somehow made my way to the door. I don't know how I did it, but I got to that front door somehow!'

My producer, Joe Wilson, and I investigated this ghost for the 'Ghosthunt' series and managed, with the help of our listeners who knew the area before the studios were built, to bring to light what appears to be a reasonable explanation for the haunting. It seems that several years ago a baker's shop and bakehouse stood on the site and, according to one listener, whose parents kept the shop for a good number of years and who had lived there as a child, the night bakers often saw a dark figure drifting across the bakehouse floor in the early hours. Apparently, early one morning, at the beginning of this century, a baker or his bakehouse assistant fell down a flour chute and died as a result of his injuries. It is thought to be his industrious ghost which now drifts through the studios in the early hours of the morning, just as he would have done in his lifetime, as a night baker!

Mr Vincent Miller of Chorley related the story of an interesting spectral workmate who haunts the Star Paper Mills at Feniscowles, near Blackburn. He told me: 'I went to work there in 1965 and was there for about eighteen months. During that time several strange sightings were reported.'

Mr Miller worked in the coating preparation department, not a very clean place at the best of times, as he worked with pulverized china-clay, starch and various chemicals which were used to age the paper. He operated an Astralux machine, for which he had to mix a rather gooey, sticky mixture, used for coating thick paper to give it a gloss finish. This was used in the manufacture of gift cartons and Christmas cards.

Mr Miller said: 'Some time before I began working there, one of the mixer-men had put his arm into a vat containing the mix for the Astralux machine, but unknown to anyone a mistake had been made and the wrong chemical had been added. It found its way into the man's bloodstream by way of a cut, and in less than twenty-four hours, the poor chap had died of septicaemia.'

Some weeks later, one of the men from the department was in a room on the third floor of the mill; a room which had to be entered from an outside iron staircase. He was surprised to see someone else in there, and his surprise turned to horror when he recognized the figure as that of the man who had died some weeks previously. Later that same week, the figure was seen by two more men on the night shift, and there is no doubt in their minds that this was the ghost of their former colleague. After this, a number of men refused to go up to this particular room on their own – particularly the night-shift workers – and some of them began to carry sharp home-made knives with them. 'Although what use a knife would have been on a disembodied spirit, I don't know,' said Mr Miller.

Although he did not often have reason to go up to the top floor, Mr Miller said that it was occasionally necessary to go there during the weekend running, and he was always aware of an eerie atmosphere about the place which was intensified by the poor lighting. Because of the number of complaints and the number of men who refused to go to the third floor, the works' management became quite concerned and asked the security police to investigate. They could discover nothing untoward.

However, round about this time the phantom worker transferred his activities to the main part of the mill. This area was very well lit and was underneath a giant machine where paper which had broken during processing was fed into a large tank of water, to be mashed up into pulp and reused. Periodically the tank had to be inspected to ensure that all was going well.

One night, the machine-minder supervisor, whilst making his inspection, saw a man standing on the opposite side of the tank, his hands on the guard-rail, looking down into the mixture of churned up paper and water. The supervisor was puzzled at first, as no one would bother going down there just for the fun of it. Then the mysterious man raised his head, and he was immediately recognizable as the man who had died weeks before.

Mr Miller concluded, 'This ghost has been seen on a number of occasions and, even now, workers at the mill still talk about it.'

Another spectral paper-worker frightened the life out of David Bullock in the old Broad Oak Printing Works at Accrington during the fire brigade strike of 1977.

David is an ordinary sort of fellow. 'Down to earth,' say his friends, 'and not the sort to be taken in by tales of ghosts and ghouls and things that go bump in the night.' However, at about two minutes to midnight one Saturday early in January 1977, something strange and unaccountable happened that left him speechless and chilled to the bone. He met a ghost – or at least part of one – and his story of a phantom icy hand which put him in a state of shock is backed up by a tape recording which seems to prove that, even if there is not a ghost, there is something strange going on at the old printing works, which is now run by a foam manufacturing company.

David, who lives in Haslingden, was at the time a tradesman's assistant at the firm of Caligen Foam, and he had volunteered for fire-watching during the firemen's strike. On this particular Saturday, he was on duty with the night-watchman, Mr Bill Whittle. He said: 'It was almost midnight and I was walking down the main passageway of the splitting department, checking that everything was all right. I whistled to myself as I walked and suddenly I felt a rush of icy air.' The back of his neck seemed to freeze and the hair in the nape stood on end, as he sensed someone creeping up behind him. 'All of a sudden, something that I can positively say was a hand gently took hold of my arm,' he continued. 'It was ice cold and I could feel the four fingers and a thumb.'

David looked down at his arm, but saw absolutely nothing there. Fear then took a hold of him and he turned and raced out of the department to find the night-watchman.

Bill Whittle had worked for the firm for about nine years at the time of these events. He said: 'David had several cups of tea and a full packet of cigarettes before he could speak. His hair was literally standing on end. Never before have I seen anyone in a state like that.'

Plucking up courage, the two men decided to investigate further and the following night – Sunday – after checking all the works machinery was turned off, they set up a tape recorder in the splitting department – and waited.

On the eerie playback, starting at midnight, they heard strange sounds which continued for almost half an hour. Bill describes the noise as the loud ticking of an old pendulum clock; David says it is more like a machine, whilst others who have heard it suggest it could be the sound of an old loom or a plating machine. Whatever it sounds like, the noises from the tape come from none of the machinery used in the splitting room.

'I've never really believed in ghosts, but this has made me think there must be something in it,' David said. 'I can tell you straight, they've never got me to go up there at night alone since.' Following this encounter with the phantom hand, other workers claim to have experienced a strange atmosphere in the room. 'I've often had the feeling since that there has been someone watching me, as if wanting to make contact. It seems friendly enough to me,' said Bill Whittle.

Herein lies a possible clue to the identity of the ghost with the icy cold hand at Broad Oak Works which, incidentally, were rebuilt in 1926. Could it be that the eerie presence is that of a very lonely man who worked there many years ago? He always wanted to talk to people and, to make them stay longer, he held on to their arm as he spoke. If that is the case, then he may have made some new friends, for not long after these events, the firm was taken over and the workforce was increased.

Raphael Street in Bolton is the scene of a haunting by a man who hanged himself and whose ghost appears to be particularly active when there are changes in the building, which once belonged to the firm of Edges, the manufacturers of the famous washday wonder, the 'Dolly Blue' bag.

In 1934 a small cottage belonging to the company was occupied by a member of their workforce called Harry Johnson, who committed suicide in one of the upstairs rooms. Later the cottage, along with the others in the row, was converted into offices for the works and it was not long before reports were brought to the notice of the management of rather strange goings-on in what used to be Harry Johnson's old home.

First, unexplained footsteps were reported and then members of the staff began to complain of being touched by a cold clammy hand. An Alsatian dog belonging to one of the security men refused to walk down the passage which cut through the old cottage, and staff claimed to have seen the figure of a balding man of slight build drift through the area. The locals soon put two and two together. This was obviously the ghost of Harry Johnson, for he was known to dislike change. Didn't his ghost become more active whenever alterations were being made or were about to be made to the area of the offices which he had once occupied?

One security man became so afraid as a result of the odd occurrences which took place in this part of the building – mysterious, furtive shadows and shapes he couldn't account for and footsteps when he knew that he was the only person in the building – that he resigned on the spot one night. The ghost had been particularly active, and had touched him with its cold, clammy hands.

An office worker heard footsteps pass her and appear to walk through a steel-lined door. Another woman said she walked into the office one morning to find the hazy figure of a man standing beside her desk, whilst another woman said she had seen the figure, and her detailed description corresponded with other eye-witness accounts and the description of Harry Johnson.

One correspondent, who had worked at the factory for a number of years, told me that although she had never seen the furtive figure, she had often felt that there was a strange chill in the atmosphere and she had heard from other workers about their strange experiences. She said that she was of the firm belief that there was something weird in the factory which defied logical explanation.

I'm told that in the late 1940s the steelworks at Trafford Park was claimed to contain a haunted crane! Footsteps were heard on the crane roof, seventy feet above the ground, something which soon began to worry the operator.

He had previously reported a defect in another crane and, at first, he thought the footsteps were those of an electrician walking on his crane by mistake. He called out to tell him that he was on the wrong job, but getting no reply he looked out – and there was no one on the crane roof, although the footsteps continued for some time. Then he began to hear the footsteps quite regularly and each time he looked, but could find no reasonable explanation for them.

Officially, the noise was put down as some form of vibration in the crane roof, but the driver was not to be taken in with that

– particularly when he later learned that some years earlier, a driver had been killed working on this same crane.

Radcliffe's old telephone exchange used to stand in Railway Street, occupying the premises of the former Commercial Hotel, built in 1850. Late in 1972, the building was demolished when the new automatic exchange at Bury was opened, much to the relief of the telephonists.

One day in 1951 the engineer in charge noticed a sudden drop in temperature and, looking round, saw a hazy and indistinct shape rise from the floor and grow until it reached the ceiling, where it then disappeared. He said at the time that, although he was a sceptic, there was something there which he could not explain. There were reports that the same phenomenon was witnessed by a number of people on several occasions, right up until the place closed.

After the Post Office moved out, the building remained empty for a short time before demolition began. Two schoolboys on their way home from school decided to explore the old, empty building. They later reported seeing a grey mist, which suddenly appeared to rise through the floor, thoroughly frightening them. It was only much later that they learned of the ghostly mist which had long had a reputation of haunting the place.

According to tradition, the ghostly form was associated with a seaman, alleged to have been knifed to death in the cellars. However, recent research seems to suggest that it could be associated with a previous landlord of the Commercial Hotel, who was murdered there many years ago.

Just as a point of interest: a portrait of a bearded man, engraved on a window and thought to be a likeness of the murdered landlord, was removed for safe keeping when the property was demolished and is now preserved in the local library.

The old Mayfield Railway Station at Manchester is a spooky, dilapidated place with crumbling walls, rusting ironwork, broken roofs and platforms festooned with cobwebs. At the time of writing, it is in use as a parcels depot, but up until about 1958 it was a terminus and shunting yard, which many railway workers said was haunted.

It did have something of a reputation. Over the years there had been two suicides – a man hanged himself in the gents' toilet and another hanged himself inside the station indicator box. A night porter opened the baggage hoist gate thinking the lift was at his level, and plunged fifty feet down the shaft to his death. So, with a history like that, it is little wonder the place gained a reputation and a spectre.

Long after the station was closed for the night and all was dark except for the light in the foreman's office, where one man was always on duty, heavy and distinct footsteps were heard approaching from the door of an office at the end of the corridor. They would pass the foreman's office, seeming to pause at the enquiry window, and then continue towards the hoist. There they would suddenly cease.

Mr Jenks, a retired station-foreman, said that he heard the footsteps on at least three occasions, and each time he went to investigate he saw nothing, although the sounds would still reverberate along the deserted platform.

An ex-shunter told me of his experiences. The first manifestation was at about three o'clock one morning, just as he was getting ready to clock off for the night. At the time he was the only person at the station, yet as he walked towards the office he heard footsteps close behind him. About two or three weeks later he heard them again, this time nearer the end of the platform, where there was a master-switch for all the station lights. Frightened, he grabbed the handle, flooding the station with light as the footsteps continued towards him and seemed to pass quite close by. Seconds later they abruptly stopped.

One tough porter said that he had been through some nasty experiences in his lifetime, but he had never come across anything like Mayfield station. He said that you often heard footsteps which didn't belong to anyone and a chilling feeling would suddenly come over you. He went on to say that one night he was sitting in the foreman's room on his own when suddenly he felt a prickling sensation up his spine. He said he somehow knew that something was going to happen. It did: suddenly, from the end of the corridor, the footsteps began.

* * *

A well-known Burnley builder and his son, who wish to remain anonymous, told me of some rather strange experiences they had whilst improving some old property at Barrowford – three late-Victorian terraced houses. Now, he is a sane, cheerful, down-to-earth character, who says he does not expect to be believed, and therefore he was able to recount quite unemotionally a number of facts about the property he was working on.

'There were certain parts of the house,' he said, 'that had a strange atmosphere.' One such area in which both he, his son and their YTS trainee were reluctant to stand for any length of time was an old ingle-nook. Another area was a very small room, rather like an exceptionally large cupboard. None of them had mentioned their feelings towards this particular spot until I interviewed them, so perhaps they would have been able to dismiss this kind of vague awareness had it not been for the more physical evidence that there was some kind of presence in the building.

Things began to move, quite mysteriously. A thermos flask placed on a windowsill would turn up later in another room. One of them would put down his hammer only to find, when he reached for it moments later, that it was not where he had left it. On arriving for work one morning, they entered the building to discover a transistor radio playing, despite the fact that the batteries were so low that the radio could only be played for about twenty minutes before the sound became distorted. Working on a pair of steps, the builder's son felt a tap on his shoulder. He turned to tell the YTS trainee to stop larking about, and fell off the ladder with shock when he discovered he was alone in the room and could hear the lad being given some instructions by his father in another part of the house.

The men told me that they felt the property was haunted by a young girl, although when I asked them what gave them this idea they were not very clear about how they had arrived at the conclusion, except that on one occasion, whilst working late to complete a job, they heard the church bells begin to ring and looking out of the window they all three saw a petite figure, dressed in black, leave the house and make its way towards the direction of the sound.

On another occasion, one of the men glanced up from his

work and saw a figure pass the window. 'Hello. We've got company,' he called out to the others – but no one arrived at the door.

'The Case of the Haunted Ghost' is perhaps one way to describe the unusual goings-on at the premises of Studio Arts in Lancaster's Cheapside. For, since first mentioning the case in *Lancashire's Ghosts and Legends*, a new and evil presence is now threatening to upset the friendly haunted atmosphere.

For years the staff there have been quite chummy with a benign spirit who drifts about the place giving off a strange aroma of lavender-water mingled with the whiff of strong tobacco. He even ruffled the hair of one of the staff in a friendly fashion and they have become quite fond of him. But now, another ghost seems to have appeared on the scene and the people at Studio Arts are worried about its effect on their friendly phantom.

Mrs Ann Dodgson, proprietor of the shop and art gallery, whose premises date back to 1720, said that since the arrival of the newcomer, she had experienced one or two rather eerie moments in the gallery. She said, 'Doors have mysteriously closed on staff, pictures have moved and there is a frightening atmosphere in the part of the gallery where the Lowry paintings are.' She went on to say that she and her staff were concerned that the friendly ghost might be frightened away. 'We don't want to lose him,' she added.

Mrs Dodgson continued: 'I must confess that I have been frightened by the atmosphere in that gallery myself, something which has never happened before.'

Mrs Valerie Foster recalled one encounter with the friendly spook. She said: 'Once it ruffled my hair and was breathing down my neck. At times there is a strong smell of lavender water – very sweet-smelling – and at other times the smell of tobacco, like that old-fashioned thick twist!' Mrs Foster said that she didn't particularly believe in ghosts, but they had lived with this one for years. However, 'The feeling in the gallery is different now and it is certainly most frightening,' she said. 'There is a very strange atmosphere up there.'

Other members of the staff said that they had also felt the

presence of the ghost and until recently had never been afraid. One theory is that a man once murdered his wife on the premises, a good many years ago, and was hanged at Lancaster Castle, a few hundred yards away. She and the staff are not sure what they can do about the evil presence other than exorcize it. 'The question is,' said Mrs Dodgson, 'is that the friendly ghost – or has the murderer suddenly appeared? We certainly don't want to exorcize the evil presence if it means our friendly ghost will disappear too. He must be the friendliest ghost in Lancaster!'

Perhaps it's the man's murdered wife, jealous of the attention he is paying to the lovely ladies who work in Mrs Dodgson's shop!

Many engineers say the old automatic exchange at Burnley is definitely haunted. It appears that this building was put up on the site of an older property and, during its construction in the 1960s, several accidents occurred, culminating in the death of a night-watchman, who died when he was trapped in his blazing hut.

Several telephone engineers have told me that since the building was completed a number of strange things have happened, usually on a particular night towards the end of the week. One man told me: 'I was once called out on an emergency repair at about two o'clock one morning. As I was quietly working alone on the fault, I heard a door open on the floor above, and footsteps crossed the full length of the building, following which I heard another door open and then close. I knew I was on my own in the place and there was no way in which anyone else could have got in. I didn't wait to find out what it was,' he added.

Another engineer told me: 'I hated having to go into that building alone at night. There was something about it which made me feel very uneasy.' He said that he wasn't particularly sensitive and that he didn't, until recently, believe in ghosts and such like, but he said, 'One Friday – or rather in the early hours of Saturday morning – there was a fault and I was called to go to the old automatic exchange and see what was wrong. I very soon traced the fault and was tidying up, when suddenly I heard a door slam upstairs.' As this was about 2.30 or three in the morning, this was the time when a couple of the town's nightspots closed. He continued: 'I thought someone had come away from the Angels, or somewhere like that, and after having a few had broken in.

'Footsteps overhead convinced me there was an intruder and I went up to tackle him. I could still hear the footsteps and as they approached the door, I suddenly threw it open, ready to grab whoever was there. Imagine my shock when I discovered the place totally deserted.' He concluded: 'I was going to tackle an intruder, with no thought for my own safety. But here was something else. I was so scared I ran out of the building, and from then on I refused to go back in the early hours by myself. Not even for a pension!'

The reason the watchman haunts the place, particularly towards the weekend, is amusingly simple. It seems that he died on the night before pay day. He had done a full week's work and died with his employer owing him for it. Now he haunts the place, presumably seeking his week's wages.

In 1972, engineer Frank Lee took over Bunkers Hill Mill at Colne, for use by his engineering firm. The mill, which was demolished in April 1986, had been built in the late nineteenth century and for over seventy years had produced specially woven fabrics. For many years, the mill was reputed to be haunted by a ghost nicknamed 'Miffy', a previous owner who committed suicide by hanging himself in one of the staff lavatories.

Frank told me: 'When I took the place over, the mill was partly converted and occupied with engineering machinery. I became familiar with the place during the evenings, as I had a sailing boat which I sailed on Morecambe Bay and which I had brought over to the factory in order to give it a refit. In fact I'd had two very large doors fitted into one side of the factory wall for the sole purpose of getting the boat and its trailer in.'

The refit took longer than anticipated. In fact Frank was working on the boat off and on, both in the evenings after the works had closed and at weekends, for about eighteen months. He said, 'What should have been a refit turned out to be a major rebuild and I spent more time on it than I should have. I was there almost every evening, sometimes leaving well after midnight, happily pottering about on the boat.' It had been suggested to him several times, particularly by former employees, that the building was haunted, but being an engineer with a practical, down-to-earth way of looking at things, he treated the whole idea with a certain amount of scepticism.

'Ex-employees of the old weaving firm, a couple of whom I had taken on, kept asking me whether I had ever met "Miffy",' he continued, 'but although I had been going in and out of the place at this point for nearly a year, staying behind to work on the boat in the evenings, nothing untoward had happened to me. I never noticed a thing.' However, Frank had a young man called David working for him who, besides being a good engineer, was rather sensitive. 'Before we had actually got into production properly, this lad came up to the works with my middle son late one evening,' continued Frank. 'Whilst there he went to the toilet, and although at the time he knew nothing of the alleged haunting, he came out rather shaken, saying that he'd never go in there again. The atmosphere was strange, he said, and it was very cold indeed.'

Frank's son went to investigate and when he came back he said that he had to agree with David. There was certainly a very strange atmosphere in that room. Frank admitted that this was somewhere he never went, but one night he was working alone and had to walk past the area where the toilet was. He said, 'I was very disturbed. Even before I got to the toilet door – at a distance of three or four yards – I could feel this terrible cold atmosphere. I'd never felt it before and wondered if perhaps it was auto-suggestion or imagination when I remembered what David had said.'

Putting the experience down to imagination, Frank went about his work, but a couple of days later he happened to mention it to a former employee, Mrs Bessie Allen, who had spent a lifetime as a weaver at Bunkers Hill Mill and who lived a few yards away on Bunkers Hill Road. She said, 'Well, I'm not surprised. That's where old Mr Smith is supposed to have hanged himself!'

Finally, 'Miffy' put in an appearance. Frank said, 'I had a chap working there in 1974 who operated a slotting machine. He was one of those people who was a stickler for time-keeping, always starting dead on time and always expecting to finish dead on half-past five. One day, much to his horror, he was told he had to work late to finish off a job which was urgently needed. At one stage in the evening, he had to use the toilet and he looked round to find someone standing next to him. He hadn't heard the door open, hadn't heard the person approach, and the room suddenly went icy cold. He said that his hair seemed to stand on end and he turned round to see whether, in fact, someone had left the door open. Turning back again, the figure had simply vanished.'

Frank went on to say that the man was terrified, and when he asked him what the figure had looked like, the man said, 'I knew it must have been old "Miffy", so I didn't hang around long enough to find out!'

According to Frank, this man was a most reliable person, who under normal circumstances wouldn't have admitted to being frightened and would have felt embarrassed at even discussing the subject of ghosts, let alone claiming to have actually seen one. Frank concluded: 'I think that is what finally convinced me the place was haunted. The fact that this particular man told me personally that he had seen something. If I was to believe anyone at all, it was him.'

Hutton Hall, on the outskirts of Preston, was demolished in 1957 to make way for the building of the Lancashire Constabulary Police Training School. However, before this – from about 1947 – the Lancashire Constabulary occupied the old Hall for use as radio workshops and by the traffic branch. It was a two-storey building, the main entrance being through the eastern part of the Hall. This led through a short passage to the main hall, containing a wide staircase which ran around three sides of the upper floor. The fourth side contained a balcony which gave access to the first-floor rooms.

One evening, engineers from a firm of outside contractors were working late on their own in the first-floor laboratory. The following day, they reported that during the night they had heard someone enter the building, walk into the main hall, and begin whistling. On going to investigate, the engineers – who had only arrived from London the previous day and had no knowledge of the Hall – were disturbed to discover no one there.

Over the years, various members of the staff were obliged to work late into the night and on many occasions they heard the sound of someone entering and walking across the main hall, whistling as they did so. The sound usually ceased when the footsteps reached the staircase, although on one occasion they were heard to climb the stairs. No one was ever seen, even though on each occasion the men working on the first floor would go out on to the balcony to see who had come in. It sounded so natural that they would go and look without thinking.

These events always took place in the evening, but late one afternoon three or four engineers were standing in the main ground-floor workshop and were surprised when the workshop door opened and closed by itself, and footsteps were heard to cross the floor of the workshop and stop in one corner of the room. The men, unable to see anyone or anything, stood openmouthed. Then they dashed into an adjoining room only to discover that too was empty. The incident provided a talking point for several days afterwards, but eventually was forgotten.

The footsteps in the main hall were so real and natural that in time they were accepted as a fact of life at Hutton Hall, not in the least frightening. Then came an incident which was frightening, and was described by engineer Jack Davies in the January 1985 edition of *Lancashire Life*.

He said, 'On the balcony was the door to a washroom which could only be secured from the inside, and which used to bang gently whenever there was a wind blowing.' About two weeks before the Hall was due for demolition, Mr Davies was working alone one evening on the first floor. In the middle of the evening, before he was ready to finish work, the door to the washroom started banging violently. There was no wind. Mr Davies said, 'When I heard this, I decided it was definitely time to go home!' To get his coat, he had to go to a small landing, part-way up the stairs, where there was a padlocked door to the traffic branch. He continued: 'As I stepped on to the landing, the padlock started to shake and rattle violently, as though someone was trying to force it open. I just grabbed my coat and ran out of the building.' Once outside, however, he regained sufficient courage to return to check that the whole building was locked and in complete darkness.

Within a couple of weeks of these events, old Hutton Hall was knocked down and construction of the new training school began. No more was heard of the phantom whistler or his footsteps – at least, that is what the people in charge of the training school today tell me!

More Grey Ladies

Melling, near Hornby, is a beautiful village of graceful old houses which appear to view the twentieth century with more than a jaundiced eye. Over the years the manor house, which stands on the eastern edge of the village, would have been second in importance only to the church, in whose shadow it stands. Life revolved round Melling Hall and today, despite its conversion into a residential hotel, things don't appear to have changed all that much.

All kinds of things go on here; the doctor holds a surgery in one of the downstairs rooms every Wednesday; the mobile public library operates from here every Friday, and every other Monday the place is invaded, not by tourists or leather-jacketed motor cyclists, but by the senior citizens of the village, who hold a pensioners' luncheon club and get-together here, under the watchful eye of Mrs Joan Rogerson, the landlady.

The hall was owned originally by the Darlington family, a family who were in many ways benefactors to the whole community. The last Lady Darlington to reside here did much to alleviate the suffering of British soldiers during the First World War, opening up the hall as a convalescent home for wounded officers. She also opened a nursing home in the village's main street where, until fairly recent years, many of Melling's sons and daughters were to first see the light of day. Lady Darlington loved Melling and its people; she also loved Melling Hall for, with her death, her gracious spectre remained behind.

One man who regularly stays at the Melling Hall Hotel is businessman John Friend. It was he who first reported sighting the ghost in room ten. He told me: 'I woke up during the night, or rather early in the morning, and looking over to the wardrobe I could see in the early morning light the figure of a woman in a long, violet or purplish dress, standing in front of the mirror combing her hair. She seemed so life-like, combing her hair back from her face, although, strangely, I was not able to make out her features.'

Mrs Rogerson told me: 'I was discussing the mysterious figure with an old lady from the village one day. She was in her eighties and had lived here all her life, so she was something of an authority on the history of the village.' It was she who told Mrs Rogerson that Lady Darlington had opened the hall as a nursing home for officers. Mrs Rogerson continued: 'I asked her whether Lady Darlington was a nurse, or whether she wore a uniform during this period, and I was told that she was not a trained nurse, but she always wore a pale purple-coloured dress!'

A second ghost which haunts the hall is not quite so easy to identify, but he too has been seen by a number of guests, although it is not known who he was, or why he now haunts the place. One guest told me: 'One night after dinner, I went up to my room and as I opened the door I saw this very strange little man, who appeared to be jumping on and off my bed in a state of great excitement. As I walked fully into the room, he seemed to disappear through the wall into the room next door.' This is not really surprising, as apparently the two rooms were originally one, which was divided when the hall was converted. The description of the figure is rather interesting. He is said to be no more than three to four feet tall, with a triangular face and pointed nose. 'The strangest thing about him, though,' I was told, 'is that his legs seem to be reversed in some strange way. His knees appear to be behind, making his legs bend backwards, rather like the legs of a bird.'

Although Mrs Rogerson and her family have not seen either of these ghosts, they have experienced the invisible phantom dog, the third in this trio of non-paying guests. 'My husband and I have often heard the animal padding around late at night, his collar-disc tinkling,' she said. 'We've searched the place thoroughly many times, but have never been able to discover where the noise came from.'

Despite these hauntings, this is one of the friendliest and most comfortable hotels I have ever stayed at, situated as it is in one of the most beautiful villages in the Lune Valley.

*   *   *

Dunkenhalgh, at Clayton-le-Moors, near Accrington, first appears in recorded history in 1285, although it probably existed long before that. In 1332 it passed into the hands of the Rishton family, who held it for 250 years, up until 1571, when it was sold to Judge Sir Thomas Walmesley. His family made considerable alterations to the property. In 1643, the house was occupied by Roundheads on the eve of their fight at Whalley. In 1712, Catherine Walmesley married Robert Petre and the house and estate passed into the hands of the Petre family, but unfortunately Robert died the following year, leaving Catherine a widow with a baby son whilst still at the tender age of sixteen.

The legend of the Dunkenhalgh boggart, or mischievous spirit, stems from the early part of the eighteenth century, when the Petre family were at the height of their status and power in these parts. Legend tells us that they took on a little French governess called Lucette, to care for their numerous offspring. One Christmas a dashing young army officer was staying with the family, and he took a fancy to the young French girl.

She, in turn, fell madly in love with the soldier, but he only wanted to have his way with her and Lucette became pregnant, at which point the young officer found he was needed urgently back at his regiment, although he did promise to return the following spring and marry her. He never did, of course, and by the summer Lucette was extremely anxious and seven months pregnant. She thought of returning home to France, but, in her condition, she was afraid of facing her strict Catholic parents.

So, she took the only way out she could think of. One stormy summer night, walking down by the River Hyndburn, which not only flows through the grounds but also under the house itself, she wandered to the old bridge – the boggart's bridge – and 'in a delirium of despair and frenzy' threw herself off the low parapet into the raging torrent of water flowing under it.

Her body was found the next morning, a little further down river, floating face downwards amongst the reeds. Gently she was wrapped in a shroud and carried back to the house. Her ghost is said to haunt the scene at Christmas time, dressed in a shroud and drifting silently amongst the trees. When she reaches the bridge, she disappears.

That is the story, anyway. However, if one researches into the family history and the history of the hall, one soon discovers that the only young girl likely to have had a governess at the relevant time was Catherine, the last of the Walmesleys, who, as we have seen, was left a widow at the age of sixteen. Most of the family records still exist, including lists of servants and their wages, and in none of these is there a mention of a French maid or governess. Yet the hall, now a residential hotel, is haunted by the ghost of a young woman which has been vouched for on several occasions. The question remains, though, who is she?

Mr Burrill, once manager of the Dunkenhalgh Hotel, told me that there have been complaints of ghostly goings-on for many years, and he himself has seen the ghostly figure of a girl on at least one occasion, in the ballroom. He said, 'Ladies often complain of an unusual atmosphere in the powder room, which is just off the ballroom. When we took the place over, it was a conservatory, which we demolished, building the ballroom on the site. One night at Christmas in 1970, I came through after a late dance, just to check that everything was all right and to put the lights out, when the figure of a girl drifted through the right-hand wall, from the direction of the park, crossed the ballroom floor and disappeared through the opposite wall, in the direction of the boggart bridge.'

One of the bedrooms, a delightful and airy room with a view across the parklands – well, it was before the motorway was built – is, like one of the haunted rooms at Melling Hall, a large room converted into two. It was a nursery in days gone by and on several occasions, guests have complained of a ghostly female appearing to walk through the wall during the early hours of the morning.

'One man,' said Mr Burrill, 'was so afraid, he left at three o'clock in the morning and spent the night in his office at Padiham Power Station, rather than have to face the ghost again. He came back the following day to pay up and pick up his belongings.'

Who the ghostly girl really is, no one knows. Dunkenhalgh, its grounds and deerpark have had a reputation for being the haunt of ghosts and boggarts for several centuries, and many fearful and furtive glances have been cast around by locals who have had to pass the place at night. Dr Whittaker wrote about the 'Dunkenhalgh Bogle' as far back as 1799. As recently as

April 1986 one old local character told me: 'I wouldn't pass that way round Christmas time. Not for love nor money.'

West Hill School at Stalybridge in Greater Manchester was originally the home of a mill owner. One night in the late 1960s, the caretaker of the school, who lived on the premises, was wakened up by the strange behaviour of his dog, a large Alsatian which everyone treated with the greatest of respect. He went downstairs to discover the animal whining and cowering in the hall.

As he was speaking to the dog, trying to calm it down, the caretaker saw a woman walking towards a blank wall. Calling to her to tell her there was no exit in that direction and at the same time thinking it was strange that a woman should be in the building at that time of night anyway, he was amazed when she walked right through the wall.

The caretaker had not worked at the school for very long and he wasn't a local man, so he knew nothing about the premises or the previous history, but his vivid description of the woman and the way in which she was dressed left no doubt in the minds of the locals that he had seen the ghost of Miss Harrison.

It appears that the mill owner who built the house was a man called Harrison and his youngest daughter, who died in the 1930s, was the last member of the family. Older residents remembered her in her 80s as a shuffling woman, usually dressed in a long fur coat and conspicuous by her scruffy appearance. She had been a spinster all her life and, following the death of her last surviving relative, she had sold the house, which was subsequently converted into a boys' school. She herself had lived for many years in a smaller house in another part of the town, although for the remainder of her life she had maintained a loving interest in West Hill.

Rectory Farm, near Southport, had a horse-box which many people claimed was haunted, and there were those who, not knowing of its reputation, often commented on the uneasy and disturbing feeling which came over them if they walked or stood anywhere near it.

Older residents living nearby spoke of the strange, shadowy

figure of a woman, wearing a white cap and carrying a basket, often seen crossing the farmyard and the road from the direction of the horse-box. For many years these stories were dismissed as old wives' tales; superstitious nonsense. Then one night Mr Rimmer, who lived at Rectory Farm and who was young at the time, went out into the yard to fetch some coal. He ran back to the house empty-handed, having met the silent figure in the yard.

From then on, neighbours began to see the shadowy figure, flitting across the road carrying her basket. One woman said that she and her friend had watched the figure of a woman from a distance of a few yards, thinking at first it was someone they knew. The figure looked back at them over her shoulder and they were both overcome with a sudden surge of fear which neither could explain, because it was not possible to see the woman's facial features. Who she was, no one knows to this day.

Still at Southport, Meols Hall has a ghost known as 'Old Nancy'.

There are several versions to the story behind this spectre but all connect her in some way with a disaster at sea. It seems that during the eighteenth and early nineteenth centuries, the ancestors of the present owner, Colonel Hesketh – one of the Heskeths of North Meols – lived at Rossall Hall, whilst Meols Hall was occupied for several generations by the Heskeths' agents, the Linakin family.

At some time during the Linakins' period of occupation, a ship was wrecked off the Fylde coast, and a box containing the possessions of an old lady who was among the survivors was taken to Meols Hall. When, in due course, the old lady went to the hall to collect her box, the Linakins denied all knowledge of its existence, whereupon the old lady is said to have placed a curse on the house and its occupants.

Accordingly she has haunted the driveway ever since her death and, according to a report published in 1934, 'Old Nancy is as genuine and authentic a spectre as any manorial ghost can ever be.' Even so, the present occupiers have said that they have never seen her, nor do they know of anyone else who has. Perhaps when the Linakins moved out the curse was lifted. Who knows?

* * *

Up until the end of the nineteenth century, the mortality rate among children in East Lancashire was very high indeed. Parish registers reveal frightful stories of whole families of children dying one after the other from poverty and the diseases it brought with it. The Industrial Revolution had brought about a large increase in child labour and made things far worse than they had been in the more gracious eighteenth century. The American Civil War, which brought about the cotton famine, also caused a great deal of poverty among the poorer classes and the children seemed to be the first to suffer.

The factories brought little prosperity to the working classes; all they offered was hard, grinding work in appalling conditions. On top of this there were many epidemics which broke out in the slums of the mill towns, and the great cholera epidemic of 1832 took a dreadful toll in East Lancashire, affecting not only the poor, but the rich as well. Children went down like flies and it is thought that perhaps this accounts for the grisly discovery made in Haslingden some years ago.

A mother and her two daughters were invited to stay in a large house in Haslingden for Christmas in 1883. The house was quite crowded with guests and their hostess asked the older girl, Mary, if she would mind sharing a room with her younger sister. During their very first night in the house, Mary woke up feeling that the child's head was resting on her shoulder. Thinking it was her younger sister, she asked her why she had climbed into her bed, wondering perhaps if the younger girl was frightened because they were in a strange house.

However, Mary got no reply and, not actually being able to feel her sister in bed with her, she lit a candle – only to discover the younger girl was sound asleep in the bed next to her. She thought she must have been dreaming and, putting out her candle, she settled down again and went back to sleep. But again she was wakened by the same feeling of a child's head resting on her shoulder. Mary again put out her hand, but there was no child there.

Deciding it was imagination, she went back to sleep. But the following night, the same thing happened again and she continued waking up, convinced that a child's head rested on her shoulder. For several nights the same thing kept occurring and she could get very little sleep, so one morning she told her hostess who, although puzzled at the strange events, moved Mary into another room. Here she slept soundly and undisturbed for the remainder of her stay.

I am told that the house was pulled down earlier this century. It had stood somewhere in the vicinity of the railway station and had been used many years ago as a home for orphans who had been brought up from the south to work in one of the large mills in the area. When it was being demolished, workmen discovered the skeletons of five little girls under the floor of the room in which Mary had been unable to sleep.

In March 1970, a widow of fifty-eight, Mabel Potter, was found battered to death in her neat flat in Northern Drive at Collyhurst. Later a man was charged with the murder, but he was aquitted and the file on the murder still remains open today.

In 1972 the flat was occupied by a family called McLeish and in November of that year their two young children were admitted to Booth Hall Children's Hospital suffering, so the records state, from a rather serious form of shock. Mrs McLeish told newsmen that she blamed their illness on the ghost which she had seen twice, and she didn't at the time know of Mrs Potter's murder. She said that the youngsters had been constantly crying and talking nonsensical chatter and she believed that they had seen the same ghost. In the end, their nerves were so badly affected that Mrs McLeish had taken them to the hospital.

She later told reporters: 'The first time I saw the ghost was around midnight one night, as I was just about to go to sleep. I opened my eyes and saw a figure of a middle-aged woman dressed in white, standing and looking at me.' She went on to say that the woman had auburn hair which was turning grey, which answered the description of the late Mrs Potter. 'As I watched, paralysed with fear, the figure came towards me, and then it suddenly vanished,' she said.

The figure was again seen by Mrs McLeish about five or six months later. This time she had been to sleep, and woke up at about three o'clock in the morning with the feeling that there was someone else in the room. Suddenly she realized with mounting fear that the figure of the woman was standing right over her. It vanished within seconds, but she was terrified.

Then, one night in November 1972, she had put the children to bed and was settling down to watch television when they both came running out of their bedroom screaming hysterically that there was someone in their room. At the time Mrs McLeish couldn't get much sense out of them, other than something which sounded like, 'She was very cross.' Every night after this, the two children, aged five and three years old, refused to sleep in their own room, becoming more and more agitated as bedtime approached.

Later, the elder of the two was able to give a reasonably coherent account of the 'white lady' they had seen. 'She had long hair, like mummy's, and she was on a cross and there was a big band playing,' she said. 'It frightened me. The bogey woman told me to wait for her in my room, then she touched me and I ran for my mummy!' It appears that the 'white lady' also touched the younger child on the mouth and it is this, more than anything, which caused the hysterics.

A house in Gladstone Terrace in Abbey Village near Chorley is also haunted by a ghost of a murdered woman. The occupants, who have asked to remain anonymous, told me: 'We came here in 1967, when there were fourteen in the family, so an eight-roomed house was very welcome indeed.' The house was built in stone with walls over two feet thick by a local quarry owner for his own use in 1874. Later the houses on either side were added for his staff, and one was in use as an office. I was told: 'We were very soon informed that the house was haunted by the ghost of a woman who was murdered at the turn for the century. Apparently, she was the wife of a Methodist minister from the local chapel. No one knows exactly why he killed her, but general opinion is that she may have been finding comfort in the arms of another.'

Whatever the reason, the minister hurried through his service one Sunday, hurried home and, finding his wife in the bath, cut her throat. 'Until quite recently we had never seen or heard anything in the house, but two of our friends swear they have seen the figure of a woman standing outside the front door,' I was told. The ghost has had an effect on the family dog, too. It is quite a tough little dog which seems afraid of neither man nor beast, but one night it ran into the bedroom round about midnight, whimpering and whining, and then went padding dowstairs again after a few minutes. Then, minutes later, it ran back up again, still whining. This went on for some time and, I was told, 'We didn't want to go out and don't mind admitting it put the wind up us!'

It appears that since that time, on several occasions various members of the family have been in the bathroom when they have heard footsteps on the stairs which have then come on to the landing and approached the bathroom door. Someone – or something – has tried the door, moved away and the footsteps have faded away. 'At first we used to think that one or the other wanted to use the bathroom, but recently it has happened on at least two occasions when there has been no one else in the house.'

About three hundred yards from the house is the gateway to an old quarry, probably the quarry owned at one time by the house-builder. Two or three people in the past couple of years have reported seeing the ghostly figure of a woman there. One person told me: 'I was going into Chorley one evening in my van and as I got to the quarry corner, there was a figure dressed in what appeared at first to be a plastic mac. As there is no bus stop in the vicinity, I wondered what anyone would be doing out here on a wet and windy night. I turned away for a second to check behind me through the wing mirror, as I intended to stop and see if I knew them and offer them a lift. When I looked back again – after only a matter of a second or two – the figure had completely disappeared.'

Manchester Road in Burnley is one of those roads which seems to go on forever. Beginning in the centre of town, it rises to about 1,000 feet in the space of less than two miles, before dropping down again into the Rossendale Valley. One of the town's major roads which once carried trams, it is wide and lined with a wonderful selection of Victorian and Edwardian houses; which give way to bleak moorland at its highest point, about one-and-a-half miles from the town centre. This one-and-a-half miles contains, to my knowledge, half a dozen ghosts, and if the truth was known, there are at least as many again.

The ghost of Lady O'Hagan, the last resident of Towneley Hall, is said to drive down Manchester Road in her pony and trap, pulling up outside the front garden of one of the houses she often visited in the latter years of her life.

She is said to drive down the hill from the junction of the Todmorden–Halifax road and Manchester Road, the hoofbeats of her sprightly pony striking the road surface quite loudly in the still night air, the carriage wheels rumbling on the long-gone granite setts. About three hundred yards from the junction, she pulls up outside the front gate of a large house, where both she and her pony and trap then disappear.

So far, I have heard the story from several of the older residents of the area, but I have yet to come across anyone who has either seen or heard her.

Further down Manchester Road, an Edwardian house is haunted by the ghost of its original owner, who moved in with her husband in 1906, was widowed during the Great War and who died just before the outbreak of World War II, following a long consumptive illness.

Several times callers to the house claim to have seen a female figure sitting in the lounge or peering through an upstairs window. She has been heard coughing during the night and often, during the daytime, she is heard pottering about the house, busying herself with the chores she would have under-taken during her lifetime. Often she is heard poking the fire, although there is no coal fire in the house today, central heating having been installed some fifteen years ago. Nor does the noise come from the house next door, where again there are no coal fires.

During the winter months, when the ghost appears most active, the smell of wintergreen often wafts through the house, and at other times the smell of baking bread or steak and onions is very strong. Once the neighbours complained to the occupants that they had been kept awake by the sounds of heavy furniture being dragged about at 1 o'clock in the morning. However much the occupants might have sympathized, there was little they could do about it, as they had been in bed since 10.30 and had slept through any noise there might have been.

Doors are said to open of their own accord; cupboard doors previously closed are often found to be open, particularly those in the kitchen; things disappear, only to turn up again in another part of the house some weeks or even months later. The volume of the television and the stereo is often turned down, particularly if there is modern pop music being played too loudly, and on more than one occasion the television set has changed channels by itself! In fact, the television set is a constant cause of embarrassment, as it often appears to go awry, yet when the repairman is called out to attend to it, he is unable to find anything wrong, something which has happened on many occasions over the years. Light footsteps are often heard in the hall or on the stairs and cold spots in various parts of the house usually inform the occupants that their friendly phantom female is about.

She has actually been seen on a few occasions and, strangely, she is seen not as an old lady who died after a long illness, but as a youngish woman wearing Edwardian clothing – usually a long slate-grey dress with leg-of-mutton sleeves, and button boots. Her hair is fashioned in the Edwardian way common to working-class people of East Lancashire at the time. But like many of the phantoms in this book, her features are indistinguishable. When she *is* seen she usually precedes good news for the family, which perhaps helps explain why she is seen as a younger woman.

Could it be that she returns in the form in which she was perhaps the most happy during her lifetime; the period just prior to the Great War, before tragedy struck in the form of her husband's death in the trenches? Who knows.

Another house in Manchester Road, built for a mill manager in about 1902, is haunted by a rather tragic-looking Edwardian child. Rita and Tony and their two children moved into the house in 1983 and it was not until they began to make a few alterations and set about redecorating that they discovered there was something unusual about it.

Tony told me: 'The first time we were aware of anything was when I was decorating the dining room. I happened to look round to the door leading to the hall and out of the corner of my eye I could see this little girl. She was dressed in what can best be described as old-fashioned Sunday best. An Edwardian child of about four or five years old, wearing lots of frilly petticoats and a white pinafore and those funny little Edwardian button boots. She was a super little girl, just standing looking across at me.'

Tony saw her again later, in the same room. His wife had left some ironing on a chair and he looked round to see the little girl looking earnestly at him. She appeared to merge in with the ironing. 'One second I was looking at a pile of ironing,' he said, 'then it seemed to disappear and the little girl had taken its place. I sort of shook my head and she vanished. I looked again, and she was there, seemingly sitting in the ironing. It was very strange.'

About two weeks later, Tony and Rita were in bed and, coming from the room in which their children were sleeping, a room opposite their own, Tony suddenly heard a child's voice pleading with his two children, saying, 'Please come and play with me.' Tony said, 'I knew it wasn't one of my kids, because obviously I know their voices. I got up and went to have a look and there was no one there – and my two were sound asleep.'

On another occasion, Tony was decorating the hallway downstairs. He said he was standing on the top of his step-ladder painting the ceiling when the ladder was actually shaken, as if by invisible hands. He said, 'The ladder was not levelling itself out, someone was actually shaking it.' Then, higher up the stairway, a large handprint appeared on the wall. Twice the size of Tony's own hand, the print appeared as a watermark and then slowly dried out and disappeared.

One of the back bedroom windows, three storeys up and very difficult to reach from the outside, has a similar but much smaller handprint on the outside. Tony said, 'It's so difficult to reach, I never get up to it on my ladder, and although it looks to me as if someone has been trying to get in to my house, it couldn't have been anyone wanting to burgle the place. Anyway, there are so many doors and windows at ground level, anyone breaking in wouldn't risk their necks trying to get in from a difficult third-storey window.'

In the bedroom now occupied by their youngest child the atmosphere suddenly changes from being nice and warm to very cold and they get some strange smells, which have been noticed by several people. The smells, which are localized and which disappear as quickly as they appear, vary from the smell of fish to the smell of urine. Tony concluded: 'I'm looking forward to doing that room and pulling the old fireplace out to see what, if anything, is behind it. It should be quite interesting to see what happens, as this is the room where a lot of the activity seems to take place. Just why it should be haunted I don't know, but I intend to try and find out more about the history of the house and what went on here in the past. There are a number of unusual things about it, and some strange structural alterations which don't seem right, somehow. I will get to the bottom of it some day!'

Thurnham Hall, at Cockerham near Lancaster, is a success story in itself. It is a fine example of architecture spanning seven centuries which was allowed to fall into disrepair and was described as far back as 1900 as semi-derelict.

When, in 1973, Stanley Crabtree sold his profitable light engineering business in Rochdale and bought the derelict old hall, people said he was mad. The façade, erected in 1823, was in danger of collapse; the iron dowels had rusted and expanded, forcing off large chunks of stone, and the walls bulged outwards. A fire had swept through the building in 1959; thieves had stripped the lead from the roof and centuries of northern weather had taken a drastic toll.

Together with his wife, Olive, and his son, David, Stanley Crabtree set about putting the building to rights, so that after five years' hard work, the hall was finally opened to the public. Today, Thurnham Hall seems to have recaptured the irresistible atmosphere of a powerful past which so many of our country houses and stately homes seem to have lost. This is real.

It comes as no surprise to learn that the hall is haunted; not that the rooms are cold, dark or eerie – the reverse, in fact – but the feeling of history is very much alive. There are reports of sightings of a Cavalier dashing along the landing, thought to be Colonel Thomas Dalton, whose family owned the hall for 450 years. Legend tells us that there is also a mysterious boggart, who scatters the sticks laid for making a fire and who whips off the bedclothes in the middle of the night.

But perhaps the best-known and most-sighted ghost is that which is thought to be the shade of Elizabeth Dalton, who walks through her old bedroom dressed in green. It was she who added the private chapel to the house in 1845, which now houses an exhibition on the Holy Shroud of Turin, bought for permanent display by the Crabtrees.

Mrs Loftus of Morecambe told me that about three years ago she and some friends visited the hall one dull afternoon. Following their tour of the building, they had some light refreshment in the old kitchen, now converted into a delightful dining room, before going on to the chapel to view the Turin Shroud. She said, 'As we came out of the chapel it was starting to rain quite heavily. One of my friends suddenly said, "Look at that young woman, she'll get wet through!" and pointed to a small slim figure in a long dark dress, running across the lawn. I say "running", but it was more like as if she was gliding, yet the bottom of her dress seemed somehow to fall into the ground. We all saw her and watched her for some five or six seconds, before she simply disappeared into the trees. Strangely, when she disappeared the rain stopped and the afternoon seemed to brighten up. But I'm sure that was only coincidence.'

Stanley Crabtree, with his trained engineer's mind, tends to view the stories of ghosts with a sceptical eye. However, one Sunday afternoon, a few days after my last visit to the hall, he telephoned me to say that this same figure, which he described as 'dressed like a nun', had been reported by two ladies who saw her again drifting across the lawn.

It would be such a tragedy if a place as fine and as lovingly restored as Thurnham Hall didn't have a ghost, if only to make its irresistible atmosphere complete.

A phenomenon which was experienced only once by Mrs Rosemary Metcalf of Burnley has remained vividly imprinted on her memory for nearly twenty years.

In 1969, Rosemary and her policeman husband, Ian, lived in an Edwardian semi-detached house at Little Hulton, near Walkden. The house stood on a reasonably busy road and had no previous history of a haunting; in fact it was a very warm and friendly house. One night in September or October of 1969, Ian was on night duty and Rosemary was in the house alone. She told me: 'I was sound asleep, and suddenly I woke up in the middle of the night. I don't know what made me wake up, but I looked across the bedroom towards the door and framed there at the top of the stairs I could see the head and shoulders of a young girl. Just the head and shoulders, nothing else. I should say she would have been about eight or nine years old, with long blonde hair.'

Rosemary went on to say that although the room was quite dark, the girl seemed to be illuminated in some way, as if the light was coming from inside her, radiating outwards with a feeble glow. The figure stayed for something like five or six minutes, just staring sadly at her, before suddenly fading away. Rosemary continued: 'Seeing her didn't seem to bother me at all. I would have expected to have felt startled or even afraid, but I didn't. I didn't feel scared or threatened in any way by her ghostly figure. Once she sort of faded away, I went back to sleep and it never bothered me.'

When her husband came in the following morning, Rosemary told him of her experience of the night before, but he dismissed it as a possible dream or even just imagination. 'But,' Rosemary continued, 'when Ian mentioned it to one of his colleagues down at the police station, he was told that the previous occupants of the house had had a little girl who had died there of pneumonia two weeks before her ninth birthday. They had lived there for about ten years and had moved away shortly after the child died.'

She said that the ghostly child was only seen on the one occasion and Ian never experienced her at all. There had been no other activities; no cold spots, nothing had disappeared and turned up again some time later, or anything of that nature. However, it was later confirmed that the child Rosemary had seen matched the description of the little girl who had died so tragically, just before her birthday.

And finally, a lovely little story which comes from television actress Pat Phoenix, who had an uninvited house guest, but one whose presence she didn't mind in the least.

'This was the spectre of an old lady who would frequently call on me in my old home at Sale,' she told me. 'I was alone when the old lady first called. My corgi sensed something in the room, its ears shot up and its hackles rose, and I looked around and saw the woman. She appeared to be holding something – a candle or a bowl of some kind. She walked out of the door and I quickly followed her, but she had vanished!'

Miss Phoenix searched the whole house, but there was no one to be found, although she said she did notice a 'cold spot' in one of the rooms. After that she saw the figure several times, usually preceded by a bang or a bump somewhere in the upper part of the old Georgian house, and usually round about ten o'clock in the evening. However, it wasn't in the least frightening and several people are reputed to have seen the figure, including Miss Phoenix's mother, 'who would talk to her as if she were one of the family'.

Eventually, Miss Phoenix sold the house and moved to a modern flat in Salford. One evening she was entertaining a couple of friends and one suddenly said, 'I've just seen a lady go down the passage, carrying a bowl of soup.' She went on to describe the figure in detail. Miss Phoenix continued: 'I couldn't believe it. This was a very modern flat and I had no idea that ghosts could follow you from one house to another. Mind you, I personally never saw her in my Salford flat.'

So who was she? Before leaving the house at Sale, Miss Phoenix had made some enquiries and discovered that this was the shade of an old-time actress called Madame Mueller, a woman who was passionately fond of dogs. She had lived in the nineteenth century and had been married to a member of a prominent family, although the marriage had failed. During her latter years, her sad and lonely figure would often be seen in the evenings, standing at the end of the driveway to the house, a little dog in her arms. She had a reputation for gathering up stray animals and could be heard talking to them until quite late at night.

An eccentric, she finally died in poverty, trying to eke out a living by giving elocution lessons. According to Miss Phoenix, 'The poor dear died there all alone, but for her dog.'

A rather sad little tale on which to end this chapter.

And More Dark, Mysterious Gentlemen

In a bustling little town like Middleton, which stands on the A664 between Manchester and Rochdale, a town of mill chimneys, industrial plants and other commercial undertakings, one does not look for, nor expect to find, ancient inns. Yet on the Rochdale Road, close to the parish church, stands the Ring o'Bells, a small inn, which is for the most part very old, with foundations which many believe go back as far as Saxon times. Certainly the cellar floors and walls are several centuries old. The main structure of the building is no earlier, perhaps, than the eighteenth century and there have been additions and modernizations over the years since. But, even so, the Ring o'Bells does have a certain atmosphere about it. The site is thought to have once held a Druids' temple and until the Reformation it is thought to have served as a refectory, monks brewing their beer here in what now serves as cellars for a more modern and certainly less potent brew.

Whatever the history of the site, the great attraction for many people is the ghost, and a historical one at that, for this sad spectre has been left behind by history, a stirring and sad part of Lancashire's history – the Civil War. By tradition, the ghost – a Cavalier – was the son of Lord Stannycliffe of Stannycliffe Hall, a staunch supporter of the Crown at a time when Middleton was a hotbed of Puritanism. The young Cavalier was said to have been betrayed to the Roundheads, who used the Boar's Head Inn a couple of hundred yards away as their headquarters. He hurriedly tried to escape by means of one of the secret passages in the cellar that led to the parish church, little knowing that Cromwell's men were doing exactly the same thing, using a similar underground passage from the Boar's Head. The unfortunate Cavalier was intercepted as he emerged near the church, was run through with a sword and left for dead. Seriously wounded, however, he managed to drag himself back to the cellar of the Ring o'Bells where he died and was supposedly buried by his friends beneath the cellar flagstones.

Although the Cavalier's remains have never been discovered, not so many years ago a quantity of helmets and pikes, dating from the Civil War, were discovered under one of the cellar flagstones, thus giving some credence to the belief that the inn was used as a secret Royalist meeting place and arms store.

On the ground floor, immediately above the cellar, is the snug and in this room the ghosts of long-dead Cavaliers are believed to sit at night, just as they sat in secret conference over 300 years ago. This room contains what is known as 'The Cavalier's Seat', and many people have claimed to have felt an unusual coldness when sitting there.

One previous landlord, a Mr Barnett, was in the cellar one day when a stone, thrown from behind him, struck him sharply on the shoulder. He later said that he was completely alone at the time and the doors and windows were closed. He kept the mysterious stone as a keepsake for years afterwards.

Another previous tenant, Mrs Harlick, said that she had sometimes heard footsteps which could not be accounted for and talked of a presence that would occasionally follow her along a passage and into the tap room. Several times she said she heard sounds of movement coming from the cellars, as though stored boxes were being moved around, yet when anyone went to investigate, the noises ceased and there was never any sign of anything having been moved.

Several licensees have, over the years, experienced the ghostly Cavalier and one former tenant frequently encountered the ghost over several years. The spectre made his presence felt many times and thought nothing of clapping a customer on the shoulder from behind. On one occasion, a person who had been tapped in this way turned round and found no one there, but a voice, seemingly coming out of thin air, was heard laughing heartily!

Mrs Pennystone had no doubts at all that the inn was haunted when she was the tenant. Although she never actually saw the ghost, she said she often felt its presence and upstairs in the music room she several times found herself playing a piece of music that she never usually played. She said it was almost as if some force were controlling her fingers and time after time she found herself playing 'Greensleeves' – a tune which the Cavaliers of the Civil War used as a political ballad.

Towards the end of the 1970s, the tenants, Mr and Mrs Ryan, experienced ghostly phenomena on the very day they moved in. During their first night they were disturbed by muffled footsteps that passed along a passage and seemed to walk into the tap-room, something which made their dog flee from the room in sheer terror.

Mrs Ryan was one of the few people to actually see the phantom form, as she was serving behind the bar one night. She said she was in the middle of serving a customer when she noticed a man in a grey suit, a short, thick-set man with a bald head, who passed by her and went into the taproom. Seconds later she went to serve him, only to discover the room was empty.

A guest saw him late one night, when she was sitting in the taproom, long after closing time. Suddenly she saw a man in a grey suit coming towards her. Almost as soon as she was aware of his presence, the figure completely disappeared. A young man spoke to the figure and when he got no reply and spoke louder, the seemingly solid figure simply vanished. The description, so far, hardly fits that of a Cavalier.

However, Mrs Peacock, who lived in an old cottage near the inn, has actually seen the Cavalier and was able to describe him. She didn't see him inside, but out in the street very early one morning. She described him as a tall figure in the dress of the period, wearing a large, floppy hat with a wide brim and a plume, a lace collar, long cloak and sword. He had dark hair hanging down in ringlets and looked very sad. In fact, Mrs Peacock said that she had the distinct impression that he was crying, although he made not the slightest sound.

Could it be that the Ring o'Bells has two ghosts; the sad and apparently shy Cavalier and a former landlord, or even former customer? As the man in the grey suit is usually seen in the taproom it would appear so. Whatever the answer, the ghost does not seem to be resented; in fact he is, on the whole, quite friendly, often heard at times going up and down stairs, sounding like some clumsy and lumbering old man. Again, this description fits that of the man in grey, a short thick-set man, rather than a tall young blade of the Civil War era. Whoever he is, he doesn't appear to have any desire to leave the Ring o'Bells!

A rather alarming phantom was seen in 1967, in an old house in Roose Road, in Barrow, by a couple who had just moved in following their return to this country from Australia.

The couple, whom I will call Jim and Vera, had been sitting for most of the evening watching television. Just before going to bed, Jim, an ex-naval man, went out to put the car away, something he did at this time on most nights, whilst Vera, having tidied up the lounge, set off to go up to bed. She told me: 'As I got near to the top of the stairs, it appeared to go very cold. For some inexplicable reason, I felt compelled to turn and look downstairs and to my horror, saw a man walking up the stairs behind me. He was so real looking, my first thoughts were that he was a burglar. Screaming, I ran into the bathroom and locked myself in.'

It was only when her husband came upstairs that Vera came out of the bathroom and, trembling, ran across the landing to the bedroom, where she explained to Jim that they were not alone in the house. 'Jim searched the house thoroughly,' she said, 'but he found no trace of anyone, nor of the locks and bolts being disturbed.'

Yet she *had* seen someone – a man of average height – and they had stood looking at each other for a second or two, he with one foot raised mid-step. Vera had noticed he was wearing two-tone brown and white brogues, and a grey double-breasted pin-striped suit with wide lapels. His hair was crinkly brown and he had what she described as 'a ferret-like face'.

About a month later, Vera and Jim were at a wedding reception and, during conversation, her sighting of the strange old-fashioned looking man who had been seen on the stairs came out. One of the guests suddenly went pale and said, 'You have just described Frankie Charles, who used to live at your house with his mother!'

Frank Charles was a well-known amateur glider pilot in the Barrow area. A founder member of the local glider club, he was killed in a flying accident. According to the guest, Vera had seen his ghost dressed in the same clothes he was wearing on the day he was killed. It further turned out, during conversation, that the bedroom in which Vera and Jim slept was where he kept the spare parts for his flying machine.

Vera said that they didn't stay in this house for very long after this; she was frightened of seeing him again, and they moved out about a year later into another old house in Barrow. It was in this house that she was to experience a second ghost which finally decided her that she had had enough of living in old houses. She said, 'It was broad daylight, my husband was at work and I had occasion to go into the lounge. As I entered, I saw a man standing in front of the fire warming his backside, who disappeared almost at once.'

She described him as wearing dark trousers and a dirty-white roll-necked jersey of the type seafarers wear. His face appeared to have been very badly burned and was twisted in a grotesque manner.

Later enquiries led her to believe that this was the ghost of a naval officer who used to visit the house and who was killed during the First World War, when his submarine was destroyed by enemy action. He had been terribly burned about the face and shortly after being picked up by a rescue launch, he died of his terrible injuries.

Sun, sea, fresh air and sparkling sand. That is what a holiday in Blackpool is all about; that wonderland of candy floss, bikini-clad beauties, pier shows, the Golden Mile and the Tower. Ghosts are the last thing one thinks about on a seaside holiday and yet, even in Blackpool, night must fall, and some rather mysterious things are likely to happen.

If Blackpool is haunted – and records show that each year more and more psychic researchers visit the resort – then surely the ghosts will not hang around empty gale-lashed beaches or the rain-swept promenades. No, they will be found behind the lace curtains of the trim, bland boarding houses where who knows what secret tragedies are re-enacted.

It was in one such boarding house that the Rigby family from Huddersfield stayed during the height of the 1981 summer season. Thomas Rigby, his wife Beryl and their young son had, as always, been looking forward to their two weeks' holiday by the sea. But this year was a little different; for a start, the lady with whom they usually stayed had sold up and moved to the Lake District, and so they had to find new accommodation. The new boarding house, which had been recommended to them was comfortable and the food homely. They had been given a bright room on the first floor, so that for the first three days they settled into a familiar holiday routine and were just beginning to relax and feel the benefits they had looked forward to all year.

Then, on the third night, things began to go dreadfully wrong. Mrs Rigby had gone up to bed before her husband, who had gone for a last stroll along the promenade. Not long after she had got into bed and put out the light, Mrs Rigby sensed a change in the atmosphere of the room. Lying in the near-darkness, tired but not able to sleep, her eyes continually strayed towards the long mirror, set in the door of the wardrobe.

Just as she seemed to be drifting off into a doze she saw what appeared to be a misty shape forming in the mirror. It seemed to ooze out at her, and she distinctly felt the pressure of ice-cold fingers on her throat. Fortunately, at that precise moment, the bedroom door opened and her husband came in, an action which caused the atmosphere to immediately lift, as if a spell had been broken. Mrs Rigby put it out of her mind, thinking it was some kind of bad dream and that she must have been asleep after all, yet dreamed she was awake.

However, two nights later their young son, who was sharing the room with them, ran screaming to his parents that a man had come out of the mirror and had tried to strangle him. Then both parents had to admit that something was very, very wrong with that room. Their holidays were only half over, but Mr Rigby said, 'We packed our bags and left the next morning. We had had enough.'

Although the Rigbys were unable to discover just who or what the ghost was, or why he should try to strangle members of the family, the author later discovered that, early in the 1920s, this had been a reasonable-sized private residence, although in all its history, there is no record to suggest that anything untoward happened here. The only tenuous link I could discover was that the last occupant of the house, a semi-recluse, had died in the room in which the Rigbys stayed, but there is no record of him dying of anything other than natural causes.

When the row of terraced houses in Providence Street at Heaton Norris, Stockport, was demolished in 1971, the *Stockport Express* brought to light an unusual haunting which had occurred only two years before and for which there has been no rational explanation.

It appears that at about four o'clock on the morning of 17 March 1969, lorry driver George Wilshaw opened the back door of his Victorian terraced house and went to the outside toilet. Returning to the house again a few minutes later he saw in the clear moonlight a huge male figure dressed in black, standing by a tree which stood between his small garden and that of the house next door. George could not make out the features of what was obviously a huge man who made no movement but who, he felt sure, was aware of his presence.

Now, anyone discovered in your garden at that hour of the morning is obviously up to no good, and George called out to the fellow, asking him what the blue blazes he was doing there. Receiving no reply, he stormed across to the figure, which was perhaps no more than two or three yards away, and, as he did so, it completely disappeared. Now George realized he was dealing with someone who was definitely up to no good, and thinking he had eluded him in some way, he dashed into the house, picked up the poker from the living-room fireplace and dashed out again to tackle the intruder. He told the newspaper: 'I walked around the back yard looking everywhere, checking the old air-raid shelters and the toilets to see if I could find the man I had seen. But I neither saw nor heard anything, not even when the figure vanished before my eyes.'

That same evening as George and his wife were quietly watching television, their dog began whimpering to go out. George opened the back door and the dog took one look outside and froze, its fur standing on end. It gave a peculiar yelp and then shot back into the house, following which the shaken George hurriedly shut the door, making sure it was bolted. He said the poor animal was in a state of terror for the remainder of the week, refusing to leave the house and giving the back door a wide berth.

Some days later, George was awake at about the same time as before and, a little hesitantly, he made his way to the outside toilet, peering nervously in the early morning light for anything out of the ordinary. He was relieved to find there was nothing. However, this didn't last long for on returning to the house he again saw the same huge figure, black and silent, standing near his next-door neighbour's coal bunker. Again George challenged the figure and again there was no reply. This time he was determined to find out who or what the thing was and he ran at it in fury, ready to attack whoever was prowling around in the back at this time of the morning. But when he got to within a couple of feet, the strange figure just simply vanished in front of his astonished eyes. As before, there was no movement and no sound.

When George returned from work later that same day, he was saddened to learn that his neighbour had died suddenly.

Discussing these events later with the newspaper reporter, George stressed the fact that he had not been drinking on either occasion, nor was he dreaming or imagining things. He said he found it difficult to accept any connection between the appearance of the figure and the sudden death of his neighbour. 'And there was the sheer size of the thing,' he said. 'That figure was twice my size. In my whole life I've never seen a human being so big. I must have been mad to make an attack on it!'

The word 'spirits' took on a new meaning for drinkers at the Spinning Jenny Club in Accrington. They believed their favourite haunt had a ghost, and one customer – a burly six-footer – was so scared that he vowed never to go into the pub's now-demolished theatre lounge again.

The strange goings-on centred around the big lounge at the rear of the building, which stood deserted for months before the brewery decided to demolish it. Landlord Ian Montgomery said, 'There is definitely something there. It sounds unbelievable, but as you walked into the back room, you became aware of a sudden drop in the temperature. Many regulars say that even on the hottest of days when the sun beat in through the theatre lounge windows, there was still an uncanny chill.'

Since the lounge was pulled down, the inexplicable happenings have spread to the rest of the pub. Machine controls have been tampered with when nobody is around and switches are constantly being turned off and on without any logical explanation. A plumber complained that a switch had been turned off five times, so he and the landlord went into a small room at the rear of the pub to make sure that nothing was wrong and turned the switch back on. After waiting for about ten minutes they went back outside – and a couple of minutes later the switch went off again.

Regular customer, John Robertson, confirmed that lights have gone off inexplicably and a woman who once worked at the Spinning Jenny fainted with shock after she felt a hand reach out from behind a curtain in the theatre lounge and touch her when the room was empty.

Sceptics scoffed and said that the pub couldn't be haunted because it was less than twenty years old. But recent research has shown that it was built on an old swamp where once there was a forest. The centre of the dance floor in the old theatre lounge was thought to mark the spot where a man committed suicide by hanging himself from a tree many years ago.

Although there has not been a sighting of the ghost, the man's spirit is thought to be responsible for the strange goings-on. Ian said that the previous landlord was so scared, he would never go into one of the back rooms and one burly customer was so frightened one night that he vowed he would never enter the place again. 'And he was a big lad, well over six foot tall,' Ian concluded. John Robertson added, 'It was the chill and the silence that got you. The roof was flat topped, so you would expect it to get quite hot in there. There was a lot of glass too, but it just wouldn't heat up – and the silence was deafening. You never heard anything.'

Speaking to the customers later, everyone agreed that anyone who wanted to go in there late at night had to be terribly brave. Needless to say, I took the hint.

* * *

The *Stockport Express* of December, 1974, carried an unusual article concerning a large old building in Manchester Road, Heaton Chapel, which was thought to have a long and sinister history and a reputation for being haunted.

During the First World War, the property was occupied by a family of Polish immigrants, who were cousins of the private secretary to the Emperor of Austria. They were not without a bob or two and had acquired a few properties in the Manchester area, settling into the house in Heaton Chapel just before the outbreak of the war.

One night, shortly after they had just settled in, one of the teenage daughters was getting ready for bed when she was astonished to see a vanity box on the dressing table opening and closing by itself. Another night, she suddenly woke up from a deep sleep to find a black figure, with a 'grotesque and ugly face,' standing at the foot of her bed, screaming something at her, which she was unable to make out.

On many occasions she and her sister saw the same form, about six feet tall, with a dark, pointed face, walking down the stairs and carrying a lantern. Sometimes the sisters would bravely follow the figure down the steps into the cellar, where it would disappear into one of the walls, after pausing beside an old well. One particular morning, the girl's father, who was a practical and hard-headed businessman, was lying in bed gazing sleepily out of the window when the bedclothes were inexplicably drawn off him, when there was no other person in the room.

Some weeks later the father was discussing the strange incidents which were occurring in the house with the local barber, who had lived and worked in the area for years and had a considerable knowledge of the history of Heaton Chapel. Thus the apparent reason for the hauntings became clear.

Years earlier, when the railway was being laid through the town, hundreds of Irish navvies were brought in to do the heavy work. They were a godless lot, always drunk and in trouble with the local constabulary. Apparently, they brought a number of Irish prostitutes over with them who by all accounts were worse than the men.

When the work finished a couple of years later, the men left the town – much to the relief of the good citizens of Heaton

Chapel – but they left behind the prostitutes and not an inconsiderable number of illegitimate children.

One of the houses the navvies had used was the Polish family's home in Manchester Road and after they had gone, the authorities moved in to disinfect it. Following this, they set about laying a new floor and found the bones of several human babies, almost at ground level. Now the question which everyone began to ask was, 'What has happened to the prostitutes?'

People in the area used to say that when the house was demolished, more human bones would be unearthed. 'The babies' bones were found at ground level,' they said. 'What would they find in the cellars? What grim secrets lurked at the bottom of the well?'

It now became apparent to the Polish family that the dark figure seen at the house on many occasions – sometimes in one of the bedrooms, but more frequently on the stairs – was certainly the killer of the babies and probably the killer of the prostitutes too.

The murderer returning to the scene of his crime long after his death, as some form of atonement, perhaps?

When the Civil War broke out in 1642, Bolton was one of the first towns in England to raise a militia under the banner of Parliament, and the history of Lancashire shows that during this period of blood-letting, Bolton and its surrounding villages suffered more from the ravages of war than most other Lancashire towns.

It is thought that an old barn on the edge of Turton Moors, to the north of the town, may have been the site of a skirmish where a Royalist was killed, or was perhaps hidden by sympathetic supporters of the King, for the ghost of a Cavalier has been seen to materialize out of the walls of old cottages here – in broad daylight. One occupant of Old School Cottages claimed to have seen a man in the house wearing a large feathered hat, similar to those worn during the period. She said she had come out of the kitchen and, as she entered the lounge, she saw a ghostly figure resembling a Cavalier standing in a corner of the room.

In 1965, soon after another couple moved into the cottage,

their dogs began to act in a strange manner, running around for no apparent reason, barking and snapping at something invisible to their owners, whimpering and snarling and generally behaving in a manner which up until then had been foreign to them. On one occasion one of the dogs suddenly woke up from a nap and snapped at something, before charging into a door in its rush to get out of the way of some invisible menace.

One bright, warm summer afternoon the cottage's occupants were in the adjoining barn, engaged in converting it into kennels for their three dogs. Suddenly they heard the unmistakable sound of soldiers goose-stepping past the cottage – yet when they went outside to investigate, the road in both directions and the moors beyond were devoid of any form of human life. Later the same afternoon, someone was heard speaking and although it was not possible to make out what was being said, two words, 'menace' and 'peril' were distinctly heard, spoken in a man's voice, but again when they left the barn to investigate, there was not a single person in sight.

To my mind, perhaps the most interesting ghosts are those which are seen by down-to-earth folk in their own homes, and which are accepted for what they are – the shades of ordinary people from the past who, just like us, carry out their day-to-day activities, despite the fact that they have moved on to another world. Typical of this is the friendly spectre which was experienced in the lovely old converted home of Mr and Mrs Younger.

Until his employers transferred him south, Bill Younger lived in a lovely converted barn on Whalley Nab. High above Whalley, it commands a view right across the Whalley viaduct, with an open prospect which, on clear days, takes in Clitheroe and the Ribble Valley. A lovely spot.

When Mr Younger bought the tumble-down old barn in the late 1970s it needed a lot of attention. It consisted of the main barn and hayloft, with a shippon alongside. Conversion took quite some time; the main double doors became a magnificent, floor-to-ceiling panoramic window. The wall to the shippon was taken down to make this into a sitting room, into which was built a beautiful stone fireplace. All in all, the finished result was sheer delight.

Whilst in the early stages of the conversion, Mr Younger was working in the building one day when he heard the sounds of someone walking on the gravel path outside, apparently trundling a wheelbarrow which, on arriving at the shippon door, was heard to stop and drop on to its legs with a little skid. Then the sound of someone shovelling something from the shippon floor and throwing it into the wheelbarrow was heard; the sound of his shovel hitting the wooden wheelbarrow sides was quite clear. At this time the shippon wall had not been taken down, so Mr Younger had to go outside and walk round to the old doorway to find out who was there and what they were doing. When he reached the shippon, the sounds ceased and there was no one at all to be seen anywhere.

On another occasion Mr Younger was working on the house, this time on a Sunday afternoon, when he again heard the noise of footsteps and the sound of a trundling wheelbarrow going past outside. This time, he rushed to the window and was just in time to see what appeared to be an old farm labourer, his trouser legs fastened around his knees with string, pushing an old-fashioned wooden wheelbarrow. He dashed outside – this time being able to go through the old shippon – but, on reaching the door only seconds later, figure and wheelbarrow had disappeared.

Puzzled, Mr Younger later discussed his experience with a neighbour who told him in a matter-of-fact way, 'Oh, that'll be Johnnie Rushton!' Apparently he had been seen on the land and surrounding areas quite often, usually seated on a log, and he had become an accepted fact of life. Everyone knew him when he was alive and it seemed quite natural for them to have him around the place still.

I'm told that one lady who used to live in the farmhouse next to the barn looked round to see his figure sitting beside her as she did her ironing; a little man in a billycock, with a loose tie round his neck. His trousers were fastened at the knees with string.

Whalley is a very ancient village and so it is natural that there should be ghosts here, although we mainly associate them with the abbey. But these old farms and outlying areas were inhabited by people who were very close to the land and close to nature. They had a close affinity with the elements – both natural and supernatural.

It is still like this today; the only problem is in getting them to talk about it, for this is an area of fiercely independent people who resent outside interference. Neither Henry VIII nor Elizabeth I could make much impression in enforcing their religious reformation on them, and when the Roundheads came this way towards the Battle of Preston they considered this to be an area where it was wise not to linger or to camp for the night without extra guards. So it was then and so it is today. Long may it remain so.

Mrs Irene Lea told me an interesting little story of an event, not dissimilar, which concerned her grandparents' house just off Stockport Road, in Longsight, some ninety years ago.

She told me: 'Almost every night, right on the stroke of midnight, something or someone tried to get out of the cellar. The locked door would shake and rattle almost off its hinges.' Mrs Lea's grandfather was an engine-driver for the London Midland and Scottish Railway and, after discussing this phenomenon one day at work, he brought a number of his disbelieving workmates home with him to witness the phenomenon for themselves. Mrs Lea continued: 'Sure enough, on the stroke of midnight the door began to rattle and shake savagely, and by the time the clock had stopped chiming, there wasn't a workmate left in the house!'

Eventually it began to get on the nerves of the occupants and so the police were contacted and asked to investigate. They were as puzzled as anyone else. They waited for the midnight rattling and when it began they quickly opened the door and dashed down into the cellar to catch the culprit – but they returned baffled. There was no one to be found, nor any way in which anyone could have got in or out of the cellar without being seen.

Now whether this was coincidence or not, no one can say, but the noises ceased in 1935 when Mrs Lea's grandfather died. She told me: 'Although he didn't have much to leave, my grandfather had made a will. However, on his death it couldn't be found.'

One night, his daughter was sitting alone in the house, when she heard grandfather's familiar footsteps coming down the back stairs, sounding just as they had during his lifetime. Suddenly his voice was heard to say, quite clearly, 'The top right-hand drawer in the dresser.'

'The following day, my father forced the drawer open – it was the only one in the whole set which had stuck – and there he found the will, leaving everything to my aunt, who my grandfather's shade had spoken to!' she concluded.

Unfortunately, the house, 33 St John's Street, just off Stockport Road, has been demolished, so it has not been possible to follow up the story, nor to discover whether other occupants were disturbed by the rattling cellar-head door. Nor is there any history of violent happenings on the site. Perhaps it was something to do with grandfather's impending death, who knows?

A Touch of Evil

Great Harwood, about three miles from Accrington, stands on the edge of what was once the vast Pendle Forest. Pendle – the very name conjures up visions of witchcraft and evil, although it is quite innocuous and means nothing more sinister than 'hill'. Yet, as every Lancastrian knows, Pendle has a significant place in the history of the occult in England.

Burns Way, Great Harwood, is lined with corporation houses built between 1949 and 1951, and it was in one of these houses that a young boy experienced a rather sinister and frightening event, which to this day remains unexplained. The boy, Steven Wood, occupied a bedroom which had a clear view over Pendle Hill. The room contained two single beds, one on each side of the fireplace, with their heads set into the alcoves.

One night in 1957 Steven suddenly woke up, which in itself was unusual because he was normally a sound sleeper. He didn't know what time of night it was, but as there was no sound inside or outside the house, he thought it must have been well past midnight. Because of the street-light outside, the room was not in total darkness and it was possible to make out familiar objects around him. Suddenly, to his amazement, Steven saw the silhouettes of five figures, gliding silently and apparently without movement of their limbs from the fireplace near his head to the wall at the opposite side of the room.

The figures were no more than about three feet in height, and although their clothing was not distinguishable, they appeared to be solid right down to the floor, as if the top halves of their bodies were in the bedroom and their legs were in the room below. They didn't appear to have any hair and the round outline of their heads suggested that their heads had been shaved.

In a strange way the inky shapes stood out clearly from the general darkness of the bedroom.

As the frightened boy watched the procession, which seemed to vary the speed of its movements, the figures came to the wall beyond the foot of his bed – and here he saw a sixth figure sitting featureless and opaque like the others, but with the shadow of a hat of some sort on its head. As each figure in the procession reached the seated figure, it handed up to him what appeared to be a jug. It then made its way back down the room, passing its companions and returning to the fireplace, where it would resume its journey once more!

Petrified by now, the boy quietly called to his sister who was sound asleep in the next bed, and who made no comment, whilst all the time the shining black silhouettes slid up and down the room with their 'offerings'. Then, quite suddenly, there was just the empty room tinged with the glow of the outside street-lamp. The figures had simply disappeared just as quickly as they had come. Nothing, no history or event, can account for the experience. Remnants of earlier seventeenth-century ritual witchcraft, perhaps? Who knows? Some funny things went on in Pendle Forest in years gone by.

A nineteenth-century terraced house in Bradford Street, Oldham, made local news in October 1972, when a young couple suddenly left it after only a few months of marriage, saying they couldn't stand the evil atmosphere any longer. They said that for the previous three months they had gone through sheer hell, and thus they moved in with relatives across the other side of town.

As soon as they had moved into the house they had begun to notice odd incidents: the electricity turned itself off and on, stamping noises were heard in the bedroom, bangs and thuds seemed to come from an old table in the kitchen and a candle began to act in a strange way, its flame bending nearly at right-angles, as if someone was blowing on it. The couple's Alsatian dog lay trembling in a corner of the room whenever these activities took place, its terrified eyes following the movement of something the couple couldn't see.

Then one day the forms of two old ladies were seen, sitting

together on the living-room settee. They were dressed in old-fashioned clothes and wore what appeared to be scarves on their heads. They disappeared as soon as they were spoken to. It was noticed that, at the time the figures were seen, the room became extremely cold, and gradually an atmosphere of evil, which was always in the house, seemed to get more and more powerful, until the couple just had to get out.

The local press got to hear of the strange events and on the night of 31 October, 1972 – Hallowe'en – two intrepid reporters were despatched to spend the night there and investigate the now-empty house, surrounded by cameras, tape recorders, thermometers and all the paraphernalia associated with a ghost hunt. In the event, all they got for their pains was thoroughly cold, as no abnormalities were experienced, no knocks or thumps were heard and no figures were seen.

Just who the two old ladies were and why they should pervade the atmosphere with evil has, to my knowledge, never been established.

Early in 1978, a young couple and their two children moved into 16 Wardle Brook Avenue, a two-bedroomed council house at Hattersley on the outskirts of Manchester. Unknown to them, the neat, end-of-terrace house had once been occupied by the moors murderers, Myra Hindley and Ian Brady.

Some twenty years ago, an early morning telephone call from Hindley's brother-in-law informed the police that a murder had been committed there. A detective, posing as a bread delivery man, managed to gain entrance to the house, where he discovered the body of 17-year-old Edward Evans in a bedroom. Later, in company of other police officers, the detective discovered photographs taken near makeshift graves high on the moors above Saddleworth of 10-year-old Lesley Ann Downey and 12-year-old John Kilbride. They also found tape-recordings of a frightened child's voice, later identified as that of Lesley Ann. In due course Hindley and Brady were brought to trial at Chester, were found guilty and sentenced to life imprisonment.

Following the trial and conviction, the house became known locally as 'the house of horror' and hundreds of ghoulish sightseers came from surrounding areas by bus and car out of morbid curiosity, just to look at it. Later, Manchester City Housing Committee re-let it, and two or three families moved in, although they never stayed for very long.

The young couple already mentioned had lived for several weeks in a homeless-family unit and were overjoyed when they were offered the keys to a two-bedroomed house in Hattersley. Unfortunately, the council chose to play down the claims of previous tenants – in fact a council spokesman told the author recently, 'We do not feel it is in the interest of our tenants to discuss the matter.' They certainly didn't mention the history of the house to the young couple, and the address meant nothing to them either. In fact, it was not until after they had moved in that people told them, 'That's the moors murderers' house.'

From the very beginning they said there was a strong feeling of evil, as if the presence of Hindley and Brady had eaten into the very fabric of the building. The night after the couple moved in, the house was burgled, and from then on things gradually became worse; strange noises, creaks and groans coming from upstairs, and, at night, mysterious tapping on the bedroom windows.

As soon as the couple knew of the house's associations, they contacted a priest who blessed it, but still the presence persisted, and it wasn't long before they too moved out.

Other couples and their children moved in and out again in succession and nearly every resident over the past nineteen years has sworn that the horror lives on.

In the summer of 1985, the last known tenants moved out, but before doing so they told me of hearing the screams of phantom children, walls that poured water and the shape of a ghostly body which impressed itself on the bed.

Unemployed Brian Dunne, like others before him, knew nothing of the history of 16 Wardle Brook Avenue, when he took his then pregnant wife, Margaret, and their three children to the area from their native Dublin. But the neighbours soon told him of the horrific history. Mr Dunne said, 'We were terrified when we heard about it. All sorts of things were happening which couldn't be explained.' He said that damp ran down the walls and the council were unable to stop it, although the adjoining houses were in no way affected. 'It's as if the house is crying in shame,' said Mr Dunne.

He said that the phenomenon of the ghostly body on the bed had happened several times, but it was the sound of children screaming and crying which was the most frightening. 'There is the sound of smashing and banging,' he continued, 'but when I go to investigate, there is never anything to be seen.' He admitted that the shape of the body in the bed was pretty weird too, and said there had been a petition demanding the house be demolished. 'It should be burned to the ground,' concluded Mr Dunne. 'The memories this place contains should be erased for ever.'

Many people agree with him and some go further, saying that Hindley and Brady should go with it.

From experience, I learned long since that some of the best supernatural happenings occur in the most ordinary and mundane settings – not in ancient halls, ruined abbeys or gloomy old castles, but in ordinary and, under normal circumstances, comfortable homes.

Number 38 Pendle Street, Accrington, was such a house. A small two-up-and-two-down terraced house which, so far as is known, had no emotional upheavals associated with it other than the normal births and deaths such as occur in all houses during their history. However, this home became the setting for one of the best-authenticated hauntings in East Lancashire and lasted for a number of years.

At the time of these events, the house was occupied by a family of normal, level-headed Lancastrians, hard-working and respected and with three lovely children. The eldest child, a girl of fourteen, had a tendency to sleepwalk, but this only occurred on rare occasions. The girl invariably woke up at the top of the stairs, or when she was a few steps down. But there was one exception; on a night in April 1965, the sleepwalking child almost reached the bottom of the stairs before she woke.

Immediately she was fully awake and she felt the tomb-like silence and blackness of the early hours of the morning. Then she felt an instant and overwhelming intangible sense of evil and danger, something which she had never experienced on previous occasions. She was terrified, yet she didn't know why. Hoping that the awful sensation would vanish, she closed her eyes to shut out the feeling in the darkness around her. A moment later, she heard a faint noise in the hall and quickly opened them again.

Instantly she experienced an intense wave of heat, as if someone had suddenly opened a huge furnace door, and then, to her absolute horror, she saw the glowing, formless shape of a figure appearing to hover about three or four feet in front of her. There were some features which she subconsciously took in; it was a male form which emanated a sense of real evil, projecting an inexpressible hatred. The girl was conscious that 'it' was standing on or just off the hall floor and 'its' face was level with her own, staring directly into hers.

There was a certain ugliness about the apparition which she could not define, but which froze her senses, and a malevolence that seemed to be directed towards her personally. Fortunately she was standing immediately next to the light switch and had the presence of mind to reach out and press it, flooding the hall with light. As she did so, the apparition vanished. Terrified, she scurried back upstairs to bed.

The incident seemed so incredible that on the following morning the youngster dismissed the whole thing as an unpleasant nightmare. It couldn't really have happened. However, some weeks later, the girl was woken up by the sound of something falling heavily from a chair in the living room below her, followed by the sound of dragging and accompanied by a peculiar scratching noise.

Thinking it was the family dog which needed to go out, she went downstairs and, as she did so, the regular scratching continued. But the moment she put on the living-room light, the noise stopped and she saw that the dog was sound asleep, apparently undisturbed. Mystified, she went back to bed.

In the months that followed she heard the same sequence of sounds on a number of occasions. Once she approached the living-room door and called quietly into the darkness; the dog at once roused itself from sleep and padded quietly towards her – but above the patter of its paws, she heard the continual rhythm of the scratching. (One thing which puzzles the author is why the dog, usually the most sensitive of animals, was in no way affected by all this.)

During the spring of 1966, her 11-year-old brother, who slept downstairs, confided that he had often got up in the night to see what was the matter with the dog, as he kept hearing a bump and the odd scratching noise. He said the only trouble was that whenever he went into the living room, the dog was fast asleep and had apparently been so all night. When his sister said that she too had heard noises, he was prompted to go further, saying that on several occasions when he had got up in the darkness he had seen a ball of light floating around the living room, but this had vanished the moment he turned on the light.

Despite much investigation and theorizing over the past twenty years, no one has come up with a satisfactory explanation, nor has any research into the history of the little house brought to light any reason why the sense of evil should have been so strong and focused on the girl. Perhaps the name of the street is significant – Pendle Street. After all, it is within sight of Pendle Hill and all its evil associations, and is in what was at one time a part of the Forest of Pendle – but I think that is stretching things a little too far.

In 1971, a family took over the tenancy of a council house in Kay Street, Bolton. It wasn't long before neighbours were gleefully describing in lurid detail how the house was not just haunted – but cursed. However, at the time the level-headed family just laughed off the idea.

But by the end of August of that year, their amusement had turned to terror and they were asking to be re-housed. They began to encounter a thick, grey mist, which seemed to come into the house almost every night and hover in a bedroom, at the same time giving the occupants the distinct impression that something was pressing against their throats, squeezing the very life out of them.

The presence – whom they nicknamed 'Charlie' – became so frightening that they asked the local vicar to bless the house, particularly when other members of the family claimed to have heard the front door opening, followed by the eerie sound of footsteps going up the stairs. On investigation, the front door would be found to be secure and there was never anyone to be found upstairs – except the thick, choking mist.

One member of the household is reported as saying, 'It was like coming face to face with death itself. It frightened me so much I had difficulty in speaking and in moving and sometimes I lost consciousness altogether. It was evil and it sapped my strength.'

It was thought that the presence was the spirit of a former occupant, who couldn't bear the thought of anyone else living there and was trying to drive them out. If that was so, he certainly succeeded.

In August 1904, the village of Upholland on the outskirts of Wigan was the scene of some unusual events which took place in a house – long since demolished – in Church Street. This old, three-storey house next door to the ancient White Lion Inn and overlooking Upholland Church and its grave containing the remains of George 'Jack' Lyon, the highwayman, was from the outside just like any other old hand-loom weaver's cottage, found anywhere in Lancashire. It was occupied at that time by a Mrs Winstanley and her seven children and before very long was to become the scene of much curiosity in the village, when crowds of witnesses gathered, night after night, to observe for themselves the strange phenomena.

It all began when Mrs Winstanley wanted to prepare a meal but was unable to get the fire going. Where the flames should have been red, they were all colours, and Mrs Winstanley, thinking that one of her brood had put paraffin on the fire, chased them out of the house in anger.

Two of Mrs Winstanley's sons slept in what later became known as the 'ghost room' on the first floor above the front door where there were curtains hanging from rods up at the window. On the day the fire would not get going, the family went off to bed at their usual time and during the course of the night the rods and curtains fell from the window on to the two brothers in bed. They put them back up but as often as they did so, the rods and curtains fell off again.

Then, one brick began to repeatedly fall out of the fireplace in the boys' room, preceded by three knocks. Lights began to flash – bright electric-type light – although there was no form of lighting in the house other than paraffin lamps and candles. It was these flashing lights which first attracted the attention of the neighbours, to whom they were clearly visible.

But Sundays were the days when the really terrifying events took place. It was soon noticed that three knocks would sound, then a brick would fall out of the fireplace, followed by what sounded like a person clearing his throat. In time, this noise came to be regarded as a signal that the 'presence', or whatever it was, wanted silence.

On one particular Sunday, a large bible lay on a bamboo table in the boys' bedroom. When quiet had been achieved by the throat-clearing sound, the large brass clasp on the bible could be heard unfastening itself, only to be followed by the sound of the pages being turned and then – most frightening of all – a voice repeating over and over, 'Whither thou goest, I will go.'

At the time these disturbances took place, the cottage was said to be well over 100 years old. It was stone-built with thick walls and low-ceilinged rooms with oak rafters.

One night the two Winstanley boys were again in bed when they heard knockings and rumblings in the walls. These noises seemed to travel in the direction of a former window that had been walled in to avoid the window tax, repealed in 1851. The window recess was in use as a deep shelf on which there were a number of knick-knacks and two large books.

The noises woke the boys up and one of them called out, 'Who's there?' When they got no response they became quite scared, something which was exacerbated by the fact that the curtains were again taken from the window by invisible hands and draped over their heads. Paper and mortar were torn from the walls and scattered about the room. Stones under the windowsill below the bedroom window were loosened and then pulled out and thrown across the room.

As news of the happenings spread, more and more people came from surrounding areas to see and hear for themselves, and, sure enough, once the light in the haunted room had been extinguished, the noises would begin and the stones, which had been put back and wedged in so tightly they could not be removed by hand, came away by themselves and were thrown angrily across the room. The *Wigan Observer* reported that the noise caused by the thumps of the stones on to the boarded floor was so great that people standing sixty yards away in the street could hear it. In time, the unseen aggressor became so dangerous that the boys had to be removed from the room for their own safety.

On more than one occasion the two heavy books, described as 'massive tomes', are said to have been flung from the window recess halfway across the room. One was a *History of England* as large as the family bible, and the other was an ancient edition of the works of Titus Livius, the Roman historian.

There seemed to be no apparent historical reason for the hauntings, which stopped as quickly as they began, and the locals put it all down to poltergeist activity connected with the two brothers. That is the way it remained until quite recently. In 1922 the house was bought by the Upholland Urban District Council and in 1927 it was demolished to make way for street widening.

It was then discovered that the cellar beams were joined together by wooden pegs and that all the dividing walls in the upper house were constructed of interlocked tree branches and built in the primitive lamb stave and daub style, which suggested that the house was not built in the nineteenth century, but was several hundred years old.

In the published autobiography of George Lyon, who was hanged at Lancaster for highway robbery in 1815, the house was mentioned and it was described as being 'a most ancient structure, built of stone, centuries old and believed to have underground passages'. The fact that the house had underground passages was dismissed as nonsense and the disturbances, as I said, were ascribed to poltergeist activity. However, in 1985, the landlord of the White Lion, which still stands next to the site of the old house, claimed that the inn was being haunted by the bad-tempered ghost of George Lyon. In the cellars, which were already known to have two secret passages, a third one was discovered that could almost certainly have led to the cellars of the haunted house – and furthermore, this same passageway could have been used as an escape route for George Lyon, who was born and had lived not many yards away.

* * *

During the 1960s a council house in Leverhulme Avenue in Bolton was occupied by Ronald and Edna Smith and their five children, aged from one to seven years of age. The evil presence in the house terrified Mrs Smith so much that in time she dared not go upstairs alone, even to put the children to bed. She wouldn't sleep alone in the house for anything and always slept with the light burning all night.

Two sightings of the ghost and a long run of bad luck convinced them that not only was the house haunted, but there was an evil curse on it too. The first actual sighting took place round about June or July 1968, when Edna saw the figure of a woman dressed in a long pink dressing gown, who disappeared after only a few seconds. She couldn't make out her features nor could she say whether she was young or old. When she told her husband of the experience, he laughed at her for being over-imaginative. However, early in September of the same year, they were both sleeping downstairs for one reason or another and Ronnie felt something brush against his head. Opening his eyes, he saw an indefinable shape standing alongside the bed, and realized the atmosphere of the room had changed, becoming what he described as 'heavy'. He tried to get up, but found himself unable to move. Something seemed to be pressing down on his chest, even giving the impression that it was actually inside him! Then, suddenly, the feeling disappeared.

Friends and relatives began to remark on the sense of evil which could be felt in the house, and the family dog was often restless and uneasy, wandering about the place and growling viciously for no apparent reason, as if it could sense something. Their young children were also conscious of some presence or other, despite the fact that their parents tried to keep the matter from them, not discussing anything about it in front of them. They became fretful and wouldn't sleep, and the two-year-old boy would scream in fear during the night. Although at the time he was not speaking, it was obvious that something was frightening him, and there was one particular bedroom which he refused to go into.

The family suffered quite a lot of illness, but the last straw in the run of ill-luck came when the youngest child, just a year old, fell from the bedroom window, suffering severe head injuries.

The Smiths didn't say it was the ghost which actually pushed him out, but they did say that this was the last straw and asked the council to re-house them.

Who or what haunted the house has never been established and when the author visited it it was untenanted, the neighbours claiming no knowledge of hauntings or curses. The local council were not willing to discuss it either.

Most modern hauntings cause something of a local sensation, but few have caused a greater one than that which affected a house in Tully Street in Salford in the late 1950s.

The occupants and their twelve-year-old son endured noisy disturbances of the weirdest description, which resulted in a thorough examination of the property by experts from the local gas board, the environmental health department and the police. Despite this, no rational explanation was ever found and no theory was advanced as to the likely cause.

The noises could be heard in almost every house in the street and they were both violent and varied. Some said it shifted between the banging of a sledge hammer and a sound as if a heavy cannon-ball was bouncing on the floor of the room above. Life in Tully Street became something of an ordeal and the residents of the house began to consider looking for accommodation elsewhere, when suddenly, after about eight or nine weeks, the disturbances ceased as mysteriously as they had begun.

The strange and evil phenomena started for no apparent reason on 24 December, 1959 and continued almost non-stop until February 1960. Experts from the Department of Psychic Research at Manchester University made a minute check of the house, carefully monitoring and studying the noises. Their report shows that they found the noises represented a possible code of some kind, suggesting that it might be an effort on the part of some supernatural agency to convey a message to members of the family. In their opinion, the couple's young son was being used as a means through which the agency could communicate, although the boy appeared indifferent to all the pandemonium going on around him.

The affair received a great deal of publicity in the local and national press and, as a result, the whole thing became the subject of popular and excited discussion locally. As in Uphol-land at the beginning of the century, crowds of eager and expectant sightseers constantly gathered in the street outside the haunted premises in the hope of seeing the ghost. But there was no actual sighting to be made.

The vicar of St James's Church at Broughton visited the by now desperate family, and heard the strange noises for himself. Indeed, when he appeared on the scene, the sounds seemed to become particularly violent and he was soon convinced that they were of supernatural origin and were the work of a restless and malevolent spirit.

The result of all this was that permission was obtained from the Bishop of Manchester to hold a service of exorcism in the house and persuade the troublesome spirit to leave the occupants in peace. A half-hour service of exorcism was conducted by the Rev. Edward Dimond, accompanied by a Manchester vicar. When word got around that the ceremony was to be held, so many people crowded into Tully Street that the police had to be called to disperse them. However, the exorcism seemed to have the desired effect, for the noises suddenly ceased and were never to be repeated. Life in Tully Steet resumed its peaceful course – the 'banging ghost' had departed forever.

Round about the time that the affair in Tully Street was making headlines, an evil presence was occupying a small terraced house in Chorley, where a young newly-wed couple underwent a terrifying ordeal.

The young couple had been settled in their little home since their marriage some eighteen months before. They had decorated it throughout, spent a good deal of cash on home improvements and furnishings, and looked forward to some happy years together. But it appears that these same improvements and decorations were to arouse the fierce resentment of the spirit of a former occupant. Life for the young couple soon became an ordeal and their hoped-for peaceful existence quickly gave way to terror.

One day, the slight grey outline of a small man appeared beside the fireplace and soon began to appear more regularly after that, usually accompanied by disturbing sounds, rather like the scratching of a dog. But most frightening of all was a low moaning sound, which rose to the high pitch of a frantic scream. Footsteps were also heard in an upstairs room, followed by the tread of someone coming down the stairs, although on investigation there was never anything there. After a few weeks of this the young couple were advised to consult their local priest.

The house was blessed and holy water sprinkled in every room, but the malignant spirit had no intention of quitting and leaving the occupants to get on with their lives in peace. Matters came to a head when the young couple went out one night and left the wife's younger sister to care for their baby. When they returned after only a couple of hours, they discovered the girl in a state of abject terror. She told them that whilst they had been out she had sat alone with the baby and the dog. Suddenly, she had been frightened by the sound of footsteps walking about in the room overhead. Footsteps which then, slowly and deliberately, came down the stairs.

Thinking it was a burglar, she sent the dog to the bottom of the stairs, only to be frightened all the more when it suddenly turned back and rushed behind a chair, cowering in terror and with its hackles raised, clearly terrified at something she couldn't see. On hearing the story, the husband went upstairs to investigate and got the shock of his life. The rooms were in a state of total chaos. Beds had been stripped and the bedclothes were scattered and draped everywhere.

These events convinced the couple that there was something here which they couldn't contend with; something which showed marked evil intentions towards them and so, for their own peace of mind and the sake of their health, they moved out and stayed with relatives for a short time, until they could find a new home. Strange to relate, the house had no previous record of hauntings and the unpleasant affair has remained a mystery right up to the present day.

According to my colleagues at the BBC, an antique shop a hundred years old in Northenden Road at Sale was the scene of an unusual haunting, which was witnessed by an assistant, a Mr Norton. He was said to have been so frightened by his experience that he resigned from his job, vowing never to go into the premises again.

Mr Norton actually lived in a little flat over the shop and one night his room suddenly went extremely cold. Thinking it was because he had inadvertently left the door open, he turned round and was surprised to see a chair, which stood against the wall, suddenly begin to waltz across the floor towards him, as if being dragged by an invisible hand. Terrified, he ran for the door, but even before he reached it, a vase of flowers suddenly lifted itself from a table and smashed to smithereens on the floor.

The terrified man telephoned the police and very soon a sergeant and a constable appeared on the scene. They later reported that as they entered the room they noticed a strange, icy coldness, despite the fact that there was a good fire going in the grate. Some photographs appeared to have fallen on to the floor and the cat and dog belonging to the shop's owner were showing signs of fright.

Mr Norton assured the local press that nothing like this had happened to him previously, although on many occasions he said he had heard footsteps late at night when he was in bed. At the time he thought it might have been the neighbours, but now he realized he had been sharing a flat with some malevolent presence.

Kindly Leave the Stage

If there is a more eerie place than an empty theatre, then I have yet to hear of it. During a performance the theatre is a place of glitter, vitality and magic. Once the audience has gone home and the building is empty, lit only by the working lights, it takes on a different aspect altogether.

One such theatre was the Victoria Theatre at Salford, which closed its doors for the last time in February 1972. At the time, there was much local speculation as to what would happen to 'Phyllis', the theatre's resident ghost.

Phyllis was thought to be the ghost of an Edwardian programme-seller, who worked at the Victoria in the early years of this century and who may have committed suicide by throwing herself from the gallery after her love for a well-known leading actor of the day was rejected. Since then, her ghostly figure dressed in white has been seen at the theatre many times over the years, mostly – but not always – by female members of the staff. Various stories surround the ghost, which not only haunted the Victoria Theatre, but was also thought to be in some way connected with the haunting of the Irwell Castle Hotel next door.

The general story seems to be that in the early days of this century, there was some trouble between a member of the staff, his girlfriend and the leading actor. It appears that the girl 'set her hat at him' and a row flared up when the boyfriend discovered them in a compromising situation in the gallery of the empty theatre, long after hours. No one is sure what happened next, but it seems that the girl either toppled over the gallery rail to her death in the ensuing argument, or that she committed suicide by throwing herself over the edge into the stalls below.

In the latter days of the theatre's life, when a repertory company was playing there, an elderly actress, who claimed to know nothing of the story, was so terrified that she ran out into the street, refusing to say what had frightened her. A barmaid ran downstairs screaming one night after she had seen a woman come through the wall and into the bar – only to walk out again through the opposite wall.

In a letter to the *Manchester Evening News* some time ago, Mr D. Cameron said that in the 1960s he had been the stage-manager at the theatre and he saw the ghost so many times that he took her for granted. He said, 'You could always tell when she was around, as there was always the smell of perfume. On several occasions I saw her and at other times heard her moving about.' He said the stage staff became quite used to seeing her, and when they were working on the sets at night, they would actually look forward to seeing her around.

Entertainer Ronne Coyles saw her when he appeared there in pantomime. He told me: 'It was during a matinée. I had noticed earlier there was an empty seat in the circle. At one point I looked up and saw a woman in white sitting in it. When I looked again a minute or two later, she was gone.'

My old friend, the late Danny Ross, had a wealth of ghost stories connected with the theatre. One he loved to tell concerned an unknown spectre who used to walk through the bar of the old Theatre Royal at Stockport – demolished in 1960 – much to the amazement of witnesses.

Danny told me a lovely story concerning a former owner, Mr J. W. Reverill, who liked a drop or two of Scotch and was in the habit of spending perhaps more time in the dress-circle bar than he should have done. One evening, when he was enjoying his usual drink at the bar, he happened to glance up, glass poised at his lips, just in time to see the mysterious figure drift across the empty bar and seemingly walk right through the wall.

The astonished Mr Reverill did what anyone else would have done under the circumstances – he ordered another double, which he downed in one gulp, and then went off to his office to dig out the original plans for the old building. He discovered that where the figure had walked out of the bar and through the wall there used to be a doorway, long since bricked up.

My own research has revealed that this was possibly the ghost of that fine character actor, Hamilton Jordan. Apparently he used to slip into the bar for a quick drink between acts, using this door, which was later bricked up when the bar was altered in the 1930s.

Whilst researching into the old Theatre Royal, I discovered that it may also have been haunted by the ghost of the beautiful Edwardian actress, Clarice Mayne, whose portrait used to hang in the ladies' cloakroom. Her ghost is thought to have haunted the stage area and, in particular, No 1 dressing-room. One lady who appeared at the theatre just after the war with Harry Korris and the 'Happydrome' show, told me recently that she heard the rustle of what she could only describe as 'silky skirts' approaching her from behind. Looking round, she saw the distinct outline of a woman in Edwardian dress, who suddenly disappeared leaving a cold, chill feeling behind her.

The Bolton Hippodrome – demolished in 1961–2 – was the scene of a rather unusual and frightening experience for the actress Penelope Gowling, who appeared at the theatre many times in the seventeen years prior to its closure.

Miss Gowling told me: 'It was a Wednesday matinée and we were doing a farce called *High Temperature* which involved me being on stage in bed, in near total darkness, at the beginning of Act II, whilst six burglars waited outside the French windows, stage right. As the curtain rose, they should have entered to steal my jewels, but what mattered was that they were not on the actual set *before* the curtain rose.'

Miss Gowling laid herself down on the bed during the interval between Acts I and II. In those days they didn't have the sophisticated lighting systems which most modern theatres have, and still used floats – in this instance a row of blue lights to indicate moonlight. She continued: 'The curtain went up and I opened my eyes and was alarmed to see one of the burglars standing at the foot of my bed, instead of outside the window, as we had rehearsed; alarmed because this would complicate the plot and necessitate alterations to the dialogue.'

Having quite a lot to say at this point in the play, Miss Gowling put this out of her mind, carrying on with the action as if nothing had gone wrong. Things seemed to go smoothly enough, despite the change. 'When, at the end of the act, the curtain came down, I charged round and berated the burglars and asked them which one had been in the wrong place,' she said. 'They were completely mystified, as they had all been outside the window. No one but I had seen anyone at the foot of the bed!'

Apparently the whole cast heard the argument and Miss Gowling began to wonder whether she was the victim of some practical joke so, because the show had to continue, she shut up and got on with the next act. 'However,' she concluded, 'back in the theatre for the evening show, someone mentioned Jimmy, a dear old stage-hand who had died a few weeks previously. I let out a shriek – of course, it had been Jimmy I had seen. I realized that I had seen the blue footlights through the figure which had been leaning on a broom, just as Jimmy did when he was alive.'

On another occasion, the company were presenting Shaw's *Candida*, with Miss Gowling playing the lead. As was the case in most theatres in those days, for the curtain call the cast had to stand in line near the footlights to sing the national anthem with the audience. Miss Gowling said, 'On the Thursday evening, the back few rows were unoccupied; G.B.S. not being exactly a riot amongst our regular audience. But in the next to back row on the aisle seat, a middle-aged lady in a gold lamé evening dress struggled and bobbed about all through the national anthem. When the curtain came down, I asked the others if they had seen her, but they said no; all they had seen was the theatre manager standing at the back as usual, ready to bid his customers a goodnight.'

She went on to say that later she had called at the manager's office and during conversation she asked why he had tolerated such activity during the singing of the national anthem. The manager was baffled. There had been no lady in the row at all.

Southport's Garrick Theatre is the venue for the next ghost in this chapter and the story comes from entertainer Ronne Coyles, who told me that of the number of theatre ghosts he has seen during his career, it was the one he couldn't see which scared him the most. He told me: 'It was Easter time and I was appearing in a show at the Garrick with Anne Ziegler and Webster Booth. It was a beautiful sunny day and I arrived early for band call. Because I was so early, I decided to iron a few of my clothes, ready for the opening of the show that night.'

The theatre had a spare dressing-room, room 14, which was given over to the company for use as an ironing-room. Because it was so warm, Mr Coyles left the door open whilst he went about his ironing. He continued: 'I felt a sort of coldness seemingly pass by me and, glancing up, noticed the door of the room was closed. So I went over and opened it again and then went back to my ironing.' A few minutes later, he again felt a cold presence of some kind and, looking up, saw that the door was again closed. He said, 'There was no draught at all and it was impossible for a well-balanced door to close by itself. My first reaction was that one of the company had come in and was playing a joke on me. I threw the door open and looked out to see who it was, but there was no one – the place was as quiet as a churchyard.' This time, Mr Coyles wedged the door open with a piece of wood and, feeling slightly annoyed, went back to his ironing. 'I looked up again after a few minutes and was just in time to see the door, with the wedge still in place, silently close of its own accord. I picked up my ironing and cleared off down to my dressing-room, as by now I was really quite scared.'

He learned later that the theatre was said to be haunted by the ghost of a Victorian woman who was murdered by a jealous lover. She had been seen quite often over the years; a small figure in a long dress, aimlessly wandering about the place. Ronne Coyles concluded: 'I would not have been half as scared had I seen her. Ghosts you can see are not all that frightening, but the ones you can't see – well, that's something else.'

Many people would be inclined to agree.

The Thameside Theatre, Ashton-under-Lyne, has a ghost whom they have nicknamed 'Ernie'. He always appears dressed in a raincoat and standing in the shadows of the upper balcony. The figure will beckon to anyone fortunate enough to sight him, but once they begin to walk towards him, he will vanish into thin air. Just whose ghost this is no one can tell and the present management seem rather reluctant to discuss it. However, *Carry On* star Jack Douglas says he once saw it when he appeared in pantomime there in 1977–8.

Mr Douglas said that as he was leaving the theatre one night he saw the figure of a man, dressed in what appeared to be a raincoat, standing under the upper circle, his features hidden in the shadows. Just as he was going to walk away, the figure beckoned him and so, thinking it was a member of the staff who wanted to speak to him, Mr Douglas walked towards the figure – and was surprised, to say the least, when the figure melted away, leaving the area deserted.

Theatre photographer and historian Ted Bottle told me that when he visited the Royal Court Theatre at Wigan, he was struck by the fact that so many people had been affected in some way by the mysterious theatre ghost resident there. One lady said that she frequently felt someone was watching her and freely admitted talking to whoever it was when alone in the building, asking if she could help in some way. She felt doubly sure that here was a soul in search of assistance. Other members of the staff have experienced cold atmospheres and noises, which are not easily explained away.

A member of the Manchester Music Hall Association told me that this was not at all surprising as, when she used to visit the Royal Court during its days as a cinema, icy blasts would suddenly sweep through the stalls when there was no obvious explanation. So common was this that members of the audience would be heard to remark, 'Ayeup. He's back again!'

I believe that this particular ghost is thought to be that of a member of a touring theatre company who, for some reason known perhaps only to himself, committed suicide prior to a matinée performance early this century.

Like a great many cinemas, the Classic at Bury was originally a theatre and it too is thought to be haunted by an old-time actor who hanged himself in an upper room many years ago.

In 1976 a police dog was terrified after a ghostlike figure had been reported, drifting across the foyer. An extensive police search was carried out in the premises but nothing was found.

Less than two hours later, the local police received another call to say that the shadowy figure had been seen again by a young couple returning from a late dance. This time an Alsatian dog was sent in to winkle out the intruder, but within a matter of seconds it came scurrying back whimpering, and with its fur standing on end. Nothing or nobody was found.

Some weeks later, a member of the staff had the fright of her life when, during the screening of the main feature film, the figure again appeared, this time amongst the unsuspecting audience, hovering about six feet above the stalls. She later said, 'I suddenly went icy cold.' The woman's description of the figure suggested it might be an old-time theatre actor dressed in medieval theatrical attire and wearing a three-cornered hat; a description which closely corresponds with that of a figure repeatedly reported over the years in different parts of the building. He seems to prefer the foyer late at night, after the cinema has closed.

Even in the old days, when the building was still in use as a theatre, the ghost, nicknamed 'Owd Sid', was often seen. If he was an old-time theatre actor, then I don't quite know what he will make of the old place today, for most of the films shown nowadays are of the X-certificate type. Perhaps that is why he is most often seen in the foyer – trying to find his way out!

Not many miles away, the Classic Cinema at Accrington was the scene of some rather curious happenings late in 1973, when a workman claimed that a pair of clammy hands went up the back of his neck and pulled his head back with a sudden jerk. At the time he was working on renovations in the ballroom bar, but he raced out of the building absolutely terrified and refused to go back.

At the time, the manager was quoted as saying that he had experienced a number of odd occurrences, such as the curtains closing of their own accord during the screening of a film. At first it was thought to have been a mistake or a joke by one of the projection-room staff, but later enquiries were to reveal that no one had been responsible and to this day, the incident remains a complete mystery.

In 1980, whilst working on the BBC radio series, 'Ghosthunt',

Gerald Main, the producer, and myself, approached the management of the Classic with a view to investigating the strange goings-on. Unfortunately we were refused permission and the management refused to discuss the incidents. Recently, however, I was able to speak to a former member of staff, who told me that some time ago a curious dark shadow in the shape of a short man was seen in an upstairs room. The shadow disappeared after several minutes. I was also told that the cinema cat was once affected by mysterious blue lights which seemed to chase it down the corridors. But, sad to relate, it has not been possible to discover who or what haunts the cinema.

About the time that these events took place at the Accrington cinema, strange noises and mysterious lights were reported by several members of the staff at the Royal Pavilion Cinema at Blackpool. Someone suggested a seance and so, early in 1973, one was held by a prominent medium in an effort to discover what was causing the bangs, raps and mysterious lights at the rear of the circle.

It wasn't long before the medium claimed to have made contact with the spirit of a former landau driver, who had worked the promenade and who had known the cinema during the 1920s. He proved his authenticity by accurately describing a former doorman and an usherette.

According to the medium, the spirit claimed to have been trying to make contact for some time, although why this was so I do not know, for he doesn't appear to have left any message. Apparently he just said that having made contact, he felt free to depart. Recent enquiries reveal that from that day there have been no further reports of disturbances.

The Forum Theatre in the Wythenshawse district of Manchester is haunted by the ghost of a 'dripping wet boy' according to Mr Andrew Bradley who, in May 1983, was playing at the Forum in Hart and Kaufman's play, *Once In A Lifetime*.

Mr Bradley told me: 'Although I wasn't fortunate enough to see the ghost myself, the stage door keeper, a straightforward family man if ever there was one, saw it late one night and had to be taken home suffering from shock.' Fortunately the man was able to resume work the following evening, but he insisted on being accompanied when he had to go into the 'void' (the area above the stage), where he had seen the ghost. 'I volunteered to go with him,' said Mr Bradley, 'hoping very much to see something. However, in the event, I was disappointed.'

This ghost has been known to move props around the stage and seemed especially delighted to create havoc during the rehearsals for the horror spoof *The Rocky Horror Show*. Mr Bradley continued: 'Perhaps the little chap didn't approve of being sent up.' It seems the presence was firmly exorcized by the stage-manager for the production, a Scotswoman who wouldn't take any nonsense from anyone, be they of this world or the next. Mr Bradley concluded: 'The stage of the Forum, especially at night, had a very eerie atmosphere about it, as I discovered one night wandering across it in an attempt to escape from a party in the Green Room.'

Unfortunately I have been unable to discover what, if anything, was on this site before the building of the Forum complex, but, as Mr Bradley suggests, the fact that the apparition appears to be dripping wet suggests there might have been a large pond or something of that nature in the vicinity. Perhaps this is the ghost of someone who was either drowned in the pond, or who was killed somewhere else and his body was dumped there, or in a nearby river or canal. Perhaps we might never discover the truth behind the ghost which is now accepted as a fact of life by members of the Forum Theatre staff.

There have been many high tides since the author worked at the Palace Theatre on Morecambe's Sandylands Promenade. As I understand it, the Palace was built over fifty years ago by John Willie Carleton, the father of Mrs Sybil Sheldon, who, until a few years ago, kept the theatre going.

The present theatre was built on the site of a wooden pierrot theatre and was possibly Mr Carleton's first timid venture into show business. Over the years, the Palace alternated between being a theatre and a cinema – movies were shown in the winter months and for the summer season typical seaside family shows were presented. Winter or summer, one could always expect a good night out at the Palace in pleasant comfortable surroundings. No fortnight's holiday was complete without a visit to

Eddie Morrell's *Starlights* on the Central Pier, and Hedley Claxton's *Gaytime* at the Palace. (There was a change of shows twice a week and matinées if it was wet or inclement.)

Summer hosts have included Jimmy Page, Bryan Burden, Colin Crompton and, in more recent years, Ronne Coyles who has done about ten seasons there and probably knows the old Palace as well as anybody. A couple of years ago it was announced that the theatre was to close and was to be converted into a theatre club, something which seems to have upset at least one resident phantom.

Ronne Coyles told me recently: 'After a show, I love to stand on the empty stage looking into the gloom of the theatre and soak up the atmosphere. Recently I was standing there, thinking of nothing in particular, when I saw in the circle a greyish, masculine figure moving about. I knew there was no one human up there, the place was empty!'

At the end of December 1982 an electrician was working up in the circle when he heard a voice which disturbed him, for he thought he was all alone. The voice was saying, quite close to him, over and over again, 'The theatre will not die! The theatre will not die!' The electrician looked around to see who was there. There was no one. Overcome with fear, he dropped his tools and fled.

As a stage-struck youngster I spent many hours alone in that old theatre and until recently I had never heard of anything untoward happening there. It seems more than coincidence that this should start to happen after the announcement that the Palace, as most people knew it, was to close, and I venture to suggest that the spirit of John Willie Carleton is disturbed that his beloved Palace is to sink along with the rest of the entertainment empire he built up in the town. He owned most of the theatres and cinemas in Morecambe at one time; now they are all closed. Perhaps the closure of the theatre he built his empire on and which he loved more than the others is more than even his spirit is prepared to tolerate.

Another incident, quite unconnected, which happened at the Palace some years ago, was witnessed by several people and is perhaps worth a mention.

On the foyer walls there were a number of pictures, their

frames screwed to the wall for security reasons, which showed various groups of artists of the Hedley Claxton *Gaytime* era. One night, for no reason at all, one photograph fell off the wall, screws and all. One act who were in the photograph were a couple I knew well, Phyllis Terrill and Stanley Massey. They were at the Palace for several seasons during the 1950s and 60s. The day after this little incident, Mrs Sheldon received a telephone call from Phyllis, telling her that Stanley Massey had been killed in an accident at Newark on the previous night.

Finally, let us take another look at the Grand Theatre at Lancaster, briefly mentioned in *Lancashire's Ghosts and Legends*. This magnificent theatre is the home of the Lancaster Footlights Club and is built within the shell of the Atheneum, which has stood on this site for over 200 years – ever since the days when Lancaster was an elegant hive of activity in the Georgian era. Grimaldi appeared here, as did Paganini and Charles Dickens. But perhaps its best remembered visitor was one of the greatest tragic actresses of the eighteenth century, Sarah Siddons, whose portrait still hangs in the circle.

Sarah Siddons was not only a great actress, she was also a great innovator, being one of the first to discard the powdered wigs and hooped skirts which were the trademark of the tragic actresses of her day. She had a great love of the theatre and besides appearing on several occasions at the Atheneum, she also had a personal interest in the place, because it was run by her brother-in-law. Even after 200 years, Sarah is still showing a personal interest, for her ghost has been quite active here.

One person who has seen her is the Lancaster Footlights Club's chairman, writer and producer Mike Church. He told me of seeing a woman in the empty theatre, watching the actors in an early rehearsal of a play of his, back in 1973. He said, 'I noticed a person sitting well back in the stalls as we went through the plot. She was smiling, as if with approval, and I assumed she was just sitting in as a member of the theatre staff or something like that.' He admitted feeling strange at the time, but it was not until afterwards when other members of the cast said they had seen no one at all, that he learned about the ghost of Sarah Siddons. The figure he described fitted the picture of Sarah which hangs on the wall in the circle perfectly.

Footlights' publicity officer, Bernard Mayo, said that other people had described things being thrown at them when no one else was there and of footsteps being heard clearly when they were alone in the building. Bernard himself admits to feeling the hairs on the back of his neck rising when he has been in the theatre alone late at night. Some women members positively refuse to be alone there at night. Bernard said, 'There is something or someone in the theatre, but I don't know what it is. A chill atmosphere does exist late at night and it is not a matter of fear or imagination.'

Another person who saw the ghost was actress Pat Phoenix, best remembered as *Coronation Street*'s Elsie Tanner. But she could not say for sure that it was the shade of Sarah Siddons.

Miss Phoenix told me: 'I was sitting, following the performance one evening, near the second row of the back stalls. The theatre lights were out and only the working lights were on. I think an electrician or someone was working backstage. There is a break between the stalls and the back stalls and it was here the apparition appeared. She crossed my line of vision and when she reached the bottom of the aisle, I saw she had no feet.' Miss Phoenix didn't realize until after the figure had disappeared that she had, in fact, seen a ghost. She said, 'When one works in the theatre, one is never surprised at anything. At first I thought it was a real person. I wasn't in the least afraid, nor cold or anything else. I only realized what it was after she had gone.'

I don't know whether the ghost seen here from time to time is Sarah Siddons, but if it is, then I'm sure she must have appreciated all the hard work that has gone into restoring this beautiful little theatre. It really is a little gem, and a credit to the efforts of the Lancaster Footlights Club. It has all the atmosphere one would expect of a building of this age, and when I was there last, I'm sure I could smell oranges up in the gallery.

Highway Horrors

The sense of the supernatural can be very real indeed in Lancashire today, despite the M6, sprawling suburbia and all the materialistic influences of an urban civilization. Probably the best time for the ghost hunter to travel through Lancashire is at night, out of season. Roads are empty for several miles on end. The countryside, moors and fells take on a different guise. The familiar becomes unfamiliar, unknown places take on an intimidating air – far beyond the warmth and security of the car lies a world which is, at once, both enticing and intimidating.

When an article appeared in the *Stockport Express* in December 1974, it brought to light an interesting ghost which haunted not a factory, crane, warehouse or railway station but, of all things, a taxi-cab.

Taxi drivers are tough characters, used to dealing with all kinds of strange passengers, but this particular black cab stood for some time at the rear of the taxi firm's office, unused because none of the company drivers would even sit in it, let alone drive it. It acquired its eerie reputation one fine November night in 1974 when the driver, going along the A6 through Great Moor after taking a fare to Whaley Bridge, casually glanced through his rear-view mirror and thought he saw some movement on the rear seat. He was more than taken aback when, looking again, he caught the reflection of a woman quietly sitting there.

The driver, Mr Brian Mohan, thought that there must be some logical explanation, perhaps a curious reflection or something and, turning his attention once more to the road ahead, he drove on past Stockport Convent.

As he approached the Davenport Theatre, he was able to take another, longer look into the mirror and he was horrified to see the figure still sitting in the rear seat: an elderly woman sitting upright, quite motionless and with a blank expression on her face. She looked real and solid enough with nothing to distinguish her from anybody else. However, Brian was really puzzled; he knew he had not picked up a fare since leaving Whaley Bridge, so where had she come from? He decided he had better find out exactly what she was up to.

Just past Stockport Grammar School, he pulled into the kerb and stopped. Then, pulling across the glass partition, he turned to face the mysterious passenger – only to discover the taxi-cab was empty. He got out, walked all around the vehicle, looking up and down the road as he did so, but there was not a sign of the elderly woman who, only seconds before, had been seated quietly in the rear seat of his taxi.

He told the reporter from the *Stockport Express*, 'I saw her both when we were in darkness – just as we passed the Convent – and when it was light, so she can't have been some kind of image. No one could have jumped into the cab without my knowledge, because the noise of the door and the interior light going on would have alerted me. I wasn't seeing things, either; I looked three times to make sure, and she was there each time!'

Brian went on to describe the figure as that of a woman aged somewhere between fifty and sixty, with long, thick hair. She wore a black coat with a pointed collar, a white blouse and a black bow. He said that if he saw her again – but he hoped he never would – he would recognize her. He concluded: 'Whoever she was, she cost me several nights' sleep and I've no intention of using that particular cab ever again. You can bet on it.'

One bright and sunny day a few years ago, Mrs Jacqueline McEvoy, her husband, and their young son were out walking near Wray. She told me: 'Our son was misbehaving and, feeling rather irritable, I increased my lead, walking ahead of them until I was two fields in front of them. I sat on a stile, waiting for them to catch up with me.'

The stile faced the last two fields before the village and a straight flat bank of the river flowed less than three or four yards from where she sat. Mrs McEvoy continued: 'My attention was drawn to a strange figure walking parallel to the river, on the opposite bank. It didn't look in my direction and I was suddenly struck by several strange things about it. For a start, whoever it was was extremely tall and painfully thin, dressed in a drab, old-fashioned looking garb: sludge-coloured like a khaki-brown mackintosh or something similar, with one of those baggy hoods. I don't know why, but I got the idea it was a woman, although I couldn't see her face.'

The figure carried two enormous old-fashioned shopping bags, which bulged as if they were full and very heavy. 'The oddest part of all,' continued Mrs McEvoy, 'was that with such huge and heavy bags, you would expect a person to plod along, but whoever it was moved smoothly along at a reasonably fast pace. So much so that the large, labrador-type dog following at the heel was almost running to keep up with the figure.'

At this point, Mrs McEvoy heard her husband and son approaching and glanced back for a second or two to see the pair of them catching up with her a couple of hundred yards away. She turned her eyes back to watch the figure again – but both figure and dog had vanished. 'Yet there was nowhere it could have vanished to. There were no walls, woods, trees, copses or any places of concealment,' she said. As it was only springtime, the few bushes had no leaves and only bare expanses of fields stretched into the distance away from the village. At first, she thought that perhaps the person had stumbled and the weight of the laden shopping bags had toppled the woman into the river, but there had been no sound of a splash, nor a cry, and it is hardly likely the dog would have fallen in as well. But to satisfy herself, Mrs McEvoy searched the bank, only to discover there was nothing. Not a sound, not a sign, not even a footprint to suggest anything had been there.

Mrs McEvoy said, 'The experience has irked me ever since. We have walked that way many times since that day, but nothing strange has happened. It wasn't a frightening experience, it was unexpected and very real, but not at all frightening.'

Less than a mile away stands a large old house, which can be seen on the distant skyline from where Mrs McEvoy sat on the stile. She says she wonders whether there was any connection between the old house and the figure she saw. At the time of this incident the house appeared to be completely unoccupied, yet at one time it must have been rather grand, with a formal terraced garden, now overgrown and in ruins. She concluded: 'Each time I have repeated that walk, I must admit to hoping that "my ghost" would reappear, but so far I have been unlucky.'

A sighting of a similar nature still puzzles Mr John Birtwhistle of Whitehaven. It happened when he was driving down the A595 near Broughton-in-Furness in broad daylight, on a summer's day in the early 1960s, when this was still a part of Lancashire.

In those days, Mr Birtwhistle and his wife lived in Manchester, but had a caravan on the coast near Broughton. They had spent the weekend there and though Mr Birtwhistle had to return to his business, Mrs Birtwhistle decided to stay on at the caravan with the children for the rest of the week, the weather having picked up. Mr Birtwhistle told me: 'I left shortly after lunch and, as the weather was so pleasant, I took a minor road south to enjoy the countryside and join the A6 at Carnforth.'

Just outside of Broughton the road was a single track for much of the way, with passing places situated at convenient intervals. It was typical of the switchback roads in the area at the time, climbing for about 1,100 feet to the summit, which gave a magnificent panoramic view. In those days it was little used by locals or summer tourists. Mr Birtwhistle went on to say, 'After some three or four miles I reached the crest of the ridge and I noticed a bright red object on the track, way ahead of me. Even after a couple of brief sightings I couldn't identify who or what it was. As I approached I began to discern the outline of a young woman in a bright red satin bathing costume. She had unusually long black shining hair, and white high-heeled sandals on her feet. Because of my low speed I was able to note all these details, including the odd fact that she did not appear to be carrying either purse or handbag, or even a handkerchief.'

The young woman took not the slightest notice of the car's approach and, in fact, to overtake her Mr Birtwhistle had to pull very close to the soft verge of the road. Drawing level, he was able to see that she was a most attractive young woman, possibly in her early twenties. Yet surprisingly, despite the fact that she had been walking steadily up a steep incline, she showed no sign of breathlessness or perspiration. Oddest of all, her white high-heeled sandals were spotlessly clean, despite walking what must have been at least two miles along a dusty road. 'She certainly couldn't have joined the road by walking over the peat and gorse,' added Mr Birtwhistle.

In spite of her immaculate appearance, his first thought was that she might have been involved in some motor accident, so, coming to a stop, he wound down the window and enquired, 'Can I be of any assistance, miss?' He received a quiet, yet firm reply, 'No, thank you.' Appreciating that she would, quite rightly, be wary of a stranger in this remote place, he asked whether he could telephone or give someone a message when he arrived at Askam, to which the girl replied, 'Thank you again, but I am enjoying this walk.' This exchange took no more than a few seconds, and as she appeared to be perfectly well and composed, Mr Birtwhistle wished the young woman a pleasant afternoon and drove on. A few seconds later, he glanced back in the driving mirror and was surprised to see that the girl had disappeared – the road was empty.

About a mile further up the road Mr Birtwhistle reached the summit, where he parked the car and walked to where he could see the track winding up the fell side, looking to see if he could find the young woman. The road was absolutely deserted, even after more than twenty minutes, when at her pace she should easily haved reached the top herself. There was not the slightest sign of life or movement for miles in any direction. Mr Birtwhistle concluded: 'Since moving up here ten years ago, I have met local people from the area and tried to find out if there was any historical or tragic connection with what I saw, but there does not appear to be any. I have never been able to work out a satisfactory conclusion.'

I wouldn't recommend a picnic in the ruins of Rivington Castle, unless you want the meal spoilt by the unknown spectre which is said to haunt it. The old castle has long been reputed to be haunted and about twenty years ago, five council workmen watched for over two hours as a white figure drifted around the castle grounds.

It was early one summer morning when one of the workmen noticed a white form on one of the higher parts of the ruins. It was, at first, as if someone were reflecting the rays of the sun in a large mirror – except there was no sun. Then, as he watched, he could make out a distinct white human-like shape, which moved from side to side, pausing at intervals.

The man called for his workmates to take a look, but they were too busy to bother and wouldn't believe him when he told them what he had seen. However, not long afterwards, another workman came running over and said that he too had seen a white figure moving about in the ruins. Then all five men went to take a look and saw the white shape, now in the castle grounds, moving in and out of the bushes at the foot of the ruined keep.

As they continued to watch, it seemed to the workmen that the mysterious white figure was keeping a look-out. It followed the same track repeatedly, going backwards and forwards from the foot of the ruins to the top, and then going back down again; sometimes it disappeared behind the bushes, but it always re-appeared, vivid white against the dirty stonework.

Then, after more than two hours, the figure disappeared behind a bush and was not seen again, nor was it seen on subsequent days. But, according to one of the workmen, they estimated the figure to be about ten feet tall, judging by the way it was clearly visible from where they were working.

Whilst in this area, keep a look-out for the figure of a monk who has haunted Rivington for as long as anyone can remember. This is thought to be the ghost of Father Bennett, who disappeared mysteriously when he was hiding the church valuables and plates during the time of the Dissolution. Legend says that he entered an undergrond tunnel leading to the old monastery at Anderton – and was never seen again in this life.

Also, keep a look-out for the ghost of the gamekeeper of Anderton Hall, who looks and seeks in vain for three milkmaids. Apparently, about 130 years ago, Joe Hill, the head gamekeeper at Anderton Hall which was demolished in 1929, was out on his rounds when he discovered the body of his dog, which had been killed by a pitchfork.

According to witnesses, three 'milkmaids' were seen scurrying away from the scene of the crime. They were, in fact, poachers wearing milkmaids' bonnets and smocks, and it is thought that

Joe never got over his faithful dog's death, and died himself shortly afterwards.

Now his ghost wanders the Anderton area of Rivington, trying to catch the men who brutally killed it.

The ruins of Wycoller Hall and its picturesque little hamlet have long been a favourite place with courting couples. Indeed, on a warm, moonlit summer's night, Wycoller is a very romantic spot – that is, unless the Black Lady just happens to be about.

According to Fred Bannister in his *Annals of Trawden Forest*, one of the Cunliffes of Wycoller Hall went to the West Indies. There he met and married a black West Indian woman. On the return voyage back to England with his wife, Cunliffe began to regret his hasty marriage, his wife's background and certainly her colour. So he arranged with a member of the ship's crew for her quiet disappearance overboard one dark night. It is now said that the spirit of the poor drowned woman followed Cunliffe back to Wycoller Hall, where from time to time she appears, as if in search of the man responsible for her death.

Whatever the legend and whoever she is, the Black Lady's ghost is real enough and she has certainly put the wind up several courting couples over the years. In fact, it was a courting couple who first reported seeing her standing by the big fireplace in the ruined Hall. She was said to have been dressed from head to toe in black silk. The apparition was completely still and silent, and after a few minutes she simply disappeared.

Some years ago a Trawden couple sitting on a bench on the opposite side of the ford from the ruins were disturbed by her and she was reported in fairly recent years by two council workmen, who saw her on the old packhorse bridge. They spoke to her and were amazed by her sudden disappearance. It was only after they had discussed her rather unusual dress that they suddenly realized they had actually seen a ghost.

One phantom I have never before heard of at Wycoller frightened the life out of a courting couple one moonlit night. It was not the woman in black, nor the legendary phantom horseman, but what they firmly believe was a phantom coach, which drove up to the Hall after appearing to pass right through the car in which they were sitting at the time. The couple, who for obvious reasons wish to remain anonymous, told me very recently that this was the most terrifying experience of their lives and that until now they had never mentioned it to anyone other than the author.

The couple had been to a dinner in Yorkshire and, on their way back to Burnley, decided that as it was such a lovely night, they would divert and spend an hour at Wycoller. I was told: 'It was just approaching eleven-thirty when I drove the car over the ford and parked on the greensward at the south end of the ruins, the front of the car facing the houses across the other side of the packhorse bridge. They were empty and semi-derelict at the time. From here we had a perfect view of a most beautiful and romantic full moon.' As a courting couple, their minds were certainly not on anything which was going on outside the car, and they certainly gave no thought whatsoever to anything supernatural.

'All of a sudden, there was this loud rumbling noise, which seemed to be immediately above the car, sounding at first as if someone were dragging chains over a corrugated-iron roof. The sound only lasted for perhaps three or four seconds.' The startled couple wondered what it was, but soon dismissed it as of no consequence. Then two or three minutes later, the same noise occurred again, louder this time. They froze, in fact, they said, 'Freezing is the right word to use in this instance. It was cold; a horrible ice-cold chill which seemed to fill the car. It really was horrible, that is the only way to explain it.'

Scalp tingling and the hair on the back of his neck beginning to bristle, the driver got out of the car to investigate. He said, 'I must admit, Wycoller didn't seem quite so beautiful all of a sudden, even though the moon was still shining and the sky was full of stars. Somehow the romantic image of the place was beginning to fade.'

The noise could not be explained in any way. There was nothing around that could have caused it and the place was deserted so, getting back into the car, he began to discuss the whole episode with his now frightened companion and tried to find some logical explanation. 'Whilst we were discussing it, the noise began again, only this time whatever it was persuaded me that the spot where I was parked at that moment was no place for me. The rumbling was still going on, getting louder and louder, sounding now more like a coach and four racing towards my car. The noise was such that I thought that whatever was causing it was going to do a lot of expensive damage to the bodywork.'

The noise persisted and reached a terrifying crescendo which the occupants found hard to bear. The car seemed full of sound, as if the coach and horses, or whatever it was, were passing right through. The cold was intense. Terrified, the driver attempted to start the car, but the engine would only fire after whatever it was had passed through. Quickly shoving it into gear, he said he sped off the greensward and across the ford far quicker than was sensible for a private car. He concluded: 'I shot away from there absolutely terrified and raced through the hamlet, over the bridge by Wycoller Farm and along the lane as if the Devil himself were after me. I really did disappear in a cloud of flying cow dung!' he laughed. 'Any chance of romance had gone right out of the window by now!'

The hamlet is thought to be haunted by a phantom coach which races up to the door of the ruined Hall on certain nights of the year. Although I have heard vague stories in the past, this is the first time I have actually heard from anyone with first-hand experience of it.

In 1974, an article in the *Liverpool Echo* claimed that the Lodge Lane area of the city was haunted by the ghost of a young woman who had been murdered there. Carol McLean was a beautiful girl, half English, half West Indian, who opened the door of her small flat to a young man and his girlfriend. Some time later, the couple pleaded guilty at Liverpool Crown Court to murdering Carol. They had gone to her flat with the intention of robbing her and had expected to find over £200, but in the event they found nothing but a few coins. Angry, they battered her with a hammer and then stabbed her several times in the chest with a small but sharp kitchen knife.

The cold-blooded killers were each given a life sentence – and the neighbours began to talk of a new terror in their flats, or rather on the landing outside their flats, for several of the people who were accustomed to hearing the tap-tap-tap of Carol's high-heeled shoes as she made her way from the club where she worked, late at night, claimed they could still hear the footsteps round about the same time that Carol came home when she was alive.

Bernie and Madge, who lived only a few yards from Carol's flat, said they were both terrified. Madge said that Carol had once asked her if she would mind listening out for her coming home each night, just until she heard her safely in the flat. Carol worked in a nightclub which had something of a reputation and she had been followed home on more than one occasion, so Madge and Bernie were only too pleased to oblige. After all, they too had a daughter and would hope that if she were in a similar position, the neighbours would do the same for her.

Night after night, Bernie and Madge lay awake until they heard the sound of Carol's high heels and her unmistakable footsteps go past the door of their flat and enter her own. After her death, they said they still heard the footsteps clearly and distinctly – almost every night at the same time. Often they would be asleep rather earlier than usual, only to be woken up again by the tap-tap and the familiar footsteps of Carol.

On a number of occasions either Bernie or Madge – or sometimes both of them – would jump out of bed and peer through the window into the well-lit passage and the street below. It was always deserted and then the footsteps, still echoing, would cease at the door of Carol's still-empty flat.

A number of tram drivers say that various stretches of Blackpool's famous tramway system are haunted. A ghostly figure walks the tracks near Bispham on dark nights, swinging a lantern from side to side. On reaching a certain part of the promenade, the solid-looking figure walks through a locked gate before disappearing. It appears that this is the ghost of an old pointsman, who joined Blackpool trams at the age of fourteen and worked on the system all his life, except for a short period of time in the army during the war.

There is also a story which tells of a ghost tram haunting the system, and several people claim to have heard it over the years, rattling along the promenade in the early hours of the morning. On one occasion, a tram-inspector was said to have heard it approaching at about 6.30 one dark morning. He looked round and saw a lighted tram approaching and held out his hand for it to stop – the tram never arrived.

Mrs R. Dugdale of Blackpool told me that one wet day she was standing at the tram-stop opposite the Claremont Hotel along with her husband and daughter. She said, 'We heard a tram coming but there was nothing to be seen. The noise increased as the tram got closer and, as it passed, we all got our feet wet from the rainwater thrown up from between the rails. Yet no visible tram passed us!' Mrs Dugdale went on to say that she and her husband had often heard the distinctive sound of a tram's air-horn as it left Manchester Square at around two-thirty in the morning. Yet again, on investigating, there was never a tram to be seen!

At the Fleetwood end of the system, an old man is said to sit beside the tracks near the lighthouse. If approached, he gets up and walks away across the tracks towards the sea wall. He stands for a few moments, as if looking out to sea, before suddenly vanishing into thin air.

Near Rossall School 'something' is said to appear from nowhere in front of the trams which, I am told, leaves an aura of ice-cold air behind, even on the warmest night. Just who or what this is I have been unable to discover. Neither have I been able to discover anything about the hauntings which are said to take place in the tram-sheds, other than that there are supposed to be two ghosts there.

If driving through Greater Manchester beware the phantom lorry which haunts the A57 at Longdendale, between Hyde and Mottram, for according to reports there have been a number of rather strange accidents here over the years. Accidents which have long remained unexplained.

Some years ago there was a nasty accident here in which a man lost his life. At the inquest that followed, the coroner, Mr Stuart Rogers, wasn't satisfied with certain explanations and so he arranged for the jury to visit the scene of the accident at midnight – the time the accident happened – in an attempt to find a logical explanation for the circumstances surrounding the unfortunate man's death. One of the difficulties was that a witness swore to having seen a lorry backing out of an entrance which, he said, had been the cause of the accident. However, the police said that there was no entrance or any other opening at that particular point in the road – and so far as they could establish, neither had there been a lorry.

It was early in 1930 that a man called Charles Ridgeway had been riding pillion on his cousin's motorbike. Early in the morning both men were discovered lying in the road badly injured; Ridgeway in fact suffered fatal injuries. His cousin, Albert Collinson, received multiple injuries, including a fractured skull.

There were no witnesses to the accident, but Collinson told the inquest that as they approached a side entrance between the local pub and the crossroads, where the A57 crosses the B6018, a large lorry had suddenly backed out in front of him. The police pointed out that there was no opening of any kind and they could find no evidence or tyre tracks to suggest any such vehicle had been there at all. Collinson was adamant, however, saying that he most definitely saw it and remembered seeing the long flat tail of the vehicle, just before the crash.

The coroner eventually had to record an open verdict and, following the report of the case in the local press, locals began to suggest that this was by no means the only mysterious accident on this stretch of road. On the contrary, in a period of two years there had been no less than sixteen accidents at this spot which had involved cars, lorries, motorcycles and pedestrians. These had resulted in three deaths, nearly thirty people injured and twenty vehicles badly damaged. In every case there had been no satisfactory explanation, yet the road is almost straight and has a good surface.

Following the reports of the latest accident, more residents came forward to report other strange incidents; things such as footsteps heard in the roadway when it was deserted and plainly empty for some distance. The licensee of the nearby inn said that he had heard mysterious footsteps for which he could find no logical explanation. He said he had heard them so often he just took them for granted, although a member of his family often screamed in the night when she was awakened by them. He said it sounded as if a heavily built man was walking up and down in the road outside. 'What is most frightening,' he said, 'is that these sounds almost invariably mean there will be a nasty accident in the road within a few days.'

Psychic researchers converged on the area and explored every possibility, but they could not account for all the strange occurrences over the years. The police blamed motorists for driving too fast along this particular stretch of road, and gradually the affair died down, as these things usually do. Or at least, it would have died down if a series of accidents had not taken place less than a year later.

A six-wheeled lorry ran into a lamp-post; a motorcyclist hit something, and was thrown head first over a hedge; two cars collided head on in a wide straight stretch in broad daylight; and a pedestrian was run down by a lorry which approached in total silence in front of him – and then disappeared. A local man who knew of the road's reputation, and therefore tended to treat it with respect, crashed into a hedge and said later that he was unable to control the car which, despite his attempts to drive straight, kept veering to the right. Police examination of the vehicle immediately afterwards could not establish anything mechanically wrong with it.

A young grocer's boy was found lying beside his bicycle a few yards from the spot where the phantom lorry was said to appear. The lad died before he was able to give an account of what had happened, and again there were no witnesses.

Today, there are still reports of strange incidents occurring here, and there has been a continual stream of accidents going back to the 1930s. Although a wall and a hedge – which some people said might resemble a lorry when seen at night – were removed, it is still an area to be wary of, particularly late at night.

And finally, less pleasant than some of the phantoms one might meet on the roads of Lancashire are those strange beasts which roam by night in many parts of the country, sometimes betokening the death of the person they meet. These beasts are not exclusive to Britain; similar creatures abound throughout Europe. I refer, of course, to the phantom black dogs known in this area as 'Trash' or 'Skriker' and better known as the 'Hounds of Hell'.

The mere thought of these animals was enough to terrify our ancestors. Tales concerning phantom dogs are told all over Lancashire, and although today they are not considered to be harbingers of death, many phantom dogs are still reported.

At Levens Hall a ghostly black dog, described as 'a black woolly time-bomb', has often been seen, dashing in and out of the legs of visitors to the house. Recently Mrs Robin Bagot told me in a television interview that she has seen it a great many times. Spectral hounds, rather like large black greyhounds, have been reported moving in and out of the traffic lights at Carnforth; and the beach at Formby has been haunted by a large dog since time immemorial.

In 1962, a photographer and two staff reporters from the *Liverpool Echo* paid a Hallowe'en night visit to the beach, in search of the animal. Later they reported that two of them heard and saw 'a huge, dark shape, which moved about clearly silhouetted on top of a sand dune'. Even as they watched, it took on the definite shape of a dog.

They moved towards it and the strange shape began to move about in circles – much as a dog would. Quickly they climbed the sand dune, but on reaching the top there was no dog to be seen. Nor were there any paw prints or other marks in the soft sand. Their report ended: 'It is impossible to describe exactly in print just how we felt. Though it might have been a trick of the imagination, or perhaps even a stray dog, we are sincerely convinced that what we saw and heard was not of this world.'

In 1957 a small black phantom dog was seen in the garden of an old house at the junction of Spath Road and Holme Road, in the Didsbury district of Manchester. It was seen on a clear, moonlit night by a patrolling police officer, as it walked leisurely across the lawn and vanished behind a large tree. When the policeman looked behind the tree, the dog was nowhere to be seen.

Intrigued, the young constable decided to investigate the mystery in broad daylight. He felt a chill run down his spine when he discovered in the garden, just where the dog had suddenly vanished, a small moss-covered stone at the base of the tree. On it he read the inscription: 'PADDY. DIED 2ND SEPTEMBER 1913'.

More Ghostly Clerics

Lancashire was one of the last bastions of Catholicism at the time when Henry VIII broke away from Rome and made himself head of the new Church of England. Despite the dangers, many priests continued to live and work in the county, often hiding in secret compartments built into the homes of Catholic families or Papist sympathizers. Nicholas Owen, the famous builder of hiding places in the late sixteenth and early seventeenth centuries, is known to have carried out a number of constructions of this kind in Lancashire in such places as Chingle, Rufford and Towneley Halls and similar large Catholic houses. Yet despite this, many priests and monks were arrested and executed for their faith: Edmund Arrowsmith, John Paslew and John Wall, to name but three. Just how many more met their deaths yet remain virtually unknown, can be judged by the number of ghostly clerics who appear throughout the county without any seemingly obvious reason.

Penwortham Secondary School stands near the A59 a couple of miles to the south-west of Preston town centre. It is typical of many schools which sprang up throughout the towns and cities of England in the 1950s and 60s, built to realize socialist dreams of providing working-class children with the education to cope with the technology and leisure unknown in the days before the Second World War.

Although the schools might have changed, the children who attend them are still pretty much the same as children have been for generations, and not all of them show an interest in every subject in the curriculum.

One such pupil was a girl of fourteen, whom I shall call Joan. She was sitting passively in class C11 one afternoon in the winter of 1968. C11 was a rarely used classroom at the end of a long corridor. The lesson was religious instruction, which bored her, and there was little to distract her attention in the classroom, other than three blank cream-coloured walls without windows, and on her left an expanse of glass which gave a panoramic view across the playing fields. On a cold wet afternoon, this was even less interesting than the blank blackboard.

About halfway through the lesson, Joan's attention was suddenly caught by a vague movement to one side of her teacher, between the door and the blackboard. Turning slightly to look more closely, she was astounded to see what appeared to be the profile of a monk seated at a writing desk. From the outset, there was no question that it was real, because the apparition was two-dimensional, a white shadow imprinted on the cream wall two or three feet from the floor. She said it was 'rather like a lifesize, moving cardboard figure'. Joan still vividly remembers every detail about him; the long nose of an elderly man and the quill pen he dipped in the inkwell at the side of his desk from time to time.

For some time she sat open-mouthed with incredulity. Then with the traditional practicality of a Lancashire lass, she began to doubt her own senses and set about looking for a logical explanation. But there wasn't one.

She checked that the light from the window was not casting the teacher's shadow on the wall – he was still droning on in the way that some teachers do – but in any case the figure was lighter than the wall, not darker as a shadow would have been. It also had life and movement quite independent of the teacher. Her logic exhausted, she was forced to admit to herself that she was looking at some form of supernatural phenomenon. Joan nudged her friend to have a look, but as the other girl turned, the apparition faded away.

A few years later, when Joan was working in Preston a new girl joined the staff who had been at Penwortham Secondary School. As is usually the case, the girls began to discuss their schooldays, looking back with not a little nostalgia, when the new member of staff mentioned that she had once seen a strange apparition on the wall of classroom C11. Joan listened without saying a word, and she heard her own experience repeated in precise detail, even to the desk in which she herself had been sitting back in 1968. Neither of them could remember any reference to monasticism in any of the lessons, so they tried to relate the apparition to the building itself.

However, so far as they could discover, the site of the school had never been anything but farmland. The author has since discovered, though, that the ruins of the old farmhouse stood nearby; in fact they were very close to the wing which contained the haunted classroom.

As far back as the sixteenth century, Tower Grange at Formby on Merseyside was described as 'an ancient building, old and ruinous'. Going further back in time, in the early part of the thirteenth century, the property was known as 'Grange Farm'. It was owned, as were the surrounding lands, by the Abbey at Stanlow and then, following the commencement of the building of Whalley Abbey in 1296, the property passed to Abbot Gregory and came under the domination of the Abbots of Whalley until its dissolution, when the farm was allowed to fall into decay.

However, in the 1890s it was rescued from dereliction and handsomely restored with old materials, thus retaining much of its original character – somewhat unusual for Victorian restoration. Today it is divided into two properties, Tower House, which is the older part of the building, and Tower Grange, the newest part of the property which was added about 1900. One of the bedrooms of Tower House has been regarded as haunted for many years and the ghost, seen only on rare occasions, is said to be a small monk-like figure, dressed in a black habit.

The first member of the household to sense anything unusual was the family dog. Suddenly it stopped short in the hallway one day, fur standing up along its back, obviously aware of something its human companion couldn't see. A year or so later, the same thing happened again and at Christmas 1976, the occupier claimed she was 'touched' by a ghost.

It appears that she thought her husband had come in, and something bumped into her, moving her to one side. She turned, expecting to see her husband, but she discovered that she was totally alone. Several visitors to the house have reported hearing noises and some have come away with the distinct impression that something is 'not quite as it should be'. On one occasion, a workman who had never been to the house before, and therefore knew nothing at all about the alleged ghosts, came away convinced the place was haunted, whilst another workman, after only spending a very short time there, positively refused to work upstairs alone.

So, is the house haunted by a monk connected with Stanlow or Whalley abbeys? Not necessarily, for during the Civil War a priest is said to have hidden there, in one of the hides in the passage. As often happened in those days, rather than spend time trying to search for him, the authorities placed guards in every room of the house so that the occupants could not feed him. Thus he would either be starved out of hiding, or he would die. Apparently this brave priest chose to die rather than submit to Puritan justice, for several years ago a skeleton was discovered behind the panelling.

On occasion a large chest, known as the 'monk's chest' which stands in the passageway opposite the priest's hide in which the skeleton was found, has been moved by unseen hands, and although a number of strange inexplicable incidents have taken place over the years, the occupants consider the ghostly priest or monk – for as yet, no one has actually been able to confirm which it is – to be one of the friendliest ghosts ever to walk.

Accrington boasts one or two interesting ghosts, but perhaps the most ancient goes back to the days when the Black Abbey area of the town was a quiet and green backwater. As anyone who knows the area will tell you, that *is* a long time ago!

This area takes its name from the abbey which flourished there many centuries ago, where the monks lived out jovial and contented lives. However, monks are only human, and one of the abbey brethren fell in love with a local beauty. Knowing only too well the possible consequences of their actions, the couple would meet in secret, using one of the rooms in one of the abbey towers as their meeting place.

Unfortunately, the girl had caught the eye of a local boy who, when she spurned his advances, discovered her secret and informed the girl's father of her association with the recalcitrant monk. On learning this, the girl's father waited until she and the monk were together one night, and then forced his way into the room, where he discovered them making love. The monk hurriedly pushed his naked sweetheart into a secret passage and then bravely turned to face her father, refusing to answer any questions about the girl.

The enraged father woke up the abbey brethren who seized the monk and put him in chains, fastening him in the room, sealing the door and finally setting fire to the tower. The hapless brother lay helpless, but as he did so he heard the voice of his lover emerging from her hiding place. Unable to free him she ignored the monk's pleas to make her escape through the secret passageway. She put her arms around him and declared they would die together. The following morning, their charred remains were found amongst the debris of the burnt-out tower.

Since those events, it has been said that at midnight on the darkest nights, the luminous figure of a beautiful young girl emerges from the site of the Black Abbey. Her long fair hair streams in the breeze and her lovely features are spoilt by an inexpressible sadness. Her right arm is withered and fleshless where, centuries ago, it was burnt through by the hungry flames. She is said to utter a horrifying shriek, which strikes terror into the heart of anyone who witnesses the scene – and then she simply vanishes, her echoing scream seemingly hanging in the still night air.

In *Lancashire's Ghosts and Legends*, I described my experiences when I spent a night in Whalley Abbey. Since then, the Blackburn Diocesan Trust, which runs and maintains the buildings, has categorically denied that the buildings or the grounds are haunted. In a recent television interview the manager, Mr Derek Hartley, said that neither he nor any member of his staff had experienced anything in the seven years that he had been there. He said, 'I can assure you there are no ghosts at Whalley Abbey.' This statement brought in an avalanche of letters from viewers who claimed to have had experiences there, so they can't all have been mistaken.

To many of our ancestors, Whalley Abbey must have appeared in the role of a great estate when the monks' bailiffs came to collect their tithes or rents. To those who lived in the Forest of Bowland and Pendle, it was a lawgiver, where in the sixteenth century the court was usually held in Whalley Parish Church and dealt with such things as probate, marriage, moral offences and drunkenness as well as such trivial offences as failing to attend church, failure to contribute to church expenses and working on the sabbath.

The abbey took well over a century to build; the first stone was seemingly laid by Henry de Lacy in June 1296, and the Abbot's lodgings, the last building to be put on the site, was completed in the 1440s. The time taken to complete it does not indicate a lack of skill of the professional masons and other craftsmen, but simply the unavailability of funds. It is difficult for today's visitors to realize just how big the abbey was. There were about forty monks, but probably as many as ninety servants, of whom twenty or so would have been attached to the Abbot's personal household. They had an obligation to support twenty-four aged and infirm persons within the monastery and there might have been other pensioners and students, plus a considerable number of guests.

Sadly, the last chapter in the life of Whalley Abbey was one of violence. So it comes as no surprise to hear from others that the spirits of the gentle monks have remained.

An elderly lady told me that on a warm summer evening, about ten years ago, she had sat entranced, listening to the ghostly chanting of monks. A reporter for the *Daily Express*, and not a person to get carried away by imagination, told me that both he and his wife had heard the chanting on a quiet summer evening. Being a reporter, he was naturally cynical and suggested the sound was coming from Whalley Church, no more than about fifty yards away. Both he and his wife went to check and discovered the church was locked and empty. There was no doubt the sound was coming from the abbey ruins.

A student told me that both she and a friend, walking in the grounds one evening after attending a theological seminar, were surprised to see a group of monks appear at the site of the old stairs. They watched for several minutes as the phantom monks walked in procession, heads bowed, to the ruined choir, where they faded away again. Boy Scouts camping in the grounds told of wakening during the night to find a pale blue light, which appeared to hover over their tents for several minutes, before silently gliding away.

Mrs J. Horrocks of Rhyl told me: 'We used to live in Rochdale, and one day my husband and I went to Whalley on a day out and visited the abbey. It was during the week, so not many people were about. Having had a good look around and being very impressed by the place, my husband went to the car to get his camera, leaving me to continue to look around by myself.' She said it was a lovely day, very quiet. She sat down on a bench just to take in the feeling of peace and tranquillity. 'As I sat there, I felt a hand placed gently on my shoulder,' Mrs Horrocks continued, 'and I turned round expecting to see my husband, but there was no one in sight. The bench was empty but for me and it was well away from the buildings, so it could not have been possible for anyone to have been playing tricks on me, and the place was virtually deserted!'

The experience of Mrs Marjorie Pilkington was a little different, however. It took place in the abbey grounds over forty years ago and has left a most chilling impression in her memory.

She said, 'In the summer of 1945, I visited Whalley with my husband and son. I remember it was in the area where the old foundations are laid out like a garden [the nave, choir and presbytery]. Suddenly I was overcome by the most awful feeling, which I find difficult to describe adequately.' She said it was a feeling of dread and horror, fear and menace, wrapped up in a sense of claustrophobia. 'That is the only way I can describe it,' she told me. 'I went terribly cold with a kind of chill that seemed to eat into my bones and my only thought was to get out of the place.' It took a large brandy to warm Mrs Pilkington through again. She had told me during the interview that in no way could she be said to be susceptible to atmosphere nor did she have an over-active imagination. 'That feeling came right out of the blue, with a force I can still recall today.'

Up until quite recently, Heskin Hall at Eccleston was owned by the Lancashire County Council and run as a management training school. It was built some time in the sixteenth century and was something of a Royalist stronghold during the Civil

War. The ghost which haunts it is not a priest or a nun, but the ghost of a young woman who died there as a result of a priest's cowardice.

Many of the families who owned Heskin Hall were Roman Catholics. During the search of the house by Ironsides, led by Colonel Rigby, the family priest was discovered in one of the many hides. To save his skin the priest immediately renounced his faith and to prove what a strong Protestant he had suddenly become, he offered to put to death by hanging the young Catholic daughter of the house – something he went ahead and did by stringing her up from a beam, which is still to be seen in the Hall at the top of a fire escape. Older folk in these parts will tell you that, as children, their parents would tell them to 'touch the beam for luck', when they visited Heskin Hall.

The poor girl's ghost is said to have haunted the Hall ever since the cowardly deed was carried out, and more than one guest has been known to leave in a bit of a hurry after a midnight encounter with the ghost in one particular room which, although centrally heated, is always quite cold.

Some people claim to have seen the ghost of the girl being pursued by a ghostly priest in the Scarlet Room, the room nearest the scene of her hanging. The forms then disappear through a wall near to where the beam is situated. A large chest used to stand at the foot of the grand staircase, and the figure of a young girl has often been seen standing near it.

This has given rise to another version of the legend, in which a Scottish bride playfully hid from her husband in the chest, but as she closed the lid she accidentally locked herself inside. It was several hours after she had suffocated that her distraught husband found her.

Whichever version you prefer, the ghost is real enough. She has been seen several times, particularly in the now-modernized kitchen, where she appears as a luminous presence. A visitor, alone in the hall one day, encountered a young woman who, he said, appeared to be so real that he spoke to her. It only emerged some time later that there were no staff on duty at that time and the warden was away on holiday.

* * *

There is a story which suggests that in 1959 the small village of Downall Green, near Ashton-in-Makerfield, was the scene of some ghostly activity which brought about something of a tourist bonanza for a few weeks at least.

Three local youngsters were enjoying a midnight pilgrimage – more bravado rather than a serious ghost hunt – in Downall Green churchyard in July 1959. They ended up getting the shock of their lives. Wandering into the familiar churchyard, they inspected every dark corner. They ran their fingers over the lettering of the headstones as they searched out the names of the long-since departed and were quite confident in their knowledge of the minute details of every nook and cranny. Indeed, they had lived all their lives here and they knew the village and its lanes, the churchyard and the school intimately, and could move around the area on the darkest of nights without so much as a stumble.

This was not the first time that they had explored the little churchyard and the dell behind it late at night – but it was almost certainly to be the last. Midnight had come and gone and for their troubles all they had collected were damp feet from the dewy undergrowth around the graves, and an occasional scratch from the encroaching brambles. Watching and waiting, each night sound amplified by the imagination, they moved from gravestone to gravestone, eyes tightly screwed in an attempt to peer through the darkest shadows.

As the clock on the church tower struck two, the sky clouded over and a light drizzle set in. The boys huddled in the church doorway, where they drank hot coffee from their thermos flasks. After a while, they stood up to ease their cramped limbs, and suddenly one boy grabbed the arm of his nearest companion, who could tell by the way he squeezed it that something was wrong. He was looking at something, speechless, and as the other two turned to look, gooseflesh rose over them, their scalps beginning to tingle and their pulses race.

Their eyes were riveted on a tall, clearly defined shape, dark and almost solid, which was slowly drifting towards them. They could make out the glint of an eye peering from under the cowl of a hood as they watched, rooted to the spot with terror. The figure continued to advance, floating forward. There was no up-

and-down gait of a pedestrian, just a steady, almost rapid drifting towards the three terrified lads.

As it approached a pile of builder's sand, the bottom half of the figure moved right through it, not over it as would a human. It came to an abrupt halt some fifteen to twenty feet away from where the boys stood, appearing to stop and stare at them. No one spoke. Blind terror took over and, hearts pounding in their chests, the three boys turned and fled.

Later the following day, the boys each drew a sketch of the apparition exactly, yet they hadn't dared to speak their descriptions, in case the words themselves became an invocation of what they had hoped to see, yet wished they hadn't. They knew they had seen a ghost of some sort and that it had moved through a pile of sand without leaving a single footprint, but even now, no one really knows who the ghost was. So far as the author is aware – and I lived not more than two hundred yards from the churchyard for two years – this spectre has never been seen again since that night in July 1959.

In Middleton, a few miles to the north-west of Manchester, there used to be a small café and bread shop at the front of a bakehouse in Long Street. The premises dated back to the 1760s, having been at one time a convent and a private residence.

The café owner's daughters, soon after they moved in, began to complain of frequently hearing strange noises, and were afraid of being left alone in the place during the evenings. They attributed the noises to the ghost of the Mother Superior and felt that a kindly presence walked the house – although this didn't serve to make them feel any less scared. Nothing of a tangible nature occurred and the adults didn't encourage any mystery, pointing out several logical reasons for the origin of the noises.

However, one night the girls' mother was alone in the house when she heard a loud noise, which sounded as if someone was dropping a load of bricks in the empty building next door. Some months later, she was in the shop at about nine o'clock one evening, when she and two members of the staff heard exactly the same noise – a loud crash resembling the sound of a load of bricks being dropped next door.

This time, one of her daughters came running downstairs

startled, wondering what the noise could be at that time of the evening. The baker and his assistant thought there must be something wrong next door; perhaps the old building was collapsing. They informed the owner, who went through the property from top to bottom. Yet nothing could be found to account for the noises which seemed to originate there.

Still in Middleton, the parish church dates back to the twelfth century and occupies what is thought to be the site of an earlier place of worship. From time to time, members of the congregation have reported seeing the figure of a tall, thin man, dressed in a surplice, wandering silently about the church during the services. He usually disappears behind a particular pillar.

One member of the choir reported sitting in a choir-stall during a service, looking towards the back of the pulpit during the vicar's sermon. To her amazement she saw there were two clergymen there – her own vicar and a complete stranger, a rather tall, thin man in a surplice who after a few moments drifted behind a pillar. She was even more surprised when no one else in the choir or in the congregation appeared to notice him.

Following the service, the woman mentioned the incident to the vicar, who told her that he had heard of other people who had seen the figure, but who it was or why it suddenly appeared, only to vanish again behind one particular pillar, no one seemed to know.

In recent years, another ghost has been seen by several people, lurking in and around Middleton Parish Church. One man even claims to have taken a photograph of her. Amongst those who have seen this spectre is lay preacher Mr Frank Ogden. He said that he saw the ghostly woman first at the front of the church, and later observed her walking into the Langley Chapel, where she disappeared as if into thin air.

This appears to be a comparatively new ghost but, again, one which wishes to retain its anonymity, by all accounts, for her features are indefinable and, so far, no one has been able to identify her, or even suggest who she might be.

* * *

Bryn Hall – now demolished – stood just north of Ashton-in-Makerfield and was once the seat of the ancient and powerful Gerard family. Built in quadrangular form and surrounded by a deep moat, it had a spacious courtyard which was entered by means of an easily defended narrow bridge, and a gateway containing two heavy iron-studded doors. According to Roby's *Lancashire Traditions* it was 'a residence of local importance and architectural attraction'. In the great hall were displayed the arms of England, surrounded by rich carvings, whilst at one side of the large room a railed gallery provided accommodation for musicians or onlookers who wished to watch the entertainments from a point of vantage. The hall maintained a chapel and a priest – for the Gerards were staunch Catholics – and it was in this connection that Bryn Hall became associated with the dead hand of the Blessed Edmund Arrowsmith.

Father Arrowsmith was a man dedicated to his faith. He was born at Haydock in 1585 and, despite the risks to English priests, he entered the Jesuit College at Douay, where he was ordained in 1612. In 1623 he was betrayed and taken under escort to Lancaster Castle for trial, where, with all the bigotry of the time, he was charged with being a Roman priest, contrary to the laws. He was found guilty and sentenced to death.

Just before his execution, he asked one of his friends to sever a hand after his death, as he was convinced miracles would be possible through his lifeless hand. Indeed a great many people were credulous enough to have faith in such an assertion and tramped miles to where it was kept, at Bryn Hall, to receive the miraculous and healing power from the dead hand.

One story relates of a wrong done at nearby Ince Hall, when one of its occupants lay on his deathbed, and a lawyer was sent for at the last possible moment to make a will. However, before he arrived the man was dead. In a dilemma, the lawyer decided to see whether the dead hand of Father Arrowsmith might have the desired effect on the corpse, and he sent his clerk to Bryn Hall to borrow it.

The body of the dead man was rubbed with the holy hand, and it was said that the inert body apparently recovered sufficiently to sign the will. However, following the funeral, the daughter of the deceased produced a will which was not signed and which left Ince Hall to her and her brother. But the crafty lawyer soon produced another will, signed by the dead man's hand and, naturally, conveying all the property to himself. The son is said to have duelled with the lawyer and after wounding him and thinking him dead, he left the country and was never heard of again. His sister also disappeared, but no one knew how or where. After many years the gardener turned up a skull in the garden with his spade – and the secret was revealed. By now the hall had long been uninhabited, for the murdered girl's ghost had made life intolerable for the dishonest lawyer, following him wherever he went. It's said he spent his last days in Wigan, the victim of remorse and despair.

There was said to be one room at the hall which was haunted by the ghost of the girl, her shadowy form frequently witnessed by passers-by, hovering in the window or over the spot where her remains were buried. No one really knows what happened at Ince Hall all those years ago which gave rise to the haunting. Over the centuries the story has become confused, but there is no disputing that Ince Hall was long famous for its ghost of a young girl.

However, back to the dead hand. For a very long time it was believed by people over a wide area of Lancashire and Cheshire that the hand had great power to heal the sick and crippled. As late as 1872, it is recorded that a woman, wholly destitute and with one side of her body paralysed, tramped some twenty-odd miles from Salford in order to have the holy hand placed on her. It was stated at the time by a member of the Wigan Board of Guardians that hundreds of persons had visited the township for the same reason.

With the demolition of Bryn Hall, the hand was first moved to Garswood and later it was placed in the Catholic Chapel at Ashton-in-Makerfield where, preserved in a white silk bag, it remains to this day.

Wardley Hall at Worsley is the official residence of the Catholic Bishop of Salford; it is also the official residence of the skull of Ambrose Barlow, created a saint by Pope Paul VI in 1970. Father Ambrose was born at Barlow Hall in the sixteenth century, the son of a noble Catholic family, friends of the Downes of

Wardley Hall. A pious man who did all he could to help the poor, providing them with hearty meals whilst he ate the leftovers, Father Ambrose entered the priesthood at the age of twenty-three.

Following the Hampton Court conference in 1604, when James I clamped down on Catholicism, Father Ambrose was advised by his friends to flee the country, but he insisted on remaining in England to continue his preaching. On Easter Sunday in 1641, following his betrayal, he was arrested at Leigh while celebrating Holy Communion and although his congregation were willing to put up a fight and allow him to escape, Father Barlow insisted on standing his ground.

Led by the Protestant vicar of Leigh, the mob seized the priest and he was hauled before a magistrate at Winwick where, during his period in custody, he apparently suffered a stroke. This did not prevent him from being taken to Lancaster Castle where he was held for four months until his trial. He was found guilty and taken feet first on a hurdle to Lancaster Moor where, surrounded by a large crowd which included his friend Francis Downes and several of his followers, Father Barlow was hanged, drawn and quartered, his remains being displayed in various parts of the town as a warning to other Roman Catholics.

Downes and his friends managed to rescue the priest's head and brought it to Wardley Hall for safekeeping. However, just being in possession of such a relic could lead to trouble for the whole family, so its identity had to be kept hidden. In order to do this, the Downes family invented an incredible story which, until about 1780, was believed by almost everybody.

According to the legend which grew up around the relic, Maria and Eleanor Downes were waiting at Wardley Hall for the return of their brother Roger from London. Fearing he might have been involved in some drunken brawl, they were surprised when a messenger arrived carrying a wooden box, which he said had come from London. Maria, feeling a little apprehensive, refused to open the box and placed it in her room where, during the night, she imagined she saw a skull grinning at her.

The following day, helped by a couple of servants, she put the box in an outhouse and, on walking away, heard a loud knocking. The servants fled and Maria, now certain that there was something evil about the box, opened it, and later claimed that it had contained nothing but straw! But that night one of the servants, unable to sleep, saw Maria go into the outhouse and reappear with something under her arm, which she then buried in the garden.

All was well and the box forgotten until one day Maria, pale and trembling, told Eleanor to follow her. Going to the staircase, she pointed to a mutilated skull in a small niche in the wall, where Roger had loved to play as a child. At this Eleanor is said to have fainted, was put to bed, but never recovered.

Francis Downes was successful in getting this story about, saying that it was definitely his son's head. He said that in London he had been in a drunken frolic and vowed to his companions that he would kill the first person he met. Drawing his sword, he staggered along until, near London Bridge, he met his victim, a poor tailor, whom he ran through with his weapon. This started a riot and a watchman struck Downes with his bill, severing his head from his shoulders, his body falling over the parapet into the Thames. His head was rescued, packed in a box and returned to Wardley Hall.

That was the legend which was accepted until the eighteenth century when, round about 1780, the Downes family vault in Wigan Church was opened up and a coffin was discovered which had on it an inscription to the memory of Roger Downes. When the coffin was opened, Roger Downes' skeleton was intact, but the upper part of the skull had been sawn off just above the eyes – an obvious attempt at an early post-mortem.

So much for legend, but what about the skull? It is still preserved in a niche in the wall of the staircase at Wardley Hall. During the past couple of hundred years or so, some weird tales have been told about it. Any attempt to remove it for burial brings repercussions in the form of violent storms and other disturbances, and although it has been burned, cut to pieces and thrown into the river in the past, it has always somehow found its way back to its niche in Wardley Hall.

The bone of the lower jaw has become detached, and there are signs of violence on it, proof that at some time in the past it has been broken up in an attempt to rid the hall of its weird happenings. In Harland and Wilkinson's *Lancashire Legends* the editor states that he visited the hall and discovered that a locked door hid the grisly relic. Inside was a square aperture which accommodated the much-feared tenant. At this time, over a century ago, two keys were provided for the cupboard, one held by the owner of the property, the Countess of Ellesmere, and the other by the party who at that time rented Wardley Hall. The tenant stated that he found it quite possible to live unconcernedly with it.

Chingle Hall

Besides having the reputation of being one of the oldest houses in the county, Chingle Hall, at Goosnargh, near Preston, holds the dubious distinction of being the most haunted house in Lancashire. Therefore, it surely deserves a chapter all to itself.

Built by Adam de Singleton about 1260, Chingle Hall stands beside the old Watling Street, a major route to the north, the site being chosen because of its close proximity to water. It is thought that a building dating back as far as the Roman occupation may have occupied the site originally. Although Chingle is comparatively small, it is a manor house of the cruciform type, originally surrounded by a moat, complete with drawbridge. It is thought that the timbers used in the construction of the house are of Norwegian oak, believed to have been ships' beams, possibly originating from the wrecks of Viking ships found in the River Ribble.

Since Adam de Singleton built it, Chingle Hall has seen many alterations. The cellars, recorded on the original plans, have disappeared; the drawbridge has been replaced by a small stone bridge and there is little trace of the moat; all that now remains is a small lily pond. Passing over the stone bridge, one is brought face to face with a massive, studded oak door, believed to be the original one and therefore well over 700 years old. Hanging on the stout oak door, is a large and heavy 'Y' knocker, again believed to be the original one and the only one of its kind remaining in the country.

The approach to this door is through a porch which has a very interesting feature on its south side in the form of a small signal window about nine inches square and containing the original glass. During times of Catholic persecution, a candle was placed in this window, which indicated to those of the faith that an illicit Mass was about to be celebrated.

The Tudor Singletons had left Chingle Hall to their younger sons, ardent Roman Catholics, and during the Reformation they harboured many priests in false walls built into the rooms and passages. Indeed, the house is riddled with boltholes, hides and escape routes.

Chingle was next inherited by the Wall family, relatives of the Singletons, and in about 1585, despite the religious persecutions, it became an active centre for the celebration of Mass. In 1620, John Wall was born here. He became a Franciscan priest, living and working in Kidderminster, until he was arrested and subsequently hanged at Worcester in 1679, becoming one of the last English Roman Catholic priests to die for his faith. After his execution, his head was said to have been taken on a grand tour of Europe before being smuggled back to Chingle Hall where it was buried in the cellars.

Cromwell is said to have stayed here, stabling his horses in Goosnargh Church, at the time of the Battle of Preston. In 1764, Chingle Hall passed into the hands of the Farington family of Worden Hall in Leyland, who kept it until 1945, when it was bought by the late George and Margaret Haworth. Originally they were tenants, but later they purchased the property as a working farm and began the loving restoration of the house in 1959.

It was during this period that many of the hides and boltholes were discovered. A pre-Reformation praying-cross was discovered behind loose plaster in a downstairs room, and manifestations began to take place which resulted in Chingle Hall gaining its title as the most haunted house in Lancashire.

One of the first reported incidents was when the Rural Dean visited the house in the early 1960s. He was sitting in the lounge – a long, spacious and pleasant room of seventeenth-century character – having finished a meal and was discussing with Mrs Haworth certain aspects of the hall and its contents. Suddenly, for no apparent reason, two pictures on the wall opposite the fireplace began to rattle violently. This struck the Dean as rather odd, because there were eight such pictures, all of them grouped together. Yet only two of them behaved in this strange manner.

It was as though invisible hands had grasped the two pictures and, for devilish amusement, were banging them against the wall. Both the Dean and Mrs Haworth were afraid the glass might break with the violent movement, but after one or two minutes the shaking stopped just as suddenly as it had begun, leaving the two startled observers speechless.

Mrs Proctor, who helped as a guide taking parties round the hall, was one of the first people to actually see the cowled figure of a monk during the summer of 1966. She was sitting on the settee in the lounge when she heard three polite knocks on the lounge door. Thinking it was Mrs Haworth returning with the tea she had been preparing, Mrs Proctor looked round and, to her surprise, she saw a face peering at her through the window. She later described it as 'pale and not human'. Over the head was what appeared to be a dark woollen cowl and the face was quite expressionless. As suddenly as it appeared, the face vanished.

Later the same week, a pageant was being held in the grounds of Chingle Hall, depicting the history of the house. Mrs Proctor looked at the figure of a monk, which she thought was someone depicting the Blessed John Wall – and, to her horror, she saw it was the same figure she had seen staring at her earlier in the week, through the window, devoid of expression.

Just after Christmas, 1967, a Chief Superintendent of the Lancashire County Police and his wife were amongst a small group of people invited to dinner at Chingle Hall. The meal over, hosts and guests adjourned to the sitting room. At about 8.45, sounds were heard directly above them; sounds of an unusual kind. First of all there was a bump, as though a heavy object had been dropped to the floor. This was then followed by silence. Everyone in the room looked at each other, as a second distinct thud was heard coming from exactly the same spot – yet they knew there was no one upstairs. All the guests were accounted for, they were all together in the sitting room. Following the bumps there came the sound of a heavy tread, as though someone was walking across the floor of the room above.

According to the police officer, the footsteps moved diagonally across the room in a south-east to north-west direction. However, it wasn't just the sound of footsteps that was heard, there was also the sound of what appeared to be something heavy being dragged across the room, accompanied by a rattling of what could have been chains. The footfalls moved backwards and forwards for some time until, at last, the men in the party plucked up enough courage to go up and investigate. However, once they reached the top of the stairs, the noises stopped and a thorough search revealed nothing.

For the next hour or so the conversation was confined to speculation over the mysterious and somewhat startling noises. At 10.45, just as the guests were having supper, this time in the dining room, the noises were heard again, exactly as before. Again the men dashed upstairs and, as before, nothing was found which might account for it.

Other inexplicable noises have been heard and on many occasions the ghost has moved not only objects, but people. A Mrs Walmsley was standing in the lounge one day when suddenly she felt a hand in the small of her back which gave her a violent push, sending her sprawling across the room. Her first reaction was to remonstrate with the person concerned, but on this occasion it proved impossible because there was no one in the room with her – she was quite alone.

Another guest, this time actually stopping at Chingle Hall, had a weird experience in the bathroom. She said that she had gone to the bathroom without any thought of the supernatural – in fact she is a sceptic. But what happened whilst she was there gave her cause for some considerable alarm.

Once in the bathroom the guest – Mrs Moorby – developed a feeling that something was not quite right. She felt that she was being watched by unseen eyes. The feeling became stronger and, although she could not actually see anything, she began to feel terrified. The room suddenly became cold and then she found, to her horror, that she could not move. With a considerable amount of effort she managed to open the bathroom door and run down the stairs and, she said later, 'I distinctly heard the bathroom door slam shut behind me!'

A Mrs Rigby, who was temporarily living in a caravan with her husband on the estate, also had a strange experience. She was sitting with Mrs Haworth in the lounge and chatting over a cup of tea when a plaque of an old wooden galleon shot off the fireplace and dropped on the carpet in the centre of the room. There was no one else in the house but the two ladies, yet the plaque hurtled towards them as though thrown by an unseen hand.

Mrs Haworth's brother saw the figure of a priest walk through the gate and into the field, but found nothing when he left the house to investigate. Miss Ann Strickland, Mrs Haworth's sister and the last proprietor of Chingle Hall, says that she has often heard knocking and tappings and the sound of footsteps, and she is convinced that there are two ghosts at Chingle Hall. If the statements of Mr and Mrs Jepson, who visited the hall as guests at a barbecue, are correct then she could well be right.

During the barbecue festivities, Mr and Mrs Jepson were asked by Mr Haworth if they would like to look around the house. Naturally they were delighted to have the opportunity and as everyone else was outside, they had the house to themselves, which gave them ample opportunity to view the place at their leisure.

Whilst they were in the downstairs room where the pre-Reformation cross was discovered, Mr Jepson was amazed to see two figures suddenly appear in front of them. Both were dressed in the habits of monks and both faced the cross as though they were in prayer. Then, gradually, both figures appeared to melt into the wall.

Following this incident, which Mr Jepson did not mention to his wife until some time later, the couple went upstairs and entered what is known as the 'Priest's Room'. After a few minutes, they left and went into an adjoining room, a bedroom over the porch where John Wall is thought to have been born, known as the 'Haunted Bedroom'. It was in this room that Mrs Jepson saw the figure of a man with pointed features and shoulder-length hair walk by the window. Mr Jepson then turned to Mr Haworth and said, 'Is this house haunted?' Mr Haworth just smiled and admitted that it was.

Mrs Jepson then realized that the figure she had seen outside the window must have been very tall – as the window is at least twelve feet above ground level! All three of them saw the apparition, but the interesting aspect about it is that neither Mrs

Jepson nor her husband knew anything about Chingle Hall and they were certainly not aware of its being haunted.

On one occasion Mrs Haworth and her husband moved into this bedroom over the porch and they experienced some very strange events. As soon as they settled in bed, the door latch lifted noisily and the door opened. This happened on several consecutive nights. One night it opened no less than six times and each time Mrs Haworth got out of bed to close it, making sure the catch was securely down.

Again it opened, and this time she was shocked to see an illuminated figure in a cloak by the wall near her side of the bed. She woke her husband and they both watched the figure for over fifteen minutes, before it seemed to grow dimmer and dimmer, until it gradually faded away altogether. 'The strange thing was,' said Mrs Haworth some time later, 'neither of us was the least bit frightened.'

With so much activity taking place at Chingle Hall, it wasn't long before various teams of psychic researchers were offering to try and discover just what was causing these phenomenal disturbances. One man who certainly deserves to have his name mentioned in this context is Michael Bingham, a young New Zealander, who flew eleven thousand miles to investigate the Chingle ghosts and spent five weeks living at the hall, recording and photographing his experiences, leaving us in no doubt whatsoever that it is well and truly haunted.

Night after night, Michael sat alone in complete silence, waiting for the bumps and bangs and other manifestations which have given the hall its reputation. On one occasion he recorded footsteps which, as they came nearer the microphone, turned into a loud buzz. Experts were later able to confirm that the sound could only have been made by an electro-magnetic force, something which explains why cameras and tape recorders fail to operate in certain parts of the house. Michael also photographed a face at the window in the bedroom over the porch, and he actually began to film an apparition walking into this room. Subsequent enquiries revealed that the film broke in the camera just at the point where the figure entered the room.

During his stay at Chingle Hall, Michael stumbled on two

more priests' hides. The first he discovered after hearing eerie footsteps in the room above the Chapel – the Priest's Room. They were heard to walk backwards and forwards across the room and then disappear into a wall. Expecting to find the remains of a priest, Michael and Fred Knowles, a member of the staff, began to knock away the plaster. In the process of doing this, they experienced an incredible phenomenon; they were charged by an invisible person, who stamped his feet loudly on the bare wooden floor. Both men turned, expecting to see someone, but the footsteps stopped and they realized that they were the only two people in the room. When they turn to complete the work in hand, the footsteps began again and only stopped when the men broke through and discovered a hiding place.

In the bedroom over the porch, Michael experienced other phenomena. Here he saw the ghost of a priest several times. When he heard footsteps in the passageway outside he stepped out and stood in its way, and instead of walking straight through him as he expected, Michael said that the ghost walked round him. At other times it moved to one side to avoid him.

In November 1980, following a BBC local radio series in which I investigated a number of alleged hauntings in the county, Gerald Main – the series' producer – and myself were invited to spend a night at Chingle Hall to record a special 'Christmas Ghosthunt'. For the previous six weeks Gerald and I had travelled across the county, trying to find phantoms, which Gerald was convinced did not exist. However, our experiences at Chingle Hall, which were heard by hundreds of listeners on Christmas Day, 1980, were to convert him from sceptic to believer in less than six hours.

That particular broadcast is history now and has been repeated several times over the past few years. Hundreds of listeners heard how, on two occasions, the temperature suddenly dropped and the room became icy cold, how the floor sprang as invisible footsteps crossed it and moved down the connecting corridor, how a spool of tape was flung from one of the tape recorders.

They heard the mysterious bangings and raps which came from behind one of the priest's hides and they heard our reaction when, just before one o'clock in the morning, we actually saw the figure of a ghostly monk walk through the wall into the passageway outside the haunted bedroom.

What our listeners did not know is what happened after we had finished recording and were preparing to leave at about 4 o'clock in the morning.

We had loaded all the tape recorders, microphones, cable and the thousand-and-one bits and pieces required for a broadcast of this nature into the Radio Lancashire van, which was parked at the end of the stone bridge. Fred Knowles had ensured that all the lights were out in the hall and that the place was securely locked up, and four of us were standing beside the van, discussing the night's events. Suddenly someone pointed to the window over the porch. It was lit up with an eerie orange glow. We all stood open-mouthed, as the figure of a man stood in the window staring out at us. We watched this in stunned silence for a full five minutes until gradually the figure appeared to melt away, and the light gradually grew dimmer, until finally the old hall was once again in total darkness, its white walls standing out eerily in the moonlight.

Of the strange experiences I have had in my lifetime, the things we encountered that night remain the most memorable. As a postscript to this story, a few nights later a young man from Blackburn who runs a mobile disco service was returning in his car from a late-night disco at Goosnargh. As he passed the driveway which leads up to the hall – actually the old Watling Street – he screeched to a halt in the middle of the road as a monk suddenly drifted out in front of his car. He told me only recently that he has never accepted an engagement at Goosnargh since.

Chingle Hall was bought late in 1986 by Mr John Copplestone-Bruce, a barrister and best-selling author. It has again been made habitable and a huge programme of development is under way. Work is being carried out to excavate the moat and further digs are to take place to try and locate the cellars and passages in which many priests were harboured. A team of archaeologists will attempt to substantiate the claim that Chingle Hall stands on an ancient Roman site.

Boggarts Aplenty

There is hardly an old house or hall of any antiquity in the whole of Lancashire that cannot boast of a boggart of one kind or another.

It was Walter Greenwood who described the boggart as 'a mischievous night-marauding gnome'. The word 'boggart' is really a corruption of the old English 'bar ghuist' or 'burgh ghuist' – 'burgh' meaning 'town' and 'ghuist' being an old North Country expression for ghost. Hence 'burgh ghuist' or 'town ghost' soon became corrupted to 'boggart'.

And there are boggarts aplenty, from one end of the county to the other. Boggarts like the one which haunted Radcliffe Tower, presumably in commemoration of Fair Ellen of Radcliffe who was murdered by order of her cruel stepmother, cut into small pieces and served as a venison pasty for her father's dinner.

The boggart at Thackergate near Aldervale terrified many a sober person out of his mind, whilst herds of four-footed boggarts were said to have once issued from a mine near Wigan, in a form resembling 'great big, black dogs, wi' great glarin' eyes as big as tay-cups'. A Burnley boggart stalked through a house near Hurstwood, stripping bedclothes off the sleeping residents, or sometimes assuming gigantic proportions and perching in snow-white vestments in an old yew tree. At last it was exorcized and 'laid' under its favourite tree.

There used to be a bridlepath from Fairfield to Ashton which was visited nightly by a boggart that took the form of a shadowy lady draped in a loose white robe. She would glide ahead of the unknowing victim for some distance and then suddenly vanish, leaving their hair standing on end, no doubt.

A more sinister boggart, posing as an old woman, could be met in the lanes around Longridge. From behind she looked normal enough; an old lady hobbling along in her shawl and bonnet, carrying a basket under her arm. She would walk quietly beside anyone who tried to pass her and would listen politely to their conversation.

Suddenly, she would turn towards the unsuspecting victim, revealing that the inside of her bonnet contained – nothing! As the victim recoiled in terror, the old woman would lift the cloth from the top of her basket and out would spring her head, shrieking with demonic laughter and snapping viciously. The head would then chase the hapless victim for several miles, bounding along behind them.

There used to be an old well in Church Brow at Clitheroe which was one of the three main supplies of water to the town, and a few yards from the well, which was enclosed by a wall, stood a few ancient cottages around Well Hall. Now it's a well-known fact that most boggarts are comfort-loving creatures and one of them forsook the wild Pennine cloughs for warmer quarters. As soon as autumn approached and there was a distinct nip in the evening air, he would look around for somewhere warm, where he wouldn't be spied on and especially where there would be no children to pester him. He knew just the place.

Arriving at Well Hall, he slipped inside unseen and watched his landlady from the safety of his hiding-place, a warm cupboard by the fireside, as she busied herself with small tasks and then wearily climbed the stairs to bed. When all was quiet, the boggart then stepped out of his hiding-place, perched himself on her spinning-stool and, singing with satisfaction, begin to spin, smiling happily as he did so.

This particular boggart was of a sociable disposition and for years he returned to the hall each winter, where he used to keep the old woman company by the fireside on the cold winter nights. But, although friendly towards the old woman, he had a wicked temper when roused, and once chained a man to the wall when he had been upset by something the poor fellow said.

There is an old saying in the Ribble Valley, 'He keeps turning up like t'Old Hall Boggart,' whenever someone unpleasant puts in an appearance. For centuries a boggart had a nightly 'beat' based on the Old Hall at Clitheroe, which stood between Castlegate and Lowergate.

Dead on the stroke of midnight, he would set out along Lowergate, up Wellgate and into the old market place, carrying on right up to the castle itself. Then he would make his way home again, howling and shrieking and making the night one of sheer terror for all the householders along his route. No one, it was said, ever tried to find out what he looked like. Indeed, they pulled the blankets over them, or covered their heads with the pillow to muffle the boggart's horrible howls. None was brave enough to look out of the window – except a small boy, who crept out of bed one night to have a peep. He saw a 'hairy creature as big as a woolsack, with eyes red and fiery, like flaming saucers'. Or so he said!

A much more friendly and cooperative boggart lived in the folds of the fells overlooking the Little Bowland area, choosing to change quarters when he felt so inclined, and moving to the lower levels of Leagram Mill, near Chipping.

When the miller, Roger Holden, made his periodic visits to Clitheroe market, the antics of the boggart were related round the fire of the Swan and Royal, providing many a good tale for his cronies.

The boggart was alert and ever willing. 'Over willing,' grumbled the Holden household, who objected to being roused and pulled out of bed every morning by this creature who was always up with the lark. Even the servants cursed him, as they were hurled out of bed and dumped on the cold bare boards of their bedrooms.

He was certainly mischievous. In less helpful moods – which were frequent – he took fiendish delight in stampeding the farm horses, when he should have led them out to work. Sometimes, he would call the cows in for milking, then tie each one in the wrong stall in the shippon, before jumping on the roof beams, grinning and cackling at the resultant consternation.

At a Greenside farm, a murder was said to have been committed in the shippon. The exact spot was known because it was impossible to securely fasten a cow in that particular bier. However carefully it was chained overnight, next morning the cow was sure to be found at large – once being discovered up in the shippon's rafters. Naturally, this had to be the work of a mischievous boggart and it was necessary to lower the cow down cautiously, with the aid of a block and tackle.

An adjoining cottage had a boggart which varied its amusements by drumming on the old oak chest, shaking the hangings of the bed or rustling amongst the clothes. The alarmed occupants would, in despair, roll up the coverlet and hurl it at their invisible tormentor. Amongst other things, the boggart would snatch up the baby, whilst it was asleep between its parents, and without wakening either parents or baby, carry it downstairs and deposit the infant on the hearthstone.

Clayton Hall near Droylsden is reputed to harbour a boggart to this day, which disturbed the inhabitants by making noises that sounded like heavy weights being dragged across the floor, or ringing bells as well as making heavy thumping noises. It snatched clothes from the beds and rattled ponderous chains through the crazy apartments. The boggart seemed especially to delight in preventing people from sleeping and, in time, his pranks became intolerable. The help of the parish priest was obtained who, with the aid of counter-spells and incantations, succeeded in laying the spirit forever, declaring that:

> Whilst ivy climbs and holly is green,
> Clayton Hall Boggart shall no more be seen.

He's only sleeping, though. Even yet, one room of this quaint, moated, half-timbered manor house retains the name of 'The Bloody Chamber' from some supposed stains of human blood on the oak floor planks.

The more humble class of boggart is in turn both useful and troublesome to the farmers of any district in which it chooses to take up residence. Sykes Lumb Farm at Samlesbury was reputed to be frequently visited by a boggart as late as the 1880s, and many of his mad pranks were remembered in the neighbourhood until recent years. When he was in a good mood, he would milk the cows, pull the hay, fodder the cattle, harness the horses, load the carts and stack the crops.

When irritated by what he considered some mark of disrespect, either from the farmer or a servant, the cream-jugs would be smashed, no butter would form in the churn, and the horses and cattle would be turned loose or driven into the woods. Two cows would sometimes be found fastened in the same stall, no hay could be pulled from the mow, and all the while the boggart would sit, grinning with delight, up in one of the cross-beams of the barn.

At other times the horses would be unable to draw the empty carts across the farmyard. If they were loaded, they would be upturned. The cattle would tremble with fear caused by something which was invisible to the human eye.

The inmates of the farmhouse fared no better. Their bedding would be violently torn off the beds, and invisible hands would then drag the occupant out of bed and down the stone stairs by the legs, one step at a time.

The famous boggart of Hackensall Hall had the appearance of a huge horse, which was very industrious if treated with kindness. Every night it was left to sleep in front of a roaring fire but, if deprived of this luxury, particularly if it was as a result of neglect, it expressed its anger by fearful outcries.

Hothersall Hall, near Ribchester, was once the scene of a boggart haunting, but this boggart is understood to have been 'laid' under the roots of a large laurel tree at the end of the house. It is said that so long as the tree remains, the boggart will not be able to trouble the household.

So what about today? Are boggarts still abroad in this computerized, nuclear-dominated, latter half of the twentieth century? Of course they are, but today we call them poltergeists, a word which, thanks to video-saturated home viewing conjures up pictures of little girls shrieking in darkened bedrooms, houses getting rattled to destruction or blood sweating from the walls. But, like the boggart, most poltergeists are considered playful nuisances, as the following modern examples will show.

One poltergeist paid naughty visits to the home of Mrs Elizabeth Whitehead of Burnley. Like all genuine poltergeists, Mrs Whitehead's was invisible, but he made his presence felt in no uncertain manner. 'It happened about twenty years ago,' Mrs Whitehead said. 'My husband had died, leaving me with a ten-year-old daughter. Every morning for about a month, the front-door bell would ring at about five o'clock in the morning. At first I used to get up and see who was there, only to find the street deserted.'

After about a week, Mrs Whitehead stopped answering the door, so the poltergeist set about making its presence felt in other ways. One night, Mrs Whitehead took off her slippers and sat down to put her feet up after a busy day. She said, 'I suddenly noticed the hair on the dog's back had bristled up, and so had the hair on the cat.' Then, to her surprise, her slippers flew from one side of the room to the other. The cupboard door burst open and all the contents came tumbling out on to the floor.

'Then, over the next few weeks, other things began to happen,' she continued. 'For example, a light-bulb came out of its fitting and landed on the top of the stairs. It smashed, of course, and the pieces lay on the strip of linoleum that bordered the carpet. I could distinctly hear glass being crunched, as if by feet.'

Mrs Whitehead and her daughter shared the same bedroom, which had two single beds in it, separated by a table with a bedside lamp on top. That same night, they went to bed and soon her daughter was sound asleep. As Mrs Whitehead reached to turn off the bedside light, it suddenly jumped up into the air and hit her on the head. She said, 'I put it back on the table but it began to rise up again and I really had to hold it down very firmly to stop it moving. The funny thing about all this is that I didn't feel frightened at all. Of course, with a young girl, I wouldn't have wanted to show any fear in case she panicked as well, but my lack of fear was genuine.'

Mrs Whitehead said that at the time of these incidents it was Lent, and she had small religious figures in every room. Just as they did in church, she had made little covers for them, and someone later suggested she should take the covers off. After that she was not troubled again. She concluded: 'People told me it was probably a poltergeist attracted by my daughter – in other words, a playful little fellow.'

A poltergeist in a house in Portsmouth Street in Walney made life difficult for a family from 1981 to 1983. For two years the mischievous little fellow had been responsible for pranks, such as the disappearance of household items, in the home of Colin and Marilyn Procter and their six-year-old daughter.

The mysterious prankster is also blamed by the family for stealing numerous socks and other items, including a £20 note, a 50p piece, two bibles and a stamp album – none of which have so far been recovered.

Although the events only began in 1981, Mrs Procter said she had always felt there was something a little unusual about their terraced house since they first moved in. She told the *Barrow Evening Mail* in November 1983: 'We have lived in the house for nearly eight years and I have always felt there was something watching. I have always felt a presence or something peculiar.'

Mrs Procter used the term 'poltergeist' to describe the presence she sensed, though she has only heard the thing on one occasion. That was early one morning, when she and the family dog were waiting for husband Colin, a shipyard electrician, to return home from his night-shift. Some time before he arrived home, she heard the 'swish' of a curtain which covered the pantry doorway, and the rustling of plastic bags containing decorating materials that were lying just inside. Later she discovered that one of the bags had been ripped apart.

Mrs Procter said, 'So many things have gone missing. Whatever it is, it seems to have a thing about socks, but it only takes one from each pair.' Every morning she said she found her aspidistra in the living room has been turned round, and once she discovered an unexplained scratch which had appeared across the kitchen wallpaper overnight. She concluded: 'To start with my husband accused me of being absent-minded and mislaying things, but now that it has happened to him, he is not very amused. Although I feel a poltergeist is responsible, Colin is keeping an open mind!'

Ghost? Poltergeist? Boggart? Who knows. But these twentieth-century stories do share an amazing similarity with the boggart tales of our ancestors. Perhaps we shouldn't dismiss them as just 'superstitious nonsense' after all.

Witches Galore

Mention witchcraft in most parts of Lancashire and the conversation soon drifts around to the Pendle witches. But there were many other women who stood trial at Lancaster, accused of the crime, and in this chapter I propose to discuss some of these unfortunates who, although not as well known today as their Pendle sisters, were feared just as greatly by their contemporaries.

Witchcraft was by definition evil. It was heresy and was denounced as such by Pope Innocent III in a Papal Bull of 1484. From then up until well into the 1700s, some 200,000 supposed witches were executed in Western Europe alone. In most cases their accusers believed they were helping stamp out a widespread heretical conspiracy to overthrow Christianity, although most modern authorities on the subject now believe that the witch-hunts were little more than a form of mass mania, which was initiated by the church and prolonged by the vested interests of people like Matthew Hopkins, 'professional witch-finders'.

The crime of witchcraft wasn't made a capital offence in Britain until 1563 and, even then, English law required proof of injury to people or domestic animals, and up until 1570 no more than half a dozen people were burnt at the stake for witchcraft. But between 1570 and 1736, when the law was repealed in England, 1,000 witches were hanged or burnt, and during this same period the figure in Scotland was some 4,400.

In both England and Scotland the popular fear of witchcraft was closely allied to the rise of the Reformed Church. Although people certainly believed in witchcraft long before the Reformation, the Catholic Church with its candles, bells and holy water seemed able, in many minds, to keep this evil at bay. Now the new Protestants denounced these rituals as Papish superstitions, believing that if man was steadfast in God, then neither the Devil nor his agents would injure his immortal soul.

They were, however, less positive about their bodies and their worldly goods, admitting it was quite possible for even the most virtuous to become bewitched. Medicine was only in its infancy, and, as was illustrated in the case of the Pendle witches, a sudden illness such as a stroke might easily be construed as the direct result of witchcraft.

It was not surprising, then, that in these troubled times the more credulous could see witches everywhere, and they secretly turned to the old defences of holy water, holy oil, herbs such as garlic, and the witches' bottle. Of course, these Papish practices were frowned on by the Protestant Church, who maintained that there was only one cure for witchcraft – the detection and death of a witch – and after about 1600 the number of prosecutions in Britain rose sharply. This was mainly due to the increasing influence of uncompromising Protestant sects and their interpretations of the 'Divers Laws and Ordinances' of Exodus 22, verse 18, which states, 'Thou shalt not cause a witch to live.'

So, by 1640, a supposed witch could be brought to trial by any anonymous, unsupported accusation – and it was extremely difficult for the accused to prove their innocence. Evidence for the defence was twisted and corrupted to suit the prosecution, and the sentence was almost invariably one of death.

In Lancashire, there are a great many places where alleged witches were brought to trial, and many of these trials have passed into folklore.

For instance, the name of Elizabeth Farclough had only to be whispered to strike fear and terror into the hearts of the good people of Wigan. She was alleged to have murdered several people, and her powers of witchcraft, coupled with a malicious and wicked tongue, held people in constant fear of their lives. Very often, it was the malicious tongues of many old women that were to brand them as witches, and which in many cases cost them their lives.

One Jane Chisnall of Little Bolton complained to the magistrates in July 1634 that her mother had been killed by witchcraft and that her brother and sister had both been afflicted by a mysterious illness. She alleged that her brother had, in the recent past, called the mother of Richard Nuttall a witch. Nuttall had warned him to be careful of what he said, or his mother would take courses with him (probably meaning she would box his ears).

But, according to the evidence, the following day Jane's brother fell ill, suffering extreme pain, and the family had to call on Mother Nuttall to ask if she would visit him and remove the spell. Mother Nuttall offered to pray for the lad and, indeed, he soon got better. Unfortunately, not long afterwards Jane's mother fell ill and within a matter of days she had died, caused, said Jane Chisnall, by Mother Nuttall transferring the spell from her brother.

Far more interesting, in my opinion, than the trials of the Pendle witches are the records of the trial of the so-called Samlesbury witches, held during the same assizes at Lancaster in August 1612. The accused were Janet and Ellen Bierley, Alice Grey, Isabell Sidegraves, Jane Southworth, Laurence Hayes, Elizabeth Astley and John Ramsden. From Thomas Pott's *Wonderful Discoverie of Witches in the County of Lancaster*, we learn that John Ramsden, Laurence Hayes, Isabell Sidegraves and Elizabeth Astley were simply bound over to be of good behaviour. Alice Grey, it appears, should never have been charged, and so only Janet and Ellen Bierley and Jane Southworth endured a full trial. Jane was a young and recently widowed daughter of Richard Sherbourne of Stoneyhurst, and the family into which she had married had been manorial lords and had lived at Samlesbury Hall for over three centuries.

The principal witness was a fourteen-year-old girl by the name of Grace Sowerbutts, the daughter of Thomas Sowerbutts of Samlesbury. Janet Bierley was her grandmother, Ellen her aunt, and together with Jane Southworth, they were accused of bewitching Grace 'so that her body wasted and consumed'. In her evidence, Grace said that her grandmother had been seen to turn herself into a black dog, which then walked on its hind legs and spoke to her, trying to persuade her to drown herself.

This same dog, it was alleged, had buried Grace in hay and straw in a barn and then, 'Laid itself atop of me 'til I lost consciousness.' She said that her grandmother and her Aunt Ellen had taken her one night to the home of Thomas Walshman at Samlesbury. There her grandmother had lifted a sleeping child out of its cradle, thrust a needle into its navel and sucked the blood from the wound, before returning the baby to its cradle, still asleep. The child had died some time later and her grandmother and aunt had allegedly taken Grace with them, at dead of night, to Samlesbury churchyard and removed the little body from its grave. Then they carried it back home and made a meal of it, boiling it in a large black pot.

According to Grace, the bones were then simmered and the women explained to her that with the fat they could make ointment, which would enable them to change into whatever form they wished. Naturally, when asked the question, Grace denied joining in the act of cannibalism.

Grace Sowerbutts went to some great lengths in describing how the three women would take her to a Sabbath every Thursday and Sunday, at a spot called Red Bank on the other side of the River Ribble. 'There, four black things, going upright, and yet not like men in the face, met them.' After some kind of ghoulish meal, they danced in pairs, before the women – and presumably Grace – allowed their partners to pull them to the ground and 'abuse their bodies'.

For once, the Judge doubted the credibility of the evidence and on cross-examining Grace, it transpired that she had been put up to denouncing the three women by Christopher Southworth, the brother-in-law of Jane. He was a Roman Catholic priest and the background to the whole case seems to rest on the fact that attempts to suppress the Roman Catholic religion had been less successful in Lancashire than elsewhere in the kingdom. It is difficult to see today just what he had hoped to gain from it. Perhaps it was Christopher Southworth's way of taking his revenge on the three women for having recently renounced their allegiance to Rome.

Beside the pathway in St Anne's Churchyard at Woodplumpton there stands a large boulder stone beneath which lie the mortal remains of Marjorie Hilton of Catforth, known to all and sundry as 'Megs Shelton, the Fylde witch'.

She was found dead one day, crushed between a barrel and a wall, and was buried here by torchlight on 2 May, 1705. Now, in those days, the death of a witch in a small community such as Woodplumpton caused a bit of a problem. Common decency demanded a respectful burial, yet the church would never allow a non-Christian – and certainly not a witch – to be buried on ground which had been consecrated.

As it happened, just before the villagers were to hold a meeting to decide how to dispose of Meg's corpse, someone came up with evidence that brought to light the fact she had been baptized a Christian. Which was very convenient.

Even so, such was her reputation that there were several people who felt that she should be buried well away from decent, respectable Christians, but in the event she was finally buried just beside the pathway. However, so many legends had grown up around Meg that stories of her crafty wiles were not going to be forgotten just because she was dead and buried. If anything went wrong on the farms, from the cream going sour to the death of a piglet, poor old Meg's spirit was to blame.

Then people began to claim they had seen her ghost, particularly near her hovel of a cottage at Wesham and in the lane by the 'Running Pump'. In the 250-odd years since her death, quite respectable people claim to have seen her.

It should not be difficult to imagine the rejoicing of the superstitious villagers when Meg's death was announced. At last there had come an end to her mischief. But because strange things still occurred in the village from time to time, it soon began to dawn on them that she was scratching her way out of her grave to continue getting up to her tricks.

So, after much deliberation, it was eventually decided that her body should be dug up and reinterred head downwards, with the boulder stone placed on top of her grave, just to make sure she stayed implanted.

But still her spirit refuses to remain quiet. About fifty years ago, she was seen in Woodplumpton by a local farmer, Major Wingard. It was not many years ago that a family visiting the area were looking around the churchyard when a small boy who was with them wandered alone into the church. After a very short time, he ran out again, frightened and screaming, and when asked what had caused the fright he said that, as he reached the lectern, a wicked old woman, dressed in old-fashioned clothes, had suddenly appeared from nowhere and had angrily chased him from the building.

Even today in Woodplumpton there are still those who are prepared to blame Meg for any misfortunes which might occur, and many a naughty child is threatened with a swipe across the backside from old Meg's broomstick.

Isobel Roby came from the Windle area of St Helens, an area now cut through by the East Lancashire Road. She was a poor woman but obviously much feared by her neighbours who, if they met her in the lane, would turn round and set off in the opposite direction rather than be fixed by her evil eye. One man convinced himself that Isobel had cursed him and that his aches and pains had been wished on him, and just because he had married Isobel's god-daughter. Twice he tried to obtain help to counteract the spells, the first time approaching James of Windle, a glover, and the second approaching someone considered to be a 'wise man' by the locals, a man called Halesworth.

As a result of various complaints, Isobel was arrested and hauled off to the assizes at Lancaster where she was prosecuted by Sir Thomas Gerard of Garswood, one of the lords of the manor of Windle. She was charged with 'having made use of her devilish and wicked arts', although we don't know who her alleged victims were. She was not accused of actually murdering anyone as a result of witchcraft, yet despite this Isobel was found guilty and sentenced to death. She was tried, sentenced and hanged all in the same day – something of a record even for the seventeenth century – yet her sentence was perfectly correct and in accordance with the law as it stood in those days. Such was the fear of witchcraft.

A ghost which haunts Clapdale Hall, just on the Lancashire–Yorkshire border near Clapham, is thought to be that of Alice Kyteller, one of Ireland's most famous witches who had the dubious distinction of being the first woman in that country to be charged with witchcraft.

Dame Alice lived in Kilkenny in the fourteenth century with

her fourth husband, Sir John le Poer, her first three having died under mysterious circumstances, leaving her a great deal of money and the power and influence that goes with it. Arrogant and hard-hearted, she was generally disliked in the district and there were many rumours about her involvement in the black arts and Devil worship.

Things came to something of a head when her fourth husband began to suffer from some form of wasting disease and one of the servants told him of the rumours surrounding his wife, suggesting she might have put a curse on him. Later, on going through her belongings, Sir John discovered a magic talisman, a book of spells and incantations and other paraphernalia usually associated with witchcraft. The church then took over the investigation, searching round for more members of Dame Alice's coven and many of her friends and servants were put on trial and imprisoned or executed.

Dame Alice, protected for a while by her noble birth and influence, eventually realized the game was up and that if she wanted to save her skin, she should make her escape from Ireland as quickly as possible. Thus she arrived at Clapham, where she sought refuge with her stepson John, and where she was to remain for many years until her death. Since then her ghost has been glimpsed from time to time, aimlessly wandering through the rooms at Clapdale Hall, a victim of her own conscience.

Legend tells us that Dame Alice had been so fond of her stepson that she was willing to sell her soul to the Devil for his sake, saying, 'I will do anything you ask me, to make sure the lad is always rich and prosperous.' The pact was duly signed and sealed and Dame Alice was given a list of tasks she must perform, if John of Clapham was not to lose his prosperity.

At midnight every night, she was seen on the bridge over the Wenning near Clapham Church, carrying nine newly killed red cocks. She would lay them in a circle which she defined with her stick. Then she stood in the centre and, waving her arms and brandishing her brush, she had to brush the waters of the Wenning back into Clapdale. Her stepson's fortunes never failed.

* * *

Most people believed that witches could turn themselves into any animals they wished, but the most common one was the hare, possibly because it was an animal difficult to capture on account of its tremendous speed over the most difficult terrain. Megs Shelton was supposed to be able to turn herself into such an animal, which was one of the reasons she was never actually caught when up to her tricks.

There is a legend concerning a ghostly white rabbit at Crank, a hamlet near the Rainford bypass, between St Helens and Billinge. The story goes back to the time of James I and the period of mass witch-mania.

During this time an old woman called Mother Pope lived in Crank and was regarded with a mixture of awe and suspicion by the villagers, for she was of foreign extraction and lived a quiet and solitary life with her granddaughter, Jenny, whose dearest possession was a pet white rabbit. The old woman was regarded locally as a witch, not only because of her knowledge of herbs and their healing properties, but because she was thought to have studied Devil worship and the black arts.

Nearby lived a man called Pullen, a small, dark and repulsive bachelor farmer, known to be something of a miser. When he found he was suffering from some wasting disease, a disease that grew rapidly worse as the weeks went by, he resorted to obtaining some herbal medicine from the old witch. Still there was no improvement in his condition, in fact it seemed to him that his illness had quickly got worse since he had begun taking the herbs. This convinced him that the old witch was trying to poison him. He resolved that the only way to break the spell was to draw some of the witch's blood, a recognized method in those days.

However, like most of his kind, Pullen was 'all mouth and trousers' and had not the courage to do this on his own. He enlisted the help of a worthless character called Dick Piers, a man who had been thrown out of the army and who now made a living by poaching and various other illegal activities.

Together, their faces covered and wearing suitable disguises, they set out one night for Mother Pope's cottage. All was quiet as they burst in and they found the old woman in bed. She sat up, startled, and the two dragged her out of bed and halfway across the floor of the room and made a large cut in her arm, from which the blood flowed freely. Their mission accomplished, our brave heroes prepared to leave the old woman, when her grand-daughter appeared, clutching her pet rabbit in her arms.

She had been awakened by the disturbance and had gone to investigate. Seeing the two men who had attacked her grandmother and fearful for her own safety, Jenny fled from the house and into the cold night air as fast as her legs would carry her. Afraid that she would raise the alarm and expose them for the villains they were, Pullen and Piers dashed after the girl. Thinking they had seen her disappearing over a hill, they gave chase. When they reached the top, Jenny's white rabbit hopped out of a hedge and approached them. With an oath, Piers kicked the defenceless little creature high into the air and when it fell at his feet, the brave Pullen continued kicking it until the dead animal rolled into a ditch. However, of Jenny they could find no trace, so they made their way home, hoping that all would turn out right.

The next morning the body of Jenny was discovered, where she had stumbled and fallen, hitting her head on a rock. Old Mother Pope recovered from the ordeal, but gave no indication of who had attacked her. She had her own way of dealing with wrongdoers. Jenny was buried and Mother Pope left her cottage quietly and moved to live in another village. Had it not been for the rabbit, the whole affair would have ended.

Dick Piers continued poaching, and some time after Jenny's funeral he was making his way home across the fields when suddenly he saw, to his absolute horror, Jenny's white rabbit hopping towards him across the field. There was no mistaking it, for there had never been another like it with its great pink eyes and enormous ears. Taking a second look, Piers took fright and ran off in the opposite direction, but he was a doomed man.

The spectral rabbit haunted him for weeks after that until he could stand it no longer. One night in the local inn, he confessed his part in the attack on Mother Pope and then, rushing out of the inn, he threw himself into the local quarry and died of a broken neck. The brave Pullen was much too afraid to confess his part in the crime, whining that he had no knowledge of the affair and that Piers was mad and had tried to implicate him because he was jealous of him. So he lived on, becoming more morose and alone, with just his conscience for company – and still his health continued to deteriorate.

One evening he was passing Mother Pope's old cottage when he caught sight of a large white rabbit sitting on the doorstep looking hard at him. Terror paralysed him for a second or two, and then with a cry of fear he took to his heels, racing across the fields towards his farm. But the rabbit could run too, and it easily kept pace with him. If he stopped, the rabbit stopped; if he turned, the rabbit turned. Desperate, he raced round the fields until he collapsed from exhaustion and, a week later, mourned by no one, Pullen died alone in his farmhouse.

Mother Pope had avenged herself.

What kind of people would denounce their neighbours and even members of their own families as witches? The records of the trials held at Lancaster in 1612 and in 1633 give us a very good insight into the living conditions in and around central and east Lancashire and especially the area around Pendle. These same conditions would probably apply to most rural districts in the seventeenth century and help to put people's attitudes into perspective.

Poverty has always been common in Lancashire; in the sixteenth century, two women from Barley had been excused from attending church, because they had no clothes to wear. The peasants were ignorant, superstitious people who could quite easily believe in the existence of evil spirits, so they would accept without question the wildest tales about the powers and activities of these poverty-ridden and usually ugly old hags, who were reputed to have personal connections with the Devil and his agents.

In those days, too, there must have been a fair number of stray animals scavenging the countryside, so it surely follows that a few would form an attachment to those human beings in a similar plight to themselves; sheltering from time to time in their hovels, snatching a scrap of food from the hearth or table.

So it would be but a short step to build up these lean, predatory creatures into manifestations of the Devil. And if – as was no doubt the case – a dog or a cat, following its human counterpart, was present when something odd occurred, then it was a shorter step still to attribute the aberration to one or the other – or both. The villages of rural Lancashire were remote and backward, with little contact with the main flow of trade and prosperity, so there was terror and belief in all kinds of supernatural – and even natural – phenomena.

The story of witchcraft from ancient times to the present is a long and often complicated one. Things were much more simple in the old days, when everyone *knew* that witches existed, had supernatural powers, and could be fought by people with equal powers in known and definite ways. To most of us today, witchcraft – that is traditional witchcraft – may seem weird and fictitious, but the memories of Lancashire's witches have become a part of our heritage and one of our greatest tourist assets.

Old Nick Himself

At the beginning of the seventeenth century, somebody wrote, 'The Devil is now 6,000 years old, of great wiliness and experience.' Belief in the Devil is still alive today and is a force to be reckoned with.

When did he usurp the power of the demons, giants and gods of our early ancestors to become all evil rolled into one? The Celts worshipped a horned deity 3,000 years ago, the stone heads of this god bearing a remarkable resemblance to medieval caricatures of Satan. The Saxons had their Scratti, the Norsemen their Nikkr and the Swedes their Neck. The early Christian priests, preaching to the Angles and Saxons, retained their familiar devils and combined them all into Satan, the Prince of Darkness. Stone-carvers began to depict evil overcome by good as the Devil in a variety of guises doing battle with Christ and being overcome. These wolf-shapes, hell-hounds and serpents can be seen on the hog-back stone at St Peter's Church at Heysham, whilst an eleventh-century artist has cut a likeness of a grinning Satan in chains in Kirkby Stephen Church.

Throughout Christian history, the Devil has appeared in many places, but has always been recognizable by his horns, his malevolent sneer, his tail and his clubbed foot. His haunts, even today, are shown on Ordnance Survey maps in such names as Devil's Elbow, Devil's Bath Tub, Hell Clough and Fiend's Fell.

He possessed enormous strength, hurling rocks with great ease and even greater accuracy. Where an ancient cross-country route, the Long Causeway, climbs between the Sabden valley and Clitheroe, the gap known as the Nick of Pendle was said to be cut by him. In a gully above Sabden he left his footprints on a rock for all to see. On the same hillside is the Devil's Apronful, where he scattered stones he had intended to throw at Clitheroe

Castle. Near Whymondhouses and at Kirkby Lonsdale one can see the Devil's thumb and fingermarks.

So, the power of the Devil, his personal appearances and the possibility of bartering the soul for temporary gain still number among the legends and traditions of the county. Repeating the Lord's Prayer backwards was said to be the most effective way of raising the Devil; but if his terms of the bargain were not to one's liking, his removal could only be affected by giving him some impossible task to undertake.

Many years ago, two threshers on a farm near Blackburn succeeded in raising the Devil through a crack in the barn floor, but on becoming alarmed at their success, they dismissed him in no uncertain terms, giving him a vigorous thrashing about the head with their flails.

The boys at the old Burnley Grammar School are said to have succeeded in raising him on one occasion. They repeated the Lord's Prayer backwards and performed some incantation which induced Satan to make his appearance through a stone flag in the old schoolhouse. As he pulled his head and shoulders through, the boys became alarmed and began to kick him with their steel-clipped clogs and hammer him about the head with a poker and tongs. This was too much, even for him, and he withdrew, howling, back to wherever it was he came from. But the black mark he left on the flag was shown as proof of his appearance until the old grammar school was rebuilt last century.

The boys at Clitheroe Grammar School heard about the exploits of the Burnley boys when someone began recounting the story after lights-out one night. They decided to have a go at raising him themselves. Rather apprehensive about reciting the Lord's Prayer backwards, they eventually overcame their reluctance and waited in the darkened dormitory for the outcome. Soon there was a roar and a rumble beneath the hearthstone, an ear-splitting crack, a gush of fire and volumes of sulphurous smoke and, bingo, there stood the Old Lad himself, grinning and capering with glee.

The lads went as white as their bed sheets and were speechless with fear. One of the boys, a little more brave than the others, shouted at the Devil to go back to where he came from. 'I'll stay here if I've a mind,' jeered the Old Lad, and called up his attendant imps from below.

Now, it so happened that the schoolmaster was just on the point of going to bed, but he had a strange feeling that something was not as it should be at the school. So, instead of taking up his candle and retiring to bed, he put on his cloak, lit his lantern and let himself quietly out of the front door and into the dark Clitheroe streets. His anxiety increased as he hurried towards the parish church, where the old school stood. Passing into the schoolyard, the schoolmaster saw a lurid red glow wavering in the windows and bursting in at the door, he was met by the smell of sulphur and a rush of terrified boys, all yelling together, trying to tell him what had happened.

The schoolmaster knew exactly what to do under these circumstances. He walked straight up to the Devil and, looking him square in the eye, said he would give him a task, and if he couldn't do it, then he must clear off back to Hell and stay there. 'No task is beyond me!' boasted the Devil, who had a short memory so far as previous failures were concerned. 'Then knot some ropes of sand,' said the schoolmaster.

The Devil and his imps laboured for days, weaving piles of sand from the banks of the River Ribble, but it was all in vain, for every time he tried to pick his rope up, the coils he had so carefully drawn, woven and plaited, disintegrated. Livid with rage and frustration, the Devil retreated to the fireplace and, with a flash, disappeared into the crack in the hearthstone, never to be seen in Clitheroe again.

Following this event, it's said he took up residence at Cockerham, near Lancaster, scaring the good citizens half to death. A public meeting was held to consider how they could free themselves of this 'fiendish persecution' and they appointed their local schoolmaster – because he was the wisest and cleverest man in the place – to do his best to drive the Old Lad away.

Using the prescribed methods, the schoolmaster managed to raise the Devil, but when he saw his large horns and tail, saucer eyes and long claws, he became speechless with fear. The Devil, feeling pleased with himself, granted the poor chap the privilege of setting him three tasks. If the Devil accomplished them, the schoolmaster would become his prey; if he failed, he would leave Cockerham forever.

The first task, to count the number of dewdrops on the hedgerows, was soon accomplished; and so was the second, to count the number of stalks in a field of grain. The third task was then proposed, that the Devil make a rope of sand, which would bear washing in the Cocker without losing a single strand.

Speedily the rope was twisted in fine sand, but it wouldn't stand up to washing, so the Devil had been foiled, yet again. In one stride, and with a howl of rage, he stepped across Pilling Moss and was gone.

Of course, even the Devil had to relax sometimes, and what better way was there than gambling at cards, particularly when you know you can't possibly lose? Unfortunately for him, the human players usually recognized him, with his tail curled round a table leg, his horns obvious beneath his high-crowned hat, and his club foot – always an embarrassment to him. The games always ended in panic.

This happened one night at the Three Lane Ends, near Chipping, when Old Nick made up a foursome at brag, with three local lads. A similar thing happened at Killington crossroads, in the upper Lune Valley, when one of the players looked down and recognized the forked tail.

Poor Old Lad. Nobody would play with him. One Sunday morning at Crawshaw Booth in Rossendale, the Devil was fresh from his morning bath in the Thrutch and, seeing a group of lads playing football, he stood on the sidelines, ready to join in if they invited him. But the lads didn't notice him, until the ball went in his direction. This was his chance. He threw his cloak over his arm, took a flying kick and up went the ball, high, high up into the sky, to disappear in the clouds. The last the boys saw of the stranger was a flash of fire as he vanished, leaving only acrid sulphur fumes in the morning air. I reckon they could use him at Turf Moor.

On another Sunday morning, he turned up at a derelict chapel at Grane, near Haslingden. Here some local gamblers were engaged in a game of pitch and toss. One threw a halfpenny up to the ceiling. It didn't come back down. Looking up, they were all horrified to see the Old Lad, clutching the coin and grinning at them from the roof beams.

Of course, even the Devil is not infallible and he has often been outwitted by sharp humans, as we have already seen. However, it was a Pendle tailor, Nicholas Gosford, who cleared him out of the Ribble Valley for ever. This is one of several versions of the same story.

One bright morning, Nicholas was stamping up and down by the riverside at Brungerley Hipping Stones, stepping-stones across the Ribble near Waddow Hall, which were in use for several centuries before Brungerley Bridge was built in 1820. He had gone down there for some peace and quiet, after a severe nagging from his wife.

He was approached by a tall, dark man in a high-crowned hat, flowing cape and shoes with long points, which in no way seemed to hamper him as he skipped across the stones. The stranger asked why Nicholas was looking so glum on such a fine morning, and the tailor replied that his wife had been nagging at him for drinking too much when there was hardly enough money in the house to buy food. The stranger – who was none other than the Old Lad himself – wheedled from Nicholas that he had a desire for quick riches, the solution to all his troubles.

A few minutes later, the Devil was waving goodbye, a signed contract in his pocket, in which the tailor had agreed to let the devil have his soul in twenty years' time in exchange for three wishes. Highly delighted, the tailor hurried home to his cottage on the Waddington road, and seeing on the table nothing but thin gruel, he shouted to his wife, 'Take that pig-swill away, woman. I want a plate of ham and eggs.' In a flash, there it was, a large oval plate of ham and eggs.

His face dropped. One wish gone. This was not what he had hoped for. His astonished wife suddenly began to laugh at the woebegone attitude of her husband and he, angry at her laughter, retorted, 'I wish that plate of ham and eggs would stick in thi gob. Perhaps that'd quieten thi.' It did, at once. Her muffled giggles ended in silence. Two wishes had been wasted – and he had to use the third to remove the dinner plate from his wife's mouth. All the wishes were wasted because of his foul temper.

From then on, Nicholas came to his senses. He stopped drinking and worked hard and long at his business. The months and years slipped by quickly and eventually the day came when the Devil arrived to collect his dues. 'But I was cheated,' complained Nicholas. 'I had nowt at all for my three wishes! Be a sport and let me have just one more.'

Well, Old Nick isn't vindictive, in fact, when the mood takes him, he can be generous to a fault, so he allowed Nicholas one last wish, suggesting he make it something good for his family.

The tailor, seeing a horse grazing outside the door of his home, pointed to it and said, 'I wish tha'd leap on yon dun horse and ride off back to Hell and let neither me nor Clitheroe clap eyes on thi again!'

The Devil gave a cry which was heard as far away as Colne, as an invisible hand lifted him on to the back of the horse, which carried him away in a trice. Horse and Devil disappeared when they reached Hell Hole Bridge. Nicholas became quite famous after this, and eventually bought himself an inn near Littlemoor, which he named The Devil on the Dun. Today the site is marked on the maps of the area as Dale upon Dun Green.

Satan appeared at all sorts of odd times in odd places and in various disguises. He was always blamed for any catastrophe, storm or drought. Johnny o' th' Pasture, a well-known Worsthorne man, made a pact with him, when the Old Lad turned up as a black dog at Hurstwood. On the day Johnny died, his funeral at Holme was literally a washout, as the area was affected by the worst storm ever known. You can still find Johnny's grave in the churchyard at Holme-in-Cliviger.

Dick o' Cinder Hill was a heavy drinker who was forever thumping someone after he'd had a few. But his drinking came to an abrupt end one evening when he had an unexpected encounter with the Devil.

Dick was a farmer who came from Worsthorne, a small village near Burnley, and he was notorious in the area for his heavy drinking. One night, he decided he would ride into Burnley to go on a pub crawl. His wife pointed out that he was already in no fit state to be on the road and that a thunderstorm was imminent. Dick replied that he would ride into Burnley, even if he had to halter the Devil.

Staggering drunkenly to the paddock, he struggled for some time, without success, to put a halter over the old horse's head. A sudden flash of lightning revealed the reason for his difficulty in harnessing the recalcitrant animal: it had sprouted horns. A second or two later, Dick was struck a violent blow and fell to the ground unconscious.

His long-suffering wife discovered him and put him to bed, and when he eventually came round some hours later, he was convinced he had tried to halter the Devil, and for this he had been struck down. Taking it as a warning, he gave up drinking and became a highly respected member of the community and a pillar of the church.

His good wife was tactful enough to avoid pointing out that he had tried to halter the bull. Not unnaturally resentful, it had given him a good kick.

We all know that the Devil built the old bridge at Kirkby Lonsdale. According to legend an old woman's cow strayed across the River Lune, but because it was swollen following heavy rain she was unable to get across to fetch the animal back. Just as she was standing on the bank wondering what to do, the Devil popped up beside her and, with a sweeping bow, he graciously offered to build her a bridge so that she could cross it the following morning and retrieve her animal – at a price, of course. The price was the soul of the first living thing to cross the bridge. The old woman agreed to the terms, signed the contract, which the Devil pushed into the pocket of his apron, and she went off home, leaving the Old Lad to get on with it.

By dawn the job was 'a good un'. The woman arrived back to find the bridge completed and the Devil impatiently waiting for his payment. She pulled a little dog from where she had hidden it under her petticoats, and from a pocket she produced a large juicy bone, which she then threw over the bridge. The dog raced after it and the Devil, howling with rage, disappeared in a bolt of lightning and a puff of smoke, leaving the air full of the smell of brimstone and sulphur. He also left behind his collar, which he had taken off to enable him to work more easily. This can still be found down-river on one of the banks, as can the Devil's Fingermarks; indentations on one of the coping stones in one of the recesses.

Built early in the fifteenth century, the bridge's central ribbed arch stands forty feet above the Lune, whilst, beneath, the dark river slides over a stratum of limestone. Steps run down to the grassy banks under tall trees. Since 1673 the bridge has borne an inscription which calls on all who use it to 'Fear God, Honour the King' and for several centuries it has been used by monks and soldiers, knights and pedlars, rich and poor alike.

Over the years, the story of the Devil's involvement in the bridge's construction has been greeted with derision. But that stopped in 1932 when the new bridge was built a little further downstream. Its construction was marred by floods and the opening ceremony was hampered by a violent thunderstorm, accompanied by hail and snow. If it wasn't caused by the coming together of dark forces, at least it added another twist to the centuries-old tale.

Nowadays the work of the old bridge is over and the narrow road is only used by pedestrian traffic. But after defying the floods of five centuries the old bridge remains today as a monument to its builder – be he human or whatever.

The Devil, it is still believed, is the supreme spirit of evil. A foe of God and man. Primitive belief ascribed all phenomena to some agency or other; for example all good things were considered to be gifts from God, whereas bad things were the work of the Devil. Since belief in the world of the supernatural has never been eradicated from man's consciousness, a belief in the Devil is still alive and a force to be reckoned with. Rural Lancashire folk will tell you that the Devil and his works can still be found in the county, even today.

More Favourite Legends

Lancashire has long held a traditional belief in the most pleasant of all supernatural spirits – elves and fairies.

The fairies have always lived amongst rural folk, and many antique tobacco pipes 'formerly belonging to the fairies' are still turned up occasionally in corners of newly ploughed fields. We all know that fairies still gambol in the early dew and that their revels are still witnessed at times by some of the more privileged inhabitants.

In all honesty, there are still people in the county, and indeed throughout England, who sincerely believe in fairies. There are those who believe they have seen them, people like Mrs Lea of Manchester who told me early in 1986, 'I have seen fairies. They were very tiny and so was I. I was about six years old at the time. They were very close to the rhododendron bushes and, although it was over sixty years ago, I am still reminded of them whenever I see sweet peas; their dresses were just like those flowers, all pale colours.'

In another letter, a correspondent referring to the chapter on fairies in *Yorkshire's Ghosts and Legends* wrote, 'I realized your chapter on fairies was written tongue-in-cheek, but I saw some as a child, although I haven't seen any since, unless they've taken on another form. I am always reminded of them when I see the delicate colours of sweet peas.'

Mrs B. Wilson of Walton-le-Dale, near Preston, told me that she had seen a group of elves or pixies when, as a child of eight or nine years old, she had lived in Mill Lane at Churchtown, Southport.

She said, 'We lived at No 8 Mill Lane and my grandmother lived at No 10. There was a passage through to the back which separated the two houses and which led to the gardens and a small orchard.' Mrs Wilson explained that about halfway down the garden there was a gate and a bank of earth about three feet high that ran the length of the remainder of the garden. Beyond this was another passage which led to some tennis courts and a wood: part of the Meols Estate and where the ghost of 'Old Nance' was said to walk.

She continued: 'Just by the gate I saw either elves or pixies dancing. They were not very tall, certainly well under three feet in height. There were six of them in a circle, one bobbing up and the next bobbing down, dancing round and round. Inside the circle was another elf, who looked as if he was in charge, who moved to each little person in turn to dance with them. There was no music, just complete silence, and I remember being very frightened at the time.'

She said that when she got to her grandmother's house, she stood on the couch, terrified. She looked out of the window and could see right across the gardens, but now there was no sign of the little people and nothing to show they had even been there. Mrs Wilson concluded: 'I'd had the fright of my life. I knew I had not been dreaming nor had I imagined them. There is no logical explanation for what I saw – and I never went that way round again.'

At Mellor Moor, near Blackburn, about a hundred years ago, a man claimed that while passing close to the remains of the Roman encampment one warm summer evening he saw a strange, dwarf-like little man, dressed in full hunting clothes, with boots and spurs, a green jacket, red cap and with a thick hunting-whip in his hand. The little creature ran briskly along the moor for a considerable distance and, leaping over a stone wall, darted down a steep bank and was lost to sight.

Popular opinion in that area for many years was that an underground city existed thereabouts, that an earthquake swallowed up the encampment and that on certain days of the year the fairies could be heard ringing their bells and indulging in various festivities. Considerable quantities of stone which remained in the ditches for years, right up until the beginning of this century, in fact, may have led to the idea of a city.

On other occasions the fairies are supposed to exhibit themselves in military array on the mountainsides, the activities conforming in every respect to the movements of foot soldiers. Such appearances were believed to portend the approach of some civil disorder and many folklorists say they were particularly common at the time of the '45 Rebellion.

Most of the Lancashire legends of old which related to fairies were, in effect, moral tales, as the following examples will show. For instance, two men went poaching and placed their sacks over what they thought was a rabbit hole, but was in fact a fairies' house. The fairies rushed into the sack and the poachers, thinking they were rabbits, grabbed the sack and set off home. One fairy, searching for another in the sack, called out in a broad Lancashire accent, 'Dick' – a rather undignified name for a fairy – 'Dick, wheer art thou?' To which the other replied, 'In a sack, on a back, riding up Barley Brow.'

The moral of this story was, of course, that the men were so afraid, they never went poaching again.

A poor peasant woman was filling her pitcher at the Fairy Well near Staining, in order to bathe her baby's weak eyes. She was mildly accosted by a handsome fairy, who presented her with a box of ointment, saying it would be a sure remedy for the baby's ailment. The woman was grateful for the gift, but somewhat mistrustful of the stranger; so she tried the ointment out on herself before using it on the baby.

Shortly afterwards, she saw the mysterious handsome little man at Preston market, stealing from people's pockets and much to his surprise, she tackled him about it. He asked her how she had recognized him, since he was invisible to everyone else, and she told him how she had used the ointment, pointing to her powerful eyes. The fairy became enraged and struck her blind on the spot. Moral: when you are on to a good thing, keep quiet about it.

A similar example crops up in the tale of the milkmaid at Thornton, who was surprised when an invisible hand placed a jug and a sixpence at her side. She delightedly took the money and over the next few weeks this was repeated every time she went into the milking shed. Eventually she could contain herself no longer and told her boyfriend about it – but the jug and the sixpence never appeared again after that.

'Do a kindness and it will be rewarded' is another moral which was brought into fairy-lore. A ploughman engaged in his labours heard a plaintive cry, 'I've broken mi speet [spade].' Turning round, he saw a little old lady, holding in her hand a broken spade, a hammer and some nails, and beckoning him to repair it. He willingly broke off his work, even though he still had a lot to get through, taking time to make a good job of the repair, for which he was instantly showered with gold coins as the old lady vanished, sinking into the earth.

Fairy funerals are said to be the heralds of sudden death and disaster. Sightings of fairy funerals at Penwortham and at Longton ended in disaster, and in 1718 Robert Parker of Extwistle Hall, near Burnley, met a similar fate. He was returning home late one night from a secret Jacobite meeting, when he saw a strange sight near Netherwood. A goblin funeral passed him by, silent and very close. On the phantom coffin he saw a name – his own.

Three months later, following a day's hunting in heavy rain, he returned to Extwistle Hall, anxious to be rid of his sodden clothing. He placed his wet coat near the blazing fire to dry out and, as his little daughters helped him to remove his boots and stockings, the hall was rocked by an explosion.

Robert Parker was killed and three of his children were quite badly hurt in the blast. He had left his powder-flask in his wet coat pocket.

Let us now look at a few other denizens of the darkness who feature prominently in Lancashire's legends. Amongst the 'demon superstitions' prevalent in the county is that of the spectral huntsman, which occupies a conspicuous place in folklore throughout the world.

This superstition is still held at Wycoller, at Rivington Pike and more particularly in the Cliviger Gorge, where a huntsman is believed to pursue the phantom white doe round Eagle's Crag on All-Hallows Eve. His hounds are said to fly yelping through the air on many other occasions. Known as 'Gabriel's Ratchets', they are supposed to bring death or misfortune to all who hear the sounds.

The 'Lubber Fiend' (Stupid Demon) still stretches his length across the hearthstones of the farmhouses around Cliviger and Worsthorne and the feats of the 'Goblin Builders' form a large portion of the popular literature of almost every Lancashire town south of the Ribble. The 'Goblin Builders' decided where churches were to be built, moving stones from their original site during the night, such as at Rochdale, where they moved the foundations of Rochdale Church from the banks of the River Roach up to their present position. Churches at Samlesbury, Winwick and Burnley all have a similar legend attached to them; at Winwick and Burnley it was a 'Demon Pig' who determined where their churches would stand.

Then there are the 'Water Sprites', believed in by our ancestors and still forming part of the folklore of both Lancashire and Yorkshire. There is hardly a stream in either county which does not possess a spirit somewhere along its length.

Prior to the bridge being built at Brungerley in 1820, the Ribble had to be crossed by the old 'Hipping Stones', said to be haunted by the malevolent spirit of Peg o' Nell, who claimed a life every seven years. It was at these stepping-stones that King Henry VI was treacherously betrayed following the Battle of Hexham by a member of the Talbot family of Bashall Hall.

'Old Scrat' is another Lancashire demon, who resides mostly around the Fylde. He would get on a cart, or other vehicle, which then became so heavy the horses were unable to move it. They would tremble and sweat, as if aware of some malevolent yet invisible presence. After a short time, Old Scrat would slip off the back of the cart and disappear with a malicious laugh.

A classic story concerning Old Scrat is that when a funeral procession was making its way to Brindle Church, the coffin became so heavy it couldn't be carried. The clergyman, who was walking alongside, is said to have offered up a short prayer and commanded Old Scrat to clear off. No sooner had he said the prayer than the excessive weight was felt no more, and the corpse was carried into the churchyard and interred without further trouble.

'Trash' or 'Shriker', the black dog of death, appears to one member of a family about to be visited by the Grim Reaper. He is said to be more or less visible, depending on how far away the death is. He is described as being as 'big as a woolsack', with very broad feet, shaggy hair, drooping ears and eyes 'as large as saucers'. When he walks, his feet make a loud splashing noise, like old shoes on a muddy lane – hence the name of Trash.

But not all our folktales are full of gloom and doom. Some weavers' tales of the last century are very funny and one of the funniest I came across whilst researching this book dwells on the age-old theme of contention between the little tackler (maintenance man) and his over-large and overbearing wife.

Maggie always knew best and she would have the last word. If her husband said Sunday, Maggie said Monday; if he said Easter, she said Christmas. Sometimes the poor little fellow grew tired of all the argument, but it seemed the only thing that kept Maggie going. They grew older and older until he was bent and she was shrivelled with a voice like a cinder under a door, but still they continued to argue, and still Maggie managed to have the last word.

One day as they sat at home, he – for Maggie never referred to him as anything but 'he' or 'him' – had been recalling a tale from their younger days, when Maggie had had a lovely bonnet trimmed with blue ribbons.

'Green ribbons,' corrected Maggie.

'No, blue, I'm sure, dear,' he replied meekly.

'Green! You said at the time it was blue, but it wasn't. It was green. We quarrelled about it then, but I know best – it was green!'

'Ah weel,' he said, 'have it thi own way! All I know is, we quarrelled about it till I took my knife out o' my pocket and cut that ribbon clean off the bonnet.'

'You did not. You used scissors!'

'Knife. Knife!'

'Scissors, I tell you. SCISSORS!'

'Well,' he said, 'we shan't settle it now, not if we're going out. Get thi coat on, missus.'

Maggie got her coat. Her eyes were flashing and he could see by the way she was working her jaw and breathing through her nostrils, bosom heaving, that she was ready to start arguing as soon as they were out of the house. Before they had even reached the gate Maggie said, 'It was my bonnet, so I ought to know what bloody colour it was. It was green and you snatched up my scissors and cut that beautiful green ribbon off!'

'I used my bloody knife!' he protested.

'Don't you use language like that to me. It was bloody scissors!'

'Knife.'

'Scissors, you great numbskull! Scissors. Scissors it was and scissors I'll say until my dying day!'

By now they were passing by the canal which cut through the town like a black, putrid ribbon. It was deep, dark and dangerous. He knew that what she said was right and that as long as she lived, she would always have the last word. So, taking a deep breath, he lunged at Maggie and pushed her backwards into the canal. 'Knife!' he shouted, as she hit the water with a resounding thwack. Down she went, but after a few seconds she bobbed to the surface, wildly thrashing her arms. As soon as she had her head above the water, she took a great gasp of air, looked towards him and shrieked, 'Scissors!'

'Knife,' he shouted back, as she disappeared again. As she rose again more slowly, helplessly flaying her arms, he yelled 'KNIFE!'

She raised her head a fraction, found him with her eyes, spit out a fountain of canal water and screamed, 'BLOODY SCISSORS!' in a voice still defiant.

The bubbles told him where to look for the third and last rising. Maggie's head was below the surface now, but her arms were still feebly moving over the dark water. He waited, carefully judging his time, then cupped his hands and bawled, 'BLOODY KNIFE!' at the drowning figure.

Slowly, Maggie began to sink, but at the last moment, her right arm rose out of the water, until her wrist and hand stood above the surface. Then she opened first and second fingers wide, closed them, then opened them and closed them, and continued to do so until, inch by inch, the arm grew shorter and the scissoring fingers disappeared forever.

The Rossendale Valley was full of characters and to many of these people, even at the end of the last century, such places as Liverpool and Manchester, Leeds and Bradford, were as foreign and unreal as El Dorado. Newspapers were as rare as £5 notes. Occasionally one would turn up and then someone who could read would place his spectacles over his rough-hewn nose and, by the aid of a tallow candle, set about murdering the Queen's English, whilst vociferating in a dialect which would be as foreign to today's valley folk as the Oxbridge accent would have been to their forbears. So distorted were the interpretations of the written word because of blunders made by the reader, that many fabulous stories were soon afloat, which have given rise to many amusing folktales and legends today.

The Rossendale Valley was considered to be one of the most sinful areas in the county; small wonder then that it was deemed to be in urgent need of religion. By the end of the first quarter of the nineteenth century, the religious teachings of the Methodists and Baptists had taken a strong hold in the area. It is from their chapels that a number of interesting and amusing stories came.

At Lumb the chapel was crowded and the excitement at its highest as Handel's 'Messiah' was rendered in good old-fashioned style. They had reached the 'Halleluja Chorus' when the conductor, who was beating time, brought his foot down too vigorously and the whole platform collapsed. The congregation thought that the chapel itself was collapsing and made a rush for the doors, the unfortunate conductor being one of the first to escape.

Once in the open he ran for dear life, never pausing until he reached his home, where he sprang into bed fully dressed, clogs and all. When his astonished wife asked him what was wrong, he replied, 'T'chapel's fallen in, an' I'm killed!' Then, pointing through the window in the direction of the building, he added, 'and there's many in the same way down yonder, too!'

Similarly, when a charity sermon was being preached at the original Wesleyan Chapel in Newchurch – since demolished – a man gazing out of a window during a particularly boring point saw a child fall into the water of the old mill lodge which stood alongside. He immediately rushed out of the crowded church to save it. The congregation thought the place was on fire and made a mad rush for the door. In the general confusion and panic that followed, one old dear wedged in the crowd thought her end had come. Raising her voice, she cried, 'Glory be to God. We're all goin' to Heaven and t'parson's coming wi'us!'

I think the best 'Chapel tale' comes from Goodshaw, where many years ago the good people of the village had to use the well in Chapel Lane as their major source of water. One evening a hysterical girl rushed into the chapel, claiming she had seen a snake in the well.

Alarm quickly spread and for several days none of the villagers dared approach, until the want of water and the problem of having to bring it from further afield led to a solemn meeting of the villagers.

The sexton of Goodshaw Chapel was one of the people present and, wanting to impress, he agreed to go to the well and shoot the snake. Armed with an ancient firing-piece, he cautiously approached the well and, seeing what he supposed was the snake lying on top of the water, he opened fire.

Careful inspection was then made, and one can well imagine his embarrassment when it was revealed that the snake was nothing more dangerous than a woman's knitted garter.

Before leaving the Rossendale Valley, mention should be made of one of its most famous characters of the early nineteenth century – Betty Treacle. She was often to be seen walking through the villages with her house key in her hand, wearing a mob cap and muttering incoherently to herself. Her prominent facial features were, in the words of one valley writer, 'enough to stop a clock'.

She had a prominent hooked nose and domino teeth and, though only half-witted, knew more about the daily doings in the valley than anyone else, and was a mine of information so far as the gossips were concerned. So famous was she in her day that it is said that a well-known portrait painter came to put her on canvas, but Betty refused to sit for him. He offered to pay her a substantial amount of cash, but still she refused. Then some village wag told him how to bribe her and she sat for hours until her portrait was finished.

The bribe? A halfpennyworth of chips.

Pub and inn signs have done much to keep alive the stories and legends of Lancashire. Many commemorate people virtually

unknown to anyone outside the county. Others are memorials
to local boys who made good or who became internationally
known, such as The Walpole at Blackburn, which honours
Britain's first Prime Minister, Sir Robert Walpole; and the Lord
Stokes at Leyland, named after the former chairman of British
Leyland, which is rather unusual in that it honours a man in his
own lifetime. But what stories lie behind the many inns with
strange names up and down the county, for instance the Yuticks
Nest in Pringle Street, Blackburn?

This, in fact, is a very good example of the application of the
local dialect. In 1862 there stood on this site a cottage which was
later extended and became a beer house. It was taken over in
about 1880 by John Fish, who was a 'drawer-in' at a nearby
cotton mill, as were his sons. For the benefit of readers who, like
me, have little knowledge of textiles, a drawer-in's work consisted of threading the needles with the appropriate coloured
threads for the pattern being worked on. The men doing this
work sat on very low stools.

Now, the word 'utick' or 'yutick' is an old Lancashire name
for a whinchat, a smallish bird which migrates here around April
or May. The whinchat builds its nest in the ground and spends a
good deal of time in what appears to be the same sitting position
as the drawer-in. So it was only a matter of time before the local
wits nicknamed the millworkers who did this job yuticks.

As John Fish was a yutick and his home (nest) was the pub, it
soon became known as – you've guessed it – Yuticks Nest.

What has the Bank of England got in common with the
Ancoats district of Manchester? Nothing, really, but this old inn
was named as a tribute to a former landlord. His honesty and
straight dealings were such that he was deemed to be as safe as
the Bank of England.

Another interesting sign is that of the Caribou at Glasson,
near Lancaster. When Glasson dock was being built at the end
of the eighteenth century, ale and liquor were sold to labourers
from an old hulk lying there. It became known as the Pier Hall
and then, for some strange reason, The Grapes, and finally,
because the owner of the hulk had attachments to the Canada
fur trade, it became known as the Caribou, a name that stuck. In
time an inn was built near the site which took the name, and

when it was rebuilt in the early 1960s it retained the name Caribou.

Visitors to Pontin's Holiday Camp at Middleton Sands, near Morecambe, will be familiar with the Roof Tree Inn. This old place was built as a farmhouse and was known for years as Roof Tree Cottage because, some years before, a tree had actually grown through the roof. One can still see the remains of part of the tree trunk embedded in the wall.

Finally, to conclude this brief history of inn signs, let us look at one which commemorates an obscure event which took place at Mereclough.

According to tradition, a cockfight was arranged between the Towneleys and the Ormerods, each of whom had a bird of tremendous fighting qualities, known throughout the whole of East Lancashire. Exceedingly large sums of money were staked on this cockfight and, according to Dr Whittaker, the eighteenth-century historian, the fate of the Ormerod estates depended on the outcome.

In the presence of a great crowd of local gentry and farmers the fight began and at length the Ormerod cock lay on the ground, seemingly beaten and dying, whilst the Towneley bird was declared the winner. Poor Ormerod, thinking himself ruined, got on to his horse and began to ride towards home, but before he got very far he was called back by one of the Towneleys, who shouted that his bird had won. It seems that with one final effort, the Ormerod bird had driven its spur into the Towneley bird's head, gaining the victory. Both birds died that day but, to mark the event, the name of the inn was changed that same night to the Fighting Cocks and has remained so ever since.

Another Fighting Cocks stood at Arnside before the days of the stagecoach. It had a widespread reputation as a cockfighting centre. After it became a coaching inn, and coaches plying between Grange and Morecambe stopped there, it was decided that a little respectability should be brought to the area – even though cockfights still took place there long after 1849, when the sport was made illegal. It was renamed The Crown, a name it retains to this day.

Not many people know it, but Clitheroe, that Queen of the

Ribble Valley, very nearly became a spa town. In the latter half of the eighteenth century a Mr Embley, who was the landlord of the Stop and Rest tavern at Shawbridge, took a lease on a sulphur spring near his inn, with the intention of making a fortune. He had high hopes of turning the spouting water into a spa to rival those at Buxton and Harrogate and proceeded to convert it into a sulphur bath, enclosed within a stone building.

He set about a massive – for those days – advertising campaign, stating that he was able to cure 'leprosy, scrofula and scorbutic complaints, with special benefits for children who did not thrive'. He said his sulphur spring, being a mild diuretic and aperient, had in the past been useful in curing bilious and cutaneous diseases. Needless to say the Trades Descriptions Act didn't apply in those days.

Patrons were able to indulge in hot and cold baths, complete with a changing-room, or take walks in pleasant gardens – and, of course, partake of Mr Embley's fine ales in his nearby tavern. However, like many a good idea before or since, things didn't work out as planned and the crowds failed to flock to his sulphur bath, so that by 1840 the poor fellow was struggling to make ends meet. He put the tavern and the spa up for sale. Today the buildings have long been demolished, but the water still flows – or rather drips – from a pipe in a stone wall at Shawbridge, where the more adventurous can still sample it today, if they have a mind to.

Crosses – market crosses, wayside crosses, churchyard crosses – all played a part in medieval life. Then the Reformation set off a wave of cross-smashing, something which was to continue off and on until the reign of Charles II. Many people were sure that some terrible punishment would come down on the heads of the perpetrators, and there are some strange stories concerned with such disasters.

For example, in 1690 Nicholas Blundell wrote of the terrible repercussions that befell a Whalley man's decision to lay out a bowling green. He ordered his workmen to remove an ancient cross. One able-bodied man reared the stone up on one end, wresting it from edge to edge. He finally managed to move it, but the heavy stone fell on him and killed him outright. No one was the least surprised, and one workman went about for days afterwards convinced that sudden death would strike him at any time.

About a mile from Hurst Green is Cross Gills Farm. On a hilltop between the farm and the River Ribble stands Cross Gill Cross, placed here in solemn ritual in about 1830. A bishop and large crowds of faithful attended the event, in which a new cross was placed on an old stone base. The Crosskill family were said to have been responsible for pulling down the original one, following which three members of the family died in quick succession under mysterious circumstances.

In about 1835 the new priest at Thornley spotted a fine cross lying by the side of the road and would not be satisfied until it was placed in his churchyard. He was most insistent, despite the reluctance of certain men in his parish, who warned him that the cross must never be removed.

However, they could not refuse him. He soon realized, though, that the removal was going to be fraught with troubles, for not one but eight horses and every man in the parish were brought in to drag the cross away with much heaving and swearing.

However, because of the trouble the cross caused in the churchyard, it was soon agreed that it should be returned to the place where it had been found. Strangely enough, this time, instead of taking eight horses and all the men in the parish to move it, the task was accomplished in less than an hour by one man and one horse.

Phantom and headless horsemen loom large in the legends and folklore of most counties and Lancashire is no exception. Perhaps our most famous one is to be found in the tiny hamlet of Wycoller, near Colne.

There is a long tradition which connects Charlotte Brontë with Wycoller, about six-and-a-half miles from her home at Haworth, and each year thousands of Brontë lovers come here in search of the Brontë spirit and to see the ruins of Wycoller Hall, which many people strongly believe to have been the setting of Fearndean Manor in *Jane Eyre*. This is the kind of place which captures the imagination and, as a result, many legends and ghost stories have grown around the place which, although not strictly true, have carried down the years as gospel. Ghost stories cling to this corner of the realm as they cling to few other parts of the north-west and it is not surprising when one considers that this half-hidden, once-deserted hamlet has always existed in isolation.

Here, on dark nights, the terrifying tales of ghostly hounds waiting in the lanes to seize the unwary, and the spectral horseman galloping down the windswept road take on real meaning. The ruined Hall, which stood lonely and empty for over a century, would be a naturally fearsome place to the timid who passed this way in the dark, their imaginations easily peopling it with the spirits of the Cunliffes.

Theirs was an important family in times gone by; their coat of arms is still emblazoned in the chancel windows of Whalley Church. Their family home was Billington before Wycoller became theirs through marriage in the late sixteenth century. But the dark shadow of ill fortune fell on them and in the days of the Commonwealth the Cunliffes paid dearly for their loyalty to the Crown. Thereafter they fell on hard times and in 1819 the last Cunliffe died, the Hall fell into a state of neglect, and rapidly became a complete ruin.

Wycoller Hall has been the setting of ghost stories for centuries, its most famous being that of the phantom horseman. Early versions tell us he appears on one night each year and 'only when the weather is at its worst with the wind wild and tempestuous'. He is said to be dressed in the costume of the early Stuart period and the trappings of his horse are 'of the most uncouth appearance'!

Basically, the story behind the legend is said to be based on an actual event, when a Cunliffe beat his wife to death with a dog-whip after seeing her in the arms of a man he thought was her lover. But he was only her long-lost brother.

Another version tells us that one of the Cunliffes murdered his wife as a result of her prediction that the family would become extinct, a prediction which was accurate, although it did take two hundred years more to happen.

Yet a third version places the event in the reign of Charles II, in which one Simon Cunliffe, squire of Wycoller, is said to have been out hunting one day when the fox ran into the hall and ran up the stairs, seeking refuge. Cunliffe, in hot pursuit, rode up the wide staircase and into his wife's room, causing her to collapse with shock. She later died as a result. There are some who say that before the staircase was removed, hoofmarks could be seen quite plainly on two of the steps.

As a result, when the howling wind is at its loudest, the phantom horseman can be heard galloping up the lanes at full speed. Sweeping into the hamlet, he crosses the narrow packhorse bridge and comes to a sudden halt at the door of the hall. The rider then dismounts and makes his way into the ruins. Dreadful screams are heard, as of a woman in agony, which subside into groans. Then, with a curse, the rider descends the stairway – which by the way, is non-existent – mounts his waiting nag and gallops wildly away.

So, which version do we believe? None of them; the whole story of the phantom horseman of Wycoller is pure fabrication. Simon Cunliffe never existed other than as a fictitious character in one of Halliwell Sutcliffe's novels – despite the fact that many people, even today, claim to have known someone, who knew someone, who saw or heard the ghostly hoofbeats as the phantom horseman crossed the packhorse bridge.

Another spectral horseman roamed the moors near Rivington Pike, above Horwich. Although the legend is difficult to swallow, a spectral horseman *was* believed to have roamed the moors and certain of the connected events do seem to have occurred, although there is still some mystery surrounding them.

According to the well-documented legend, three men and their servants, having been up on the moors on a grouse hunt, were returning to a small inn for the night. A storm which had been gathering for some hours suddenly broke, and they were forced to take shelter in a nearby tower. One of the party, a man called Norton, seemed strangely disturbed by the storm and as the dogs became uneasy, growling and barking, so he became more uneasy. Suddenly, horses' hooves were heard approaching the door of the tower, and when Norton opened it a man on a black horse stood silhouetted against the dull skyline, eerily illuminated by the occasional flash of lightning.

Norton said he recognized the stranger as his uncle who had vanished on these same moors some twelve years before. As the stranger rode away, Norton mounted his horse and followed him. His friends were about to do likewise but were advised by one of the servants not to go – for this was the legendary spectral horseman, often seen in the district.

Then the servant told a story of a night exactly twelve years before, when his father had gone out poaching. He had waited for his return, but only the dogs came back, alone and dirty. It was several hours before his father returned in a very distressed state. The father had told him that he had been approached by a small man on a huge black horse, who had asked to be taken to a pile of stones which marked the spot where two shepherd boys had died, known as The Two Lads. On arriving at the site, the horseman told him to lift up the stones, but the father remembered the tales of the spectral horseman and, where the stones had been, he saw to his horror a large stinking black pit. At the approach of another stranger, he was knocked unconscious and when he finally came to, the stranger was gone and the stones were as they had been before. He went home and never went on to the moors again.

After listening to this story, Norton's friends returned to the inn, only to find that he had not gone on ahead of them. Worried, they set off in the direction of The Two Lads to search for him, eventually finding him laid out at the foot of the pile of stones, apparently dead. He looked as though he had been in a terrible fight, lying with his hands tightly clenched. Carefully they lifted him across a horse and returned to the inn, where after sending for a surgeon, they were informed that Norton was both physically and mentally exhausted.

He remained unconscious for several weeks. When he finally recovered, he said that his uncle, who had appeared that night as the spectral horseman, had made him promise to stay by The Two Lads, and at midnight he would reveal the purpose of his visit. His uncle thus returned on the stroke of midnight, saying that he would possess Norton, at which stage a violent struggle ensued. Norton was now convinced that his uncle was the stranger who had approached the Devil and the servant's father at The Two Lads on that night twelve years before.

To the day he died, Norton was certain that his uncle was allowed to return only on condition that the Devil's spirits which possessed him re-entered someone else. As this condition was not fulfilled when Norton refused to submit to him, the spectral horseman was never seen again.

One of the most famous – and some say, finest – Penny Blood serials of the nineteenth century was *Varney the Vampire*, written by Thomas Prest and published in 1847. The serial was issued in penny weekly instalments and ran to 220 chapters. For years, this story was believed to have been a work of fiction, but in recent years researchers have come to believe that it may have been based on a case of ghostly vampirism which took place during the reign of Queen Anne. So, to finish this book, I should like, if I may, to step across the border into South Cumbria and tell a fascinating tale of vampires.

During the reign of Queen Anne, there were several reports from North Lancashire, Cumberland and Westmorland of a spirit which attacked its victims and left scratch marks on their bodies. Such a vampire was thought to have attacked a woman in Kirkby Croglin, near Ulverston, in quite recent years, and during the 1930s, a woman living at Troutbeck, a couple of miles north of Windermere, was quite savagely attacked. According to the records the young woman, from a well-to-do family living just south of the village, was attacked by the vampire and was then sent abroad by her parents to recover from her terrifying experience.

On her return home some months later, the vampire was said to have melted the lead from her bedroom window and gained entrance to the sleeping woman's room. She awakened to find a gaunt and evil-smelling figure bending over her and screamed out for help. Her brother, sleeping in the next room, heard her screams and dashed into her bedroom, firing a pistol at the figure and hitting it in the leg.

As the figure fled, the brother followed and was amazed when it led him to the local graveyard and seemed to dissolve into a particular grave, which the young man was bright enough to mark with stones.

The following day, the girl's family informed the vicar of

Troutbeck of the incidents of the previous night and the girl's brother was able to show him the grave, into which the figure had seemed to disappear, and which he had marked. On the instructions of the vicar, the body – or what now remained of the body, for it was little more than a skeleton – was disinterred and it was found, to the horror of all concerned, to have a recently fired bullet in its leg.

It is recorded that the vicar laid the vampire by cutting the head from the body and breaking its back. Then, whilst saying suitable prayers of exorcism, he ordered the remains to be burnt. I'm told the young woman survived her ordeal and was never again troubled by the vampire of Troutbeck. Local people say this story is perfectly true; it happened no more than fifty years ago, and the young woman lived on into her seventies, only dying in 1981.

Index